NEVER SAFE, ALWAYS FUN!

Tours & Tales of the Everglades

Graham Mitchell

© 2014 by Graham Mitchell

All rights reserved.

No part of this publication may be reproduced, distributed, or transmitted in any form or by any means, including photocopying, recording, or other electronic or mechanical methods, without the prior written permission of the publisher, except in the case of brief quotations embodied in critical reviews and certain other noncommercial uses permitted by copyright law.

Although every precaution has been taken to verify the accuracy of the information contained herein, the author and publisher assume no responsibility for any errors or omissions. No liability is assumed for damages that may result from the use of information contained within.

The rights of Graham Mitchell to be identified as author of this work has been asserted by him in accordance with sections 77 and 78 of the Copyright, Designs and Patents Act 1988.

Cover Design: Everkai Media

Interior Design: Everkai Media

Publisher: Everkai Media

ISBN: 978-1-4996-0684-3

Printed via Createspace

10 9 8 7 6 5 4 3 2 1

1. Travel 2. Everglades 3. Memoir

Dedication

I dedicate this book to my wonderful, beautiful, intelligent, and talented daughter Kaira, of whom I am so proud, and love more than anything. I also wish to send love and gratitude to all the wonderful people that welcomed me into their lives, and supported me during my time living in the Florida Everglades. A special thanks and love to Owhnn, Edwin, Nichol, Brandon G, Drew, Rustin, Teresa, Harriett, Sarah, Lilly, Bob, Susie, Kristy, and many more.

Also, to two good friends who have since passed; Richard and Rebecca. RIP.

Finally, thanks and love to my mum.

Contents

Biography 9

Preface 11

Introduction 15

CHAPTER ONE – Hostel & Tours 21

    The Everglades International Hostel 21

        Miami Vice 22

    The Tours 28

    Tour Seasons 32

CHAPTER TWO – The Everglades 37

    The Everglades 37

CHAPTER THREE – Heading Out 47

    Into the Wild 47

        German Grape Smugglers 50

        Incarceration on Vacation 53

CHAPTER FOUR - Arrival 57

    Arrival 57

        Taylor Slough Canoe Sail 61

        Savory Sawgrass 66

CHAPTER FIVE – Royal Palm 77

    Royal Palm 77

        Car Club 79

    Anhinga Trail 84

        Baby Food 84

  Damn Trashcans 88

  Mind the Rope Don't Bite You 91

  Don't Drop Your Camera 100

 Gumbo Limbo Trail 103

  You Never Know What's Round the Corner 105

CHAPTER SIX - Pineland 107

 The Pinelands 107

 Long Pine Key 111

 The Pinelands Trail 113

CHAPTER SEVEN - Cypress 131

 Cypress Forest 131

 Cypress Domes 132

 Pa-Hay-Okee 134

  Sunset Supper 135

  Ignorance & Priapism 136

 The Movie-Dome 137

  Guarding Hades 140

  All in A Day's Work 143

  Not So Tough 147

 The Cottonmouth Dome 149

  Toxic Toilet Paper 150

  Venomous Babies 155

  A Snake Dinner 165

  Areegay-tor! 170

CHAPTER EIGHT - Paddling 175

Brackish & Paddling 175
Nine Mile Pond 179
 Lost for Words 180
 When you have to go, you have to go! 180
 Tour with Croczilla 182
 That was lucky 184
 Country Roads, Take Me Home 186
 Even the Guide Tips 188
 Tough Mudder 190
Noble Hammock 193
Hells Bay 195
West Lake 197
 Recidivist Crows 198
Coot Bay and Coot Bay Pond 201
 Up S*** Creek without a Paddle 201

CHAPTER NINE – Flamingo & the Bay 205
Flamingo 205
 Don't Feed the Wildlife 208
 Headcount 209
Florida Bay 218
 Mating Bull Sharks 220
 Sweet Caroline 222

CHAPTER TEN – Tales 227
Traveling 227
 Machine Guns, Mayhem and Madness 227

Beef Bombs	230
Arrested on a Plane	232
Immigration Interrogation	236
The Hostel	237
Budweiser, Bike Sheds and Body Sweat	240
Putrid Pee & Pillow Pooh	241
Firefighters & Firecrackers	243
Sandals, Socks & Strange Germans	245
Boo! & the Blubbering Baby	245
Summer Boredom	248
Airports & Aluminum	249
Pool Balls and Banjos	249
World Cup and Watches	252
Why Are You Following Me?	252
The Island	254
Psilocybin Pasta, Raccoons, Crabs and Testicles	255
Coconut Grove & Biscayne Bay	260
Espadrilles, Elvis and a Ferrari	260
Frozen Delights	263
The End	264
Final Thoughts	265
Suggested Reading	269
Index	270

Biography

Graham Mitchell was born in the UK in 1973. He grew up on the Isle of Wight, a quaint and popular tourist attraction located off the South Coast of the UK.

From early 2000, he spent a considerable amount of time in the Florida Everglades, working as a wilderness guide. During his time spent in the USA, he conducted tours of the South Florida wilderness for travelers, scientists, college groups, and journalists from across the globe. He has now retired from guiding, and lives back on the Isle of Wight, UK.

Graham is a certified professional in IT, specializing in security, penetration testing and ethical hacking. He also spent many years working as a trainer and consultant. His various certifications and accreditations include CISSP, CEH, CompTIA, MCSE, MCT and MBCS to name a few.

He enjoys chess, reading, writing, walking, and anything in the outdoors. He is qualified in hand gliding and paragliding with the BHPA, close-protection/bodyguard certified, a member of MENSA, first aid, survival & bush craft, enjoys collecting various other memberships, titles, certifications, and abhors acronyms.

He now spends his time as a mature student studying for an MEng in Computer Science at the University of Southampton. He is also working on a few other writing projects, which should be coming out shortly, including:

How I Wrote This Book: A Step-by-Step Guide to Self-Publishing.

Hacking 101-1: Network Security

Hacking 101-2: Web Security

Hacking 101-3: Application Security

There is also a work of fiction planned for the future.

Author Note

If you were on a tour, and wish to find out if there are any photographs available, or just want to get in touch, then you can email the author at the following address:

neversafealwaysfun@hushmail.com

This book is also available for the Kindle with color photographs.

Preface

I once read that a preface is in a sense an apology, an explanation or defense. Therefore, I sincerely apologize for cheating you out of the systemic and visceral experience that is the Everglades. The Everglades are a wild and poetic landscape that is largely indescribable. Sadly, my words will never be enough to do them justice.

To steal a quote from the 1951 movie, *An American in Paris*, originally describing Paris:

"[The Everglades] is a mood, a longing you didn't know you had until it was answered. [The Everglades] is like love or art or faith, it can't be explained, only felt."

I wrote this book because few people have ever heard of the Everglades. If they have, they don't know where it is. If they do, they don't understand what it is. Most of the locals have never even been into the Everglades, nor could the majority tell you much more than a half-truth about it.

So just what are the Everglades?

They lay on the tip of South Florida, USA. Occupying around a one-fifth of their historic size, the Everglades remain today as a federally protected wilderness within the boundary of the Everglades National Park, established in 1947. Becoming a park helped to preserve what remained of a rapidly disappearing wilderness due to drainage and development in South Florida. The Everglades diverse plant and wildlife historically struggled for survival, and still do today, as the pernicious creep of agriculture, and development of the concrete jungles eat into their very existence. Irreparable damage occurs daily, from the chemicals and phosphates used for agriculture, and from channeling and redirection of its symbiotic fuel source, the water. Thanks to the concerted efforts of conservationists, scientists, ecologists and environmentalists alike, the restoration project is well under way. This fragile wilderness is not out of the woods yet though, as the corporate and governmental oligarchy seeks opportunities for control and wealth through overzealous development and myopic decision-making.

The Everglades hold a special place in my heart, and so I decided to document my experiences, as well as share with people a little of this magical place.

I discovered as I wrote this book, there are neither enough, nor adequate verbs nor adjectives that exist to convey the experiences of the individual. The unique perspective, feelings, and sensory stimuli that mold our memories all become lost in textual and verbal translation. We do not remember what something looked like so much, as we remember how we felt when we saw it. Accurately describing a place, experience, or feeling when you were there, is an impossible task, especially when describing such a uniquely majestic, prehistoric, and diverse wilderness as the Everglades.

I have tried my best where possible, to abstract the complex from any science, as I try to present the Everglades to the reader. This has been no easy task however. The Everglades is such a complex array of ecosystems, filled with both such beautiful and interesting flora and fauna that they would render Darwin aphasic. I am neither a scientist nor a naturalist. I was a guide, and part of a guide's purview is to interpret, and not overwhelm or confuse through dogma and hyperbole.

The time I spent in the Everglades was an important part of my life. I learned to live in the world, and not just on the world, something that we should all strive for as we go through our daily lives.

As we tour the Everglades through these pages, you may find that an interesting place or experience attracts you. My recommendation is don't just read about it, go and live it. Maybe not verbatim, but at least make the conscious choice to live your life, and not just exist.

To quote Mark Twain:

"Apparently there is nothing that cannot happen today."

I have found those words to be so true. Our lives can change in an instant. Fate brings us choices, and then we choose our fate. You do not need to be something special to do something special. Ordinary people can achieve remarkable things.

I have some amazing friends that remain in the Everglades and the USA, some of whom may have moved on geographically, and sadly, a few have passed. Regardless of their place in the physical or spiritual world, they will all hold a special place in my heart for all time. I miss them all dearly, and I appreciate every moment I spent with them. I will be eternally grateful for them welcoming me into their lives.

In its vernacular, the 'Glades', the people, and my experiences, will always remain part of my soul, and part of me will always remain within its untamed and wild embrace.

I hope you enjoy the tour.

Introduction

Imagine you had your own *Jurassic Park*, a subtropical wilderness, with nine distinctly different ecosystems. Ornately beautiful orchids, bromeliads, carnivorous water plants, venomous snakes, golden cobwebs, panthers, and modern-day dinosaurs roaming freely. Clear and calm waters, murky depths, scarlet skies, and golden sunbeams, torrential rains, blistering sun, sky blackening bird flocks, and mammals, reptiles, and insects that cover the land.

For six months of the year, the ground lays submersed below a shallow sheet of slow-moving, warm, freshwater, drizzling southwards to the salty waters of the Gulf. During the other six months, it lays dry and arid, gasping for a heavenly reprieve.

Here, the grass can cut you, the sun can bake you, the rains can drown you, the trees and plants can poison you, and the animals could eat you. This place exists, and we know it today as the Everglades. It is a subtropical water wilderness, which once occupied roughly eleven-thousand square miles in the state of Florida, USA.

I feel blessed that I lived and worked as a wilderness guide in the Everglades. Over many years, I would get to take people from all over the world on an interpretive tour of this endangered landscape. The tours would range from half-day to full day, including overnight backcountry trips up to ten days in length.

This book is a tribute to the Everglades. I will be forever grateful for the experiences and memories that I was lucky enough to take away with me.

I have tried to combine three different styles of book into one; an armchair guide, companion travel guide, and a memoir of anecdotes. I intend to give you a complete experience, whether you have visited the Everglades or not or maybe never intend to. It should be informative and educational, as well as at times offer a little comedic value provided by the short stories of my experiences and travels. I would also like to point out for clarity, though I am British, I have opted to use USA spelling, and a mix of both British and USA colloquialisms where applicable.

Chapters 1 and 2, cover a little background about the Everglades International Hostel from where the tour business itself operates, and how I came across the hostel, and employed as a wilderness guide. After this, what follows is a description of the different tours that we offered, and some background on the Everglades. If you were on the tour, this is something I would do early on, as we traveled towards the Everglades and during a little discussion, as we entered at the side of the road overlooking the park. You could choose if you like to skip these chapters, though they lay the foundation, and frame of reference for the remainder of the book.

Chapters 3 through 9, offer the reader a chance to experience a virtual tour of the Everglades. They should also act as a companion guide, should you ever decide to visit. At times, I take a short break to recount a short tale in context.

The bulk of the chapters are in the form of a guided tour through the Everglades National Park. We will be following a typical itinerary, as I would conduct a full day immersion tour.

We begin at the main East Coast entrance, and travel the 40-mile road that cuts the National Park in half. We will stop off for the fun stuff wherever I can, whilst providing an ecological interpretation of each major location, or point of interest in context. We will finish the tour at the end of the park where the Everglades vanishes off into the brackish and salty waters of Florida Bay, and into the Gulf of Mexico.

Chapter 10 includes material that may not relate directly to the tours, such as time at the hostel, traveling, and different locations in and outside of the National Park boundary. Chapter 10 is anecdotal, and written like the inline stories and tales contained in the rest of the book. If you only want a few laughs then Chapter 10 is just that.

As a short disclaimer, they say you should write about what you know. Well, I have a collection of professional certifications that would buckle the legs of a Nepalese Sherpa. However, not one of them relates to the natural sciences. I am not famous, infamous or otherwise significant over anyone else. John Muir once described himself as an *"unknown nobody."* I am that unknown nobody.

I am not a geologist, hydrologist, herpetologist, botanist, plant biologist, or any other type of natural scientist. However, I am an experienced and certified wilderness guide, with many skills and certifications such as first aid, navigation, watercraft, and wilderness leadership. By trade, I am an IT security specialist, and penetration tester (ethical hacker).

If I am not a scientist or a naturalist, why do I think that I am qualified to write a book on the Everglades?

Well, this book is not a definitive scientific text or publication on the diverse biological life, or geological aspects of the Everglades. It is an interpretive journey based on my own experience, as well as an anecdotal collection of stories and memories. However, you can rely on the wealth of encyclopedic information contained herein, although it is difficult at times to impart such knowledge without being able to show that to which I refer.

When it comes to the sciences of the Everglades as with most things, I am an autodidact. Thanks to years of experience leading interpretive tours into the Floridian wilderness, and reading everything that I could, I am confident, without hubris, or arrogance, that I have my facts straight. However, more than anything, it is thanks to my experience gained from my time spent in this misunderstood wilderness.

A true wilderness tour of the Everglades is about embracing the environment, and becoming one with it. Taking home with you a few less breaths, and leaving with a lot more memories. It is about getting wet, hot, cold, dirty, scared, unnerved, shocked, educated and enlightened. Taking a guided tour of the Everglades with a knowledgeable guide is educational, exciting, and will be a trip to remember.

There will be tales of snakebites, boat-tipping tourists, mangrove swimming, moonlit swamp walks, mating bull sharks, biting dolphins, and bleeding testicles. There will also be hallucinogenic raccoon hunting, blowing up guests with firecrackers, canoe paddling through agitated blue bioluminescence, and many more tales.

If you want to experience standing waist deep in a swamp, during the night, with eight petrified Japanese girls who don't understand English, the only slivers of light are from the moon as it breaks through the dense canopy above, surrounded by bone crunching alligators, snakes, mosquitoes and pythons, then this book is for you.

Life as an Everglades wilderness guide can be as difficult or as easy as you make it. What I can tell you is that it has the best office in the world, with the best views, and can be ever so rewarding. It can also at times be extremely tiring, painful, repetitive, often thankless, and the office air conditioning needs fixing.

Being a good wilderness guide requires qualities that are difficult to surmise. From observing others, I think that being a leader, calm, confident, skilled in wilderness first aid and backcountry living, and able to interpret, are essential qualities to have. They must possess an intimate understanding of their surroundings, and an unshakable comfort. A guide that is unsure or lacks confidence, inexperienced, or who lacks knowledge, will soon fail to please and deliver.

Paying tourists want bang for their buck, so forget about the crushing jaws of alligators, as the unsatisfied discord of disgruntled tourists is what a guide needs to fear the most. It is not always about being able to answer a question, as you cannot know everything. However, a guide should be able to divert the question, so that they can find out the answer later. This not only increases your own knowledge, but more importantly, it satisfies the paying tourist.

It is also useful to be able to speak various languages. I am no polyglot, but I do speak a little Japanese, French, some Spanish, and the odd word from other languages, usually for beer, food, sex, and toilet, not necessarily in that order though. I am certainly not fluent, and you may even think I struggle with English after reading this.

The wilderness guides' that I have met are all unique individuals, with many skills, and a broad knowledge base. However, more importantly, I think it is about having a clear passion for the wilderness and its conservation, and wanting to share that with others. I know both past and present guides' who are as passionate as I am about the Everglades and the wilderness, all with a wealth of knowledge and experience behind them, every man (and woman) an emperor.

I guess it's time to start our journey. Remember to bring plenty of water, bug repellent, sunglasses, sunscreen, change of clothes, but more than anything bring a sense of humor, humility, and a sense of adventure.

"Survival in the wilderness is a matter of heart not hardware." – Hank, *Survival Quest* (1988)

Don't be too scared. My mantra is 'Life will kill ya', and if you remember this, then you will learn to let go and enjoy fear more. In the wilderness, fear is your friend, but it needs to be controlled. Fear is not a weakness, in the wilderness it is strength, and will keep you alive.

"Expose yourself to your deepest fear. After that, fear has no power, and the fear of freedom shrinks and vanishes. You are free." – Jim Morrison

I hope, through my words, that I can convey some of the beauty of the Everglades to you. Maybe, you can catch a short glimpse of this rare, fragile, and endangered landscape.

An afternoon tour would usually leave around 13:00-14:00 PM and return around 17:00-18:00 PM, however, these times were always flexible. The tour would consist of a short boardwalk at Anhinga Trail, to catch a glimpse of all the wildlife, a short canoe trip, and a 'swamp tromp', which is a term used to describe walking in the water. During these 'swamp tromps' the water can range from chest deep, ankle deep, to bone dry, depending on the time of year and rainfall.

I would often find myself taking a morning tour, an afternoon tour and then a night walk, or full moon trip, all in the same day during the busy tourist season. After a few days of such a mentally and draining schedule I could become a bit of a grouch, although the beauty of the Everglades never lost its appeal.

Full Day Tour

09:30-17:00

The full day tours were the staple of the tour business when I was a guide. They were my favorite type of tour in preference over the half days, except of course for the multi-day and overnight trips.

The full day tour lasted around eight to nine hours, from around 09:30 AM to 17:00 PM. If I could arrange it, then I would plan to leave at twilight, so the tour would return around 14:00-15:00 PM. Often I would be heading out again a few hours after for whatever evening tour was scheduled.

The full day tour is a full immersion tour, or a complete Everglades experience. The tour travels the length of the park through all the major ecosystems, from freshwater marl prairies, pineland forest, cypress forest, and finishing up in the brackish mangrove forests, and finally the saltwater that meets the Gulf. The tour would conclude with an hour sleep for the weary tourists, as I drove them back to civilization, leaving the wilderness behind them. After a full day in the Florida sun, it was hard for me to keep my eyes open. It is no easy task after conducting ten full day tours back to back, combined with some night walks and possibly a few full moon trips. Regular high doses of caffeine were my staple. I do apologize to those few unfortunate souls that perhaps caught me on a tour where I was grumpy, usually due to lack of sleep, and working back to back for ten days or more with little rest.

Night Walk

20:00-22:00

The night walk tour had come about from the need to give tourists a short and unique introduction to the Everglades. Conducted at night under the illumination of the stars from the well-defined Milky Way, along with flashlights, and offering a very rich experience in a short amount of time.

The night walk allowed last minute arrivals, people seeking a short wilderness foray, and brief overnighters, a chance to gain a little knowledge and an experience packed boardwalk tour in a tourist free park.

Full Moon Tour

19:00-04:00 - Dependent on moonrise

The full moon tour was an idea that I came up with to create the ultimate alien experience for the Everglades explorer. Typically lasting four hours or so, the departure and return times varied depending on the moonrise timings. This tour of course would only go out at certain times of the month, the day before, on, and after the full moon, and so three days or more every month.

A full moon tour consisted of a canoe trip and a walk in the water, or swamp. This trip is nothing short of poetic, and I have no doubt as I write this, that there are people all over the world who will carry that experience with them their whole lives.

Imagine sudden splashes from alligator tails as you brush them with your paddle, whilst paddling silently (aside from giggles and occasional screams) through the mangroves, or jumping fish that dive into the boat, flailing around on the bottom. It is simply breath taking. You might even brush their tails with your foot if you are walking in the water. That is an unforgettable experience!

Paddling or wading through the still waters of the Everglades under the moonlight, surrounded by prehistoric creatures, has an eerie and surreal feel to it. However, every minute of the trip will massage your soul.

Overnight & Multi-Day Camping Trips
Ranging from one to ten days

Often not following any marked trails, and heading into pure untouched wilderness, these tours are for the adventurous, and designed for those who want to experience everything that the Everglades have to offer.

We would take everything we needed in the boats for up to ten days or so, and venture off into pristine wilderness, where for days all you will see is water, sun, wildlife, and vegetation. Overnights in the Everglades can be a real bonding and memorable experience with those you go with, or if you go alone, it will become your best friend for life. If you go with a partner, it will either make you or break you, as we do not call canoes the "divorce boats" for nothing.

Overnight and multi-day trips are for those who don't mind peeing into a bottle or over the side of a boat, and enjoys sunburn, extreme heat, and mosquito bites. There will be warm drinking water, sleeping in the haunted mangroves, or on wooden platforms (chickees) perched precariously above alligator, crocodile, and shark infested waters. In addition, there will be torrential rains, waterspouts and hurricane winds. These trips are nothing short of spectacular.

Finally, an important consideration for any traveler, the guide, and will affect the activities on a tour, but never the quality, is the weather.

Personally, I would enjoy taking tours out in all weather, regardless of the impending meteorological doom, and often did so. The only time weather would cancel a tour would be if the National Park closed for safety reasons such as during a hurricane, which they often do.

If a tour was out and it began to monsoon then you got wet. The weather in South Florida and certainly in the Everglades is extremely changeable. In a matter of seconds, I have seen it go from glasslike calm water, blue skies and blazing sun, to the dark clouds of Voldemort, with torrential rain, howling winds and white caps, all in the time it takes to say:

"Don't touch that, it's poisonous!"

Tour Seasons

South Florida has two seasons, which will affect any visit dramatically; the seasons are either wet or dry! It is that simple, but yet upon examination a lot more complex. This seasonal dichotomy is a result of a subtropical climate, though often closer to a tropical one, especially the further south you travel, such as in, or near the Florida Keys.

Florida is located in the temperate zone (between the Tropics and the Polar Regions), yet it experiences near tropical weather. This is a result of being close to the equator, with the cold Atlantic to the east and the warm Gulf of Mexico to the west. During a typical year, South Florida can experience devastating hurricanes, a defined rainy season, tropical storms, and is one of the most tornado prone states in the USA. Not to mention enough lightning to generate an amount of Gigawatts that could send a whole fleet of DeLoreans back to the future.

The wet season refers to a six month or so period, typically from May–November, and the dry season from November-May, approximately. This varies based on the weather systems from year to year. That is right, summer is wet and the winter is dry, so remember that before you book a ticket. You would not believe how many tourists have no idea about the climate of their destination, and have arrived in summer expecting perfect weather, only to find boarded up homes, businesses, and flooded highways.

During the summer months, or wet season, it is hot, but extremely wet. There are lots of blood sucking mosquitoes, high water levels, and dispersed wildlife, making it the least preferable time to visit the Everglades. During the dry season in the winter months, or what South Florida and the Everglades National Park just calls 'season' (referring to the tourist or busy season) it is milder weather. There are little to no mosquitoes, abating humidity, with low and gradually depleting water levels. There is also concentrated areas of wildlife as the dry season settles in, making it what most people see as the best time to visit.

Personally, I prefer the wet season, but I am a masochist when it comes to the Everglades. I like the heat, the mozzies don't bother me, and I prefer the increased chance of less people frequenting the backcountry and trails. However, this is how the Everglades should be, both wet and humid. Water is the Everglades venous fluid, without which the Everglades begin to die. You need to go and visit during both of the seasons to really appreciate and experience the Everglades, and preferably, during each month, to see the remarkable transitions it makes during an average year.

Through adaptation over many thousands of years, the plants and wildlife share a synchronicity with the vicissitudes of the seasons. The seasons are distinct, yet you may notice the seasonal change in just a sudden drop or rise in temperature, and the effects are often gradual and subtle. The gradual transition from the wet to dry season results in the high water levels evaporating and draining into the aquifer below. The wildlife slowly begins to seek out areas where the water remains, and the river of grass becomes a dry, arid, mud caked desert, with only 'gator holes' and unnatural depths such as from excavation remaining hydrated.

If you visit in November, which is the beginning of the tourist season, then you will have the start of the milder weather. There will be less mosquitoes and higher water levels for extended paddling, though you will not get to see anywhere near the amount of wildlife that you may see if you visit in March.

In March most of the water has dried up, and the wildlife sits, lays, and chatters away with the sounds of a cocktail party at the various remaining watering holes. Some of these watering holes are popular tourist attractions, such as the Anhinga Trail. Remember, every month is different within the Glades, in fact, changes are often a quotidian experience, but you can certainly see dramatic visual differences in the landscape as each month passes.

Although the winter months may sound attractive, when the water levels deplete it means the paddling becomes shorter or harder as you try to maneuver your craft through liquid mud, or walk in knee-deep gelatinous gloop. Conversely, if you choose to come in the middle of August or September, then the water levels would be almost chest deep in some places. Paddling can last forever, but you will struggle to catch anything more than a few glimpses of wildlife, as they spread throughout the entire drenched landscape. I can guarantee that you will get your Everglades blood drive "I'm a donor" badge for kindly contributing a good supply of blood to the Everglades Mosquito Air Force.

Mosquitoes hatch their eggs after the rainfall. Then they fly and buzz around, sucking blood from any mammal that they can find. They are probably the most irritating factor about visiting the Everglades. The skies can blacken with squadrons of these thirsty vampires, and I have seen grown men panic and flail as if being chased by a grizzly bear, as they struggle to get back in their vehicle. I did too on a few occasions, but I built up a good tolerance over time. On a positive note, it means you are part of the ecosystem. They need your blood for protein, which in turn results in more eggs, and eventually more mosquitoes, and so the cycle continues as they provide food further up the food chain.

With all the talk of the heat and humidity and the word tropical, you may be surprised to find out that it can get extremely cold in the winter months. I have personally taken tours out during December and January where a severe cold front has passed through, leaving my legs red and numb from the cold water for hours. There was even a time when thin sheet ice covered shallow puddles of water, and iced droplets hung from the bromeliads and cypress needles. This certainly is not the norm. The key to surviving the Florida climate, whatever time of year you decide to visit, is to come prepared.

In fact, a few years ago, temperatures dropped so much, and remained sustained for a period that resulted in the deaths of many manatees, crocodile, and almost every inch of the water packed full with dead fish. The Everglades turned into pungent chowder, lasting for quite a few weeks. Remember that the vast majority of wildlife here is tropical, or certainly used to warmer temperatures, and so when cold fronts come through it can have a devastating effect on their survival.

I no longer work as a guide for the hostel nor conduct tours in the Everglades. My opinions and the information presented about the hostel and its tour business only reflects that of my own personal experience, and the facts known to me during my time employed there. For more up to date and accurate information, I suggest that you contact them directly.

The contact details for them are as follows:

The Everglades International Hostel
20 SW 2nd AVE Florida City, Florida 33034
(800) 372 - 3874 | (305) 248 - 1122
FAX: (305) 245 – 7622
www.evergladeshostel.com
www.toursintheglades.com

CHAPTER TWO – The Everglades

"Something will have gone out of us as a people if we ever let the remaining wilderness get destroyed ... We simply need that wild country available to us, even if we never do more than drive to its edge and look in." - Wallace Stegner

The Everglades

Take a moment to imagine an ancient ocean, bursting at the seams with a myriad of sea creatures. Over many millennia those creatures died, becoming petrified into what we today call calcium carbonate, or more commonly, limestone. This calcium carbonate is the main component in eggshells, seashells, bones, teeth and many marine organisms. It is this limestone bedrock, which forms the foundation of Florida. Florida is essentially a huge slab of this limestone seabed, which sits just above sea level.

Geologically speaking, Florida began to take shape around five hundred and fifty million years ago, deep beneath the ocean. Around twenty-five to thirty-five million years ago it emerged from this ocean as a land mass, but its limestone foundations were laid in the millions of years preceding this, through the petrifaction of the demersed masses of organic matter.

Today, Florida is a biologically diverse landscape that contains some of the most beautiful and uniquely rare species of both plants and animals that you will find anywhere on Earth. It is home to some of the Earth's most endangered species, living within many different ecosystems, most of which were created because of changes in elevation, climate and hydrological levels. The Floridian landscape can change in the blink of an eye, as you travel through all the cardinal points. It is towards the bottom of the Florida Peninsula in South Florida, where we can find the remaining wilderness of the once flourishing, Florida Everglades.

My first few moments in the Everglades, happened at sunrise. I stood catatonic from the beauty and awe in front of me. From a creation vs. evolution point of view, I am a rational empiricist with a lean towards the romantic. However, when spending time in this wetland wilderness, with all its subtle science, cotton candy skies, and rare beautiful plants and animals, it does leave you pondering the possibility of an omnipotent deity, admiring their work from a heavenly afar. Nature is definitely a great argument for intelligent design.

Surprisingly, very few people have ever heard of the Everglades, and those that have usually have some wild and wonderful, though, skewed view of what they think it is. Most of the locals that live in the surrounding suburbs and local cities have never even ventured out into the Everglades, nor could they tell you a single reliable fact about it, at least not without some embellished rhetoric. Yet the National Park receives over a million visitors per year on average, and of those visitors, a very small percentage ever get out of their vehicle, not even to explore a short, and usually, safe boardwalk trail.

A few years ago, I bumped into an old friend back here in the UK, and he asked me what I had been doing with myself. I told him that I have been living and working in the Everglades as a wilderness guide. He told me that he and his wife had been to Florida the previous year. They had drove into the Everglades, down the road about twenty miles and then had got bored of the grass and trees, so they turned around and went to the Keys instead.

This is a not an uncommon experience for many visitors to what is the third largest National Park in the contiguous United States. You see for some reason, for many people, the term Everglades conjures up this idea of a jungle or a swamp. Somewhere in there, the term alligator will usually always pop up too. These terms are the most common to come up, along with airboats, when over the years I have asked people to tell me what they think the Everglades is. They are, however, soon shocked to find out and discover how wrong they were.

If it is famous for anything at all worldwide, then it is usually for the airboats seen during the credits of *Miami Vice* or *CSI: Miami*, or for its famous reptile, the American alligator (*Alligator mississippiensis*). Airboats are light skiffs with huge fans on the back, allowing them to hover at great speed across the open waters and sawgrass prairies of South Florida. The infamous American alligator, which is the "keeper of the glades", is a prehistoric reptilian that is a member of the twenty-three species family of Crocodilians. There are two species (three, counting the odd caiman) that live in this Jurassic jungle.

The Everglades National Park is not as ostentatious as the Grand Canyon or Yellowstone National Parks. The Everglades is far more subtle, its beauty creeps up on you, but when it does, you will fall in love. The Everglades are much more than its common misconceptions, and a total far greater than the sum of its parts. Both historically and today, it remains undiminished by the majesty of other parks, and wilderness. It stands alone and proud, and needs no excuses. Amongst all its wonder, activity, harsh terrain, weather, and the potential danger of its creatures, hides a softness, poetry, and fragility.

Pa-hay-okee or 'grassy waters' is the term that the South Floridian Indians (who survive today as the Miccosukee) used to describe the Everglades. The Everglades has a few names, usually just referred to as the glades, or sometimes the 'River of Grass', which was a term given by Marjory Stoneham Douglas, and is the title of her famous book on the Everglades; *The Everglades: River of Grass*.

Marjory Stoneham Douglas was an environmentalist, best known for her advocacy and defense of the conservation, restoration and preservation of the fragile wilderness we know today as the Everglades. The preserved Everglades we have left is a result of her and others lifelong efforts.

The term Everglades was first recorded cartographically in 1823, but was originally noted as "River Glades" and then later on it was assumed that "River" had replaced "Ever", although each are equally valid.

A glade is an open space within a forest. Historically, in the

Everglades, forests of pine trees opened up to flooded prairies of grass that seemingly went on forever as far as the eye could see.

Understanding what the Everglades is and why it is, is where most people stumble when asked. However, it does not need to be so misunderstood, so let us go back to the limestone for a minute to see if we can get a clearer picture.

Imagine you have a long slab of limestone in your hand. You drill a reasonably large depression into the middle of it, but not all the way through. If we fill that depression with water, and slightly tilt the slab of limestone, so that the water tips over the edge of the depression, running towards the tip, we can then see why the Everglades is what it is, both historically, and today.

In the middle of the Florida Peninsula, there is a large body of freshwater known as Lake Okeechobee. The lake covers an area of around seven hundred and thirty miles, and has a maximum depth of approximately 13-feet. Those stats place it as the seventh largest freshwater lake in the USA. The lakes natural source is from both the Kissimmee River and the summer rainfall. When it becomes full it then overflows (typically and historically during the wet season) due to the northern rains arriving. This overflow would then both gently and imperceptibly make its way towards the salt-waters of Florida Bay, and out into the Gulf of Mexico, all due to the tilt of Florida as it extends southwards.

As you can see then, the water flows southwards from its headwaters at Lake Okeechobee, and thus by definition the Everglades is technically one big river. This river is around fifty miles wide to one-hundred miles long. It is a capacious aqueous expanse, which is a slowly moving, shallow sheen of freshwater. This movement is thanks to the gradual descent of Florida as you move south, which is approximately 14-feet from Lake Okeechobee down to Florida Bay. Elevation and water are responsible for the existence of the Everglades, and South Florida in general.

There is of course a lot more to it than this, but if you remember for now that the Everglades is a river, it will go a long way to help you in understanding more about this amazing collection of ecosystems.

The ecosystems here range from the sawgrass filled freshwater marl prairies, which you can see instantly upon the entering the park. The sloughs, of which there are two in the Everglades National Park; Taylor Slough and Shark River Slough, where you will find often deeper water levels than their surrounding areas.

Pinelands, where slash pine (*Pinus elliotti*) dominate the landscape, along with saw palmetto (*Serenoa repens*), that hide the many highly venomous eastern diamondback rattlesnakes, or where the rare honey blonde Florida panther stalks its prey.

Hardwood hammocks (deriving their name from the fishnet style bed strung between trees) refers to a raised area of ground, kept dry from the impending floods of the summer rains and flow of water. These hammocks are tree islands, filled with both evergreen and deciduous hardwoods such as mahogany (*Swietenia mahagoni*) to gumbo-limbo (*Bursera simaruba*), terrestrial and epiphytic orchids, and industrious hordes of insects, making hammocks a real jungle within a jungle (although not a jungle).

There are vast areas of cypress forest, where cypress trees (*Taxodium*), dominate the landscape, standing proud in the water, whose base act as a forest clepsydra, where the waterline rises and falls through the seasonal changes in water level. The cypress forests are home to the feared, yet misunderstood, and apparently malevolent venomous snake, the water moccasin (*Agkistrodon piscivorus*) or cottonmouth.

However, I have had the pleasure to come up close and personal with these beautiful creatures and they are certainly not evil, nor are they looking to waste their valuable venom on human prey. Of course, they certainly will strike if you are stupid enough to step on one (and I put myself in that category), or even worse, decide it is safe to pick one up, and yes, people will pick them up.

Finally, amongst these various habitats, though certainly not exhaustive, we have the mangrove forests. These are vast halophytic prairies of red mangrove (*Rhizophora mangle*), that is one of four within the species found in Florida. These provide a maze of waterways and thoroughfares, for alligators, crocodiles, pythons, water snakes, and of course the watercraft explorer, or even on foot, as we will experience later.

These habitats among others not mentioned, make up the vast wilderness that is the Florida Everglades, and all of them suffer at the hand of the varying water levels, as do their inhabitants. Historically, South Florida was just an uninhabitable swamp as far as most people were concerned. However, as settlers and colonists began to explore, the Everglades became a prime target for development and the pervasive agriculture that comes with colonialism.

The world over, the Everglades are seen as a swamp, though you can see that term is incorrect, as a swamp is stagnant water with no flow. However, the Everglades have a source, flow, and drainage. That said there are many areas that appear like a swamp, as some areas have little or no flow throughout the year, and so they do exhibit swamp like properties. However, for now think of the Everglades as a river, though I will at times use the word swamp when it suits the context.

Depending on the changes in elevation, which are often very subtle, and the varying water depths, then different habitats or ecosystems will occur, often overlapping and struggling for territory. Throughout the Everglades, there is certainly a vast collection of biological and ecological complexity. Many of the various habitats are easily visible and differentiated from each other. Others can be harder to pinpoint or separate unless you are some form of natural scientist.

Historically, the ecosystems that made up the Everglades covered pretty much the whole of South Florida. The Everglades at one time

Which I think meant that if we cannot learn the lessons that the Everglades is trying teach us then we have no hope for the survival of our planet in general.

We are all too aware of the curse of technology and plutocratic modernity. Explosive energy sources fuel our world, slowly depleting our natural resources, yet we continue to do so, and put little effort towards implosive sources such as photovoltaic technologies or other green fuels. Even pre-dynastic Egyptians were far more advanced in these areas than we are today, yet we consider ourselves as evolved and technologically advanced, or superior over our ancestors. Sadly, what we really are is a destructive, ignorant, and arrogant capitalist society driven by material gain, when all the riches we could imagine are out there for free in the natural world if only we would open our eyes.

The wilderness is out there, and it is struggling at the hands of the most destructive force in the universe: humanity. Nevertheless, it is holding out an olive branch for us, and it has a lot to say if we would stop and listen. I hope that I can introduce you to some of the valuable lessons it has to teach us throughout my story of this biological nirvana known as the Everglades.

CHAPTER THREE – Heading Out

"No man should go through life without once experiencing healthy, even bored solitude in the wilderness, finding himself depending solely on himself and thereby learning his true and hidden strength." - Jack Kerouac

Into the Wild

Miles of dusty farmland filled with rainbows, sun charred migrant workers, squished squash, feral dogs, coiled pythons on canal banks, and a vast and fast looming wilderness horizon. All this and more is the journey into the Everglades.

Whether you begin in North Florida, head down from Miami, or head up from the Florida Keys, if you intend to enter the main East Coast entrance to the Everglades National Park, you will need to travel through, or close to Florida City. If you choose to venture into the Everglades on your own, without a guide, or as part of a tour, then you will require your own transport. At the time of writing it does look however, like there will be some public transport soon offered from Florida City to the Everglades. Your own vehicle is handy anywhere in South Florida due to its long straight roads and the long distances between places. Florida City also has a somewhat shady criminal element, and many a stray dog with a *Cujo* complex, so the safe haven of a vehicle is a good idea if you are not a local.

People often come to Florida City thinking they can take public transport (which may be an option soon, though only to the entrance) into the Everglades National Park, or stay at a nearby hotel, or the hostel, and then walk into the Everglades. The main entrance to the park is roughly ten miles from Florida City, through hot and dusty agricultural land, with no pedestrian pathways. If cycled through, this means breathing in the chemicals from the "rainbow makers" which are water sprayers that spray the fields with chemically enhanced hydration. The term rainbow makers comes from the Florida sun refracting through the water droplets from the farmers sprayers, then tiny rainbows are formed across the fields, that can be stunning.

There are options such as renting a bike from the hostel, and using them as a shuttle service, although they will only drop you at the entrance to the park. The park road is then another fifty or so miles long if you want to see it in its entirety (the road that is, and not the whole park). To be honest, the only way to enter and see the Everglades is by car, or on a tour. Preferably with a canoe or kayak strapped to your vehicle, another item which you can rent from the hostel (but not if you have a cabriolet, obviously). The options of cycling through, I will not cover, and assume you are in receipt of a vehicle, and hopefully some type of watercraft (though not required, but it is a wetland after all).

I mentioned the main East Coast entrance, which is the only vehicular access to the park. There is another entrance about an hour north of Florida City, just off from the Tamiami Trail at Shark Valley. Shark Valley is a paved fifteen-mile loop that you can cycle, walk, or ride the guided tram tour around and only shows you a limited selection of the ecosystems within the park boundary. I would definitely recommend it as an addition or alternative, depending on your itinerary and logistics of travel. There is another entrance, at the northwest edge of the park boundary, though it only offers access to the saltwater areas of the park and the Gulf, but is a great starting point for multi-day trips that may finish off at Flamingo or the Florida Keys. The 'Wilderness Waterway' would be a good example of this, which is a ninety-nine mile wilderness trail that takes around seven days to paddle. The main East Coast entrance to which I refer in the majority of this text is how most of the million or so visitors per year enter the National Park. It is also the one which will give you access to the most diverse array of ecosystems and wildlife, at least in a short time or by car and on foot.

Heading west on Palm Drive, which is the main thoroughfare through Florida City, and upon which you will need to get onto to head towards the Everglades National Park, you will drive past the hostel on your left hand side at SW 2nd Avenue. You will need to keep heading west (with some twists and turns) to arrive at the park entrance. I would suggest stopping at one of the many gas stations along the way to get fuel (as it will be at least a 100-mile round trip) to the end of the park road, along with any additional detours that you may take.

You should stock up on plenty of water, snacks and mosquito repellent. Personally, mosquitoes don't overly bother me, they may suck my blood from time to time, though rarely, and if they do, then it doesn't bother me with too much swelling or itching. I would however recommend only one repellent (don't bring one from your own country) and that would be 'Deep Woods Off' which comes in a green or orange can, and is the only one toxic enough to help at all.

DEET (*Diethyl-meta-toluamide*), which is the chemical found in most of the effective repellents, is seriously unhealthy for you to dowse your skin with (and you will). The US Army originally developed this nasty toxin, and they tested it as a pesticide for use in agriculture. DEET can eat through plastic overtime, so imagine what it does to your skin and insides. I have seen people lose their watch faces to this stuff, including my own. It would destroy the inside of the tour van, when for some reason tourists would spray it as you pulled away, only to end up choking on the toxic fog, and there isn't even a mozzie in sight yet. It is best not to apply it at all until they bother you, or are about to enter an area where you are likely too. In the dry season I don't think it is needed at all, but pale white skin, smelling sweetly, varies from person to person, so take some with you just in case. I made a deal with the mozzies, so that as long as I brought them fresh meat to feed upon regularly then they would leave me alone. It worked out well, as I usually had a couple of sweet tasting alabaster skinned donors with me. There are many "myths" about what does and doesn't attract mosquitoes. They are just that: myths. The laws of attraction for mosquitoes are still largely unknown and a well-funded research project. To date, DEET seems to be the only consistent combative method.

Once stocked up with all the necessary sundries, such as repellant, water, candy, and you have all the necessary clothing you need, it is off to the park. Choice of clothing varies from tourist to tourist, but one thing that is important, is the choice of footwear. Teva style sandals are great, but can lead to tiny stones sticking in your feet. For walking in the water, we found that old training style shoes (sneakers) were best, though people wore allsorts.

German Grape Smugglers

Actually, I have had tourists wear everything imaginable. Once, a German traveler, who decided that wearing nothing but skintight yellow grape smugglers, a pair of German military para boots and a ten-gallon Stetson, was appropriate attire for a swamp tromp with six Italian girls along for the laugh.

The mosquitoes soon sorted him out though, and he wore a shirt with long pants for the rest of the day. I wish I could include a photo but I do not want to keep anyone up at night from the nightmares.

As you approach the end of the built up area of Palm Drive, there will be a US Postal Service building on the right hand side. The gas station preceding this is your last chance to make that valuable fuel and supply stop, if you have not done so already. After a short drive and past the USPS building, you will enter agricultural land, where on both sides it will be green and plush, or maybe with yellow squash ready for harvesting, or dry mud, ready for the next crop. Migrant workers may be picking the fruit and vegetables all the way in towards the park entrance.

The process of being able to grow crops in South Florida is both difficult and easy. Obviously, the sun is beating down the majority of the year, and there is no shortage of rain during the wet season. However, the soil is next to zero, and any soil that you do see is a mix of ground up limestone (a process known as scarifying or scarification) and combined with topsoil. Agricultural processes here use a vast amount of phosphates, which then poison the water table of the Everglades, and uses gallons of water drained from the Everglades, that results in your yellow squash, tomatoes and green beans, amongst many others. I am of course pragmatic enough to understand the need for food, though not necessarily supportive of some of the processes used to bring it to the dinner table. They pump the water across these fields by tapping directly into the aquifer below, which is around twenty feet down.

I can remember a few times when I have run the 20-mile circuit from Florida City to the park entrance and back. The blistering and fluid draining humidity that results in dripping wet clothing, and covered in the agricultural dust, and god only knows what toxins. The brown slime of sweat mixed with dirt, camouflaging my skin with a disruptive pattern, and soaking my shoes in a thick sludge, all of course in the pursuit of health and fitness. The only time I found to be the most suitable, and with less field dust was around 4 AM, so if you are looking to get active around Florida City, then you should prepare for an early rise. I actually once ran the 50-mile ultra-marathon distance from Florida City to Flamingo at the southern tip of the National Park. Even with a hydration pack, electrolytes, and calories along the way, and with food at the end, I had still managed to lose around 2lbs.

Passing this first patch of agricultural land after leaving the concrete blot of Florida City, you will approach a junction that is famous to both the locals and tourists.

Mentioned in all good travel guides such as Lonely Planet, is the site of 'Robert is Here'. Established in 1959 by Robert himself, this fruit and vegetable stand extraordinaire is run by Robert and his ever-growing family. When he started out, he was only six-years old and stood on this corner selling his father's cucumbers. His father disappointed with his initial sales decided to give Robert a sign to place above him saying 'Robert is Here'. This business has been a bustling and commercially rewarding venture for Robert ever since.

It has now grown into a fully stocked farm, a veritable cornucopia of assorted tropical fruits and vegetables. Most of the produce you may never have heard of, such as the sapote (chocolate pudding fruit), or the monstera, dragon fruit, magic fruit, Jackfruit, mamey and so many more. He has regular live musicians playing, and the store is busy and bustling with tourists, even in the off-season it is busy with the locals.

If there is only one reason to stop here then it has to be the milkshakes. I can say with hand on heart that you will never taste a milkshake like it, made with fresh tropical fruits of your choice right before your eyes, along with iced milk (a mix of low fat ice cream and yoghurt). They are a decadent elixir that is sexual gratification through a straw. My personal favorite is the combined chocolate, key lime and strawberry, though it is not on the menu.

The milkshakes were a welcome treat upon returning from a long day in the glades, along with a chance for my tourists to get themselves a few treats for dinner, or to take home, such as preserves and chutneys and various other goodies. If you get the chance, then you must stop here, if only for a milkshake, or to sample (free of charge) the weird tropical fruits that are up for grabs.

From this junction you can head in one of two directions to reach the park entrance. The best way is to follow the large brown signs guiding you to the park, and turn left at this junction, or what would be south from Roberts car parking lot, and down Tower Road, SW 192nd Avenue (towards 9336 the Old Ingraham Highway). As you reach the junction towards the end of SW 192nd Avenue, about one and a half miles down on your left hand side, you will see one of Florida's all too familiar community settlements; a gated community. Actually, I jest. The gated community I am talking about is the Dade Correctional Institution, which is a penal fortification that has been there in the humid and dusty farmland settlement since 1996. It houses adult male inmates as part of the Miami Dade Correctional system.

If you were to travel straight on at this junction another few miles and continue down Tower Road, you would reach the Everglades

Alligator Farm. The farm is a popular tourist attraction, and often the only way for someone to catch a glimpse of the Everglades without venturing into the National Park, perhaps due to time, financial or physical constraints, or even just by choice. The farm is a great opportunity to take an airboat ride, if that is something you wish to experience. The farm is also a good opportunity to try alligator meat if you fancy it. However, most South Florida restaurants serve it. In fact, along this same road before you reach the prison, there is a small sandwich and burger joint called the 'Gator Grill', where you can get a tasty gator burger. Alligator meat tastes like a fishy, chicken, and pork combination for want of a better description, but more so of whatever taste accompanies it, such as the deep fried batter or chili lime sauce. People say it tastes like chicken, but it really doesn't, there is a chicken taste and texture to it I suppose, but it really has its own flavor. Nevertheless, everything they serve here is tasty and plentiful.

Incarceration on Vacation

One of the things I loved about Florida was that it is a great place for running. I found that the heat made it very enjoyable. Although for conditioning purposes the lack of undulation, make it less than ideal.

One of my favorite routes from within Florida City was through the farmlands situated southwest of the hostel grounds. The majority of this land is private acreage, split between various farms, all growing palm trees of one species or another. To get into this area requires running about one mile through crazy stray dog country, and then you are into blisteringly hot palm groves. The heat made worse due to the reflection back onto your skin from the white limestone below you. This reflective underfoot accounts for the majority of the ground and trail.

The area is abundant in wildlife from rat snakes, pythons, spiny-tailed iguanas, Nile monitors, and egrets, to roseate spoonbills and more. The route ran behind the prison, which was a route I had run for years.

On this one occasion, I was wearing nothing but a pair of shorts and training shoes with my mp3 player and nothing else. I had been running for about 5-miles, and was now on my return back past the prison towards home.

As I ran, I looked over and could see a white truck driving towards the rear of the prison, doing its continuous loops checking for escapees. After a few minutes, I got the sense of something going on around me, though I couldn't hear clearly due to my ear buds blasting out U2 music. Suddenly I disappeared into a cloud of dust, and the white truck came screeching to a halt in front of me, forcing me to reach out my arms to its rear, to prevent me from smashing straight into it.

The prison guards who were driving the truck jumped out to find out who I was, and what I was doing. It soon became apparent that they had assumed that I was an escapee, and because I had no ID, they detained me until they could conduct a headcount back at the jail.

They took me to the main gate to question me, and nobody seemed to understand my desire to run in the Florida heat, or in the dusty fields and trails at the back of the prison. One of the guards when questioning me after I had told them I was from the UK (as this was before a time when I became a legal resident) said to me:

"You ever heard the phrase, come here on vacation stay in incarceration" followed by a laugh.

Eventually the headcount came back as complete and I was able to leave, though the strange events of the day were not yet over it seemed.

I was walking back to the hostel after losing my running mojo, and had just left the palm groves when yet another truck came screeching to halt before me. This time it was nothing to do with the prison or me though. The driver jumped out of the truck, ran off into the woods, and then a few moments later emerged from the bushes with a big duffle bag. Looking at me, he said:

"Gotta hide your stash somewhere right!" while jumping back into his

truck and then speeding off.

I was sure that the heat had impaired my sense of reality, however I got back to the hostel grabbed a cold beer and slumped in the hammock, pondering the last few hours. Yet another surreal day spent in South Florida.

Leaving the prison behind, you will head into the park by taking a right at this junction by the prison. You will pass through field after field of various produce and migrant workers picking away, scarified limestone topsoil baking in the sun like the top of a peach cobbler, ready for the next crop. You will also cross the many canals that control the water flow in and around the park. These canals are a great place to find alligators, caiman and the odd python, if you are lucky.

After a short time, ahead, and in the distance, you will see stretching across the horizon, a green wall of pine. This pine wall marks the parks boundary. The approach ends, arriving shortly at the entrance to the Everglades National Park.

Everglades National Park East Coast Entrance

CHAPTER FOUR - Arrival

"Life is not measured by the number of breaths that we take, but by the moments that take our breath away" - Unknown

Arrival

The pine horizon shrinks to hardwood hammock walls and open sawgrass prairies. There are mixed aromas and a stifling heat that hits you like an ascent into deprived oxygen. You are now in the Everglades.

I would usually drive with the windows open, foregoing the air conditioning, and as soon as we hit the park boundary, you can smell the change in the air. I think there is a unique atmosphere to the Everglades. It is a combination of smells, visuals, and feelings, that all add substance to memories. Arriving early morning was my favorite time, the dew on the grass, and the early light and heat creeping in, an indescribable freshness that leaves the olfactory receptors tingling with joy.

One of the things that would always raise eyebrows upon entering the park is the sign with a black panther on it. This of course refers to the Florida panther (*Puma concolor*), which is not black at all. In theory the panther could be spotted anywhere throughout the 1.6 million acre expanse. There are areas that some seem to frequent, and the signs are placed relating to the tracking data for this rare and endangered species.

There are constant reminders about the speed restrictions, which are strictly enforced. You will often see a ranger vehicle pulling someone over for excessive speed. These speed restrictions are of course to protect the wildlife as well as the tourists.

Immediately on both sides, as you clear the initial vegetation from the main entrance, there will be a wide expanse of sawgrass and muhly grass, along with pine trees and interspersed hardwood hammock islands. Depending on the time of year this may be flooded, but a little more about that shortly.

At the side of the road, you will notice small clearings located at equidistant points, these are culverts. Culverts are concrete tunnels that run under the road from one side to the other, allowing the water to flow underneath them. This prevents flooding, and allows the continual flow of water southwards, as the road is essentially one large dam preventing the historic Everglades from ever existing as it once did.

These culverts, though often unassuming, and easy to miss, are a great place to stop and see what you can find, especially during the early to late springtime. As the water levels of the Everglades recede during the dry season these culverts will hold the water a little longer and so wildlife will happily spend every day there, especially alligators. The very first culverts you go over as you enter the park are annually home to one alligator hogging what little water remains, often including some babies. Yes, that's right, baby alligators. Unbelievably, they do have babies. I say that sarcastically, after the question by a stunned tourist who didn't think alligators could have babies. I still to this day have no comment in reply to that question.

There is a lot more going on out there than you can imagine. In fact, the Everglades can seem very bland at first glance, this I suspect is due to the lack of any major elevation, and so it is not instantly aesthetically appealing. It would appear to be just grass and trees if you only take a casual glance. The whole of Florida is essentially flat, but thanks to the small changes in elevation, the landscape can, and does change almost instantly from one to another. When I say small changes, I mean from inches to only a few feet.

As you enter, you will see on the right, a large building. This building is the Ernest F. Coe Visitor Center, which also contains the offices for the park headquarters. The visitor center is a great stop before, or after you enter the park. I would suggest visiting before you enter however, so that you can give yourself an overall insight to the Everglades. There is a great little store with some fantastic books available, along with various other collectibles and gifts. They also have a large collection of educational displays and a movie that plays at regular intervals, which is worth the fifteen minutes of playtime if you can spare it. It is of course fine to choose not to spend time in this center at all, there is another similar center located at the end of the park road at Flamingo, which I will talk about later.

If you continue traveling the road, you will then come to what is actually the main gate, though you are already in the park boundary itself, you still have to pay, which is what comes next.

There will be staff operating the gate twenty-four hours a day during the busy season. Although during the quiet season it is often unmanned, especially during the night, as there are not many visitors, if any at all that are entering the park at that time of year, though it is my preferred time. The rangers' here are friendly and very helpful, and they will provide you with a nice color map for your visit. The receipt you get here is also good for seven days, so you can come and go as you please.

You are now officially in the Everglades and one of the million or so visitors that it receives each year. Drive slowly and take it in, stop where you can, and keep an eye out for anything that looks interesting. Treat the park and its inhabitants with respect and take all warnings seriously. Above all though, allow yourself the chance to connect with it, and let the experience flow over and through you.

At this point, I would hand a map to everyone in the van and let everyone know I would soon be pulling over to give a short talk about the Everglades. It is now that the tour really begins, whether you are on a guided tour, in a car, on a bike, or even on foot. Don't forget the culverts as you move along the road, you might find something amazing.

From here, you leave the pineland area where the main gate is situated. This pineland is also the home to the employee accommodation, which is a quaint bunch of cabins in the woods for those seasonal employees who come down from the colder north to work through the dry tourist season. As you depart the pineland of the main gate, you will enter into one of the major ecosystems that you will experience throughout the park.

Looking at the map given to you at the entrance there are essentially nine major ecosystems, all color-coded on the map, with the legend towards the top. The ecosystem at this point is a freshwater marl prairie. It is the one that is most often associated with the Everglades, in that is a vast open expanse of sawgrass. During the wet season, this will be flooded from the summer rains, and the flow from Lake Okeechobee. In the dry season, it becomes a dry and crispy prairie. This grassy and wet expanse is what you see the airboats skimming across the top of in movies and on TV shows.

I mentioned previously that the Everglades are mainly famous for two things, airboats and alligators. You will almost certainly see some alligators, seasonally dependent of course, and will vary from one to a few hundred possibly throughout your day. It is unlikely, however, that you will encounter an airboat, and there is a simple reason for this. In the park boundary, park staff, such as rangers and scientists, are the only people who can legally operate airboats, there is no public use allowed.

If you travel along Tamiami Trail (Highway 41), you will encounter an airboat tour almost every 50-feet (slight exaggeration). They are quite common in South Florida, except the tours are on privately owned land outside of the park boundary itself. Within the park interior, they are reserved for use by the park scientists and rangers only. It is unlikely you will ever see one. Although, you may hear one in the distance, especially near the park entrance, or at the Royal Palm Visitor Center, as nearby is the staff accommodation and offices located in the pineland area, where there is an airboat launch.

You are welcome to take a tour on one outside of the park. There is a good one located at the Alligator Farm, just down the road from the correctional institute, but not in the Everglades National Park, where you can forget them. Besides, they are noisy, and destroy the landscape and scare wildlife away anyway, so good riddance in my humble opinion.

Driving along the road you will initially be heading in a north-westerly direction, though ultimately heading southwards, as the road will later take a turn in that direction. The freshwater marl prairie (marl being mud and limestone) that you are driving through is Taylor Slough (pronounced slew), and it runs under a few bridges along this area of the road, and through the culverts. A slough is like a river inside a river. It is slightly deeper than its surrounding areas of marsh, and tends to have a slow, yet measurable current. Taylor Slough is moving at around 100-feet per day, thanks to the decline of Florida as you head south. Although anywhere you look, the water never seems to move or flow in any direction, it is unperceivably slow.

There are two major Sloughs within the Everglades National Park, Taylor Slough and Shark River Slough. Shark River Slough is much larger, and responsible for the vast majority of water flow in the western and southwest part of the park. The headwaters of Taylor Slough provide the main flow of water to the eastern part of the National Park.

Historically, Taylor Slough had the nickname "dead pecker slough", referring to its affect upon male genitalia when wading through the cold water during winter, frogging for pig frogs by spear in the moonlight. Battered pig frog or frog kebabs, are still popular today, and very tasty, as long as you can keep them on your plate. That may sound like a jest, however, frogs legs do still move around when grilling, so you feed one leg through the other at the knee joint to prevent too much movement.

Talking of wading through Taylor Slough, I can take this opportunity to tell you about an amazing wilderness trip that I took through Taylor Slough with some friends from the hostel and the National Park Service back in 2003.

Taylor Slough Canoe Sail

Back in 2003, Rustin, Drew, Owhnn, some others, and I, including some Everglades National Park employees, set out to take a multi-day expedition off trail, through the Everglades. This was something we tried to do regularly, but this particular trip had its own particularly memorable story. These types of trip were separate to the hostel overnight and multi-day trips, and didn't include paying customers, this was our own time well spent.

These kind of trips involved sticking everything you need in your canoe and getting from point A to point B, and dealing with whatever you encountered along the way.

We spent three days pushing our canoes fully loaded through sawgrass, with a few brief chances to get in and paddle, or sail, as we had a sail attachment that we could rig up in our specially adapted canoe.

Pushing the canoes is no easy task though. Imagine ankle to waist deep water and mud, the depths of which vary with each step, combined with pushing or pulling a 17-foot (70lb.) canoe. We were also fully laden with enough food for ten people for three days, including a large cooler, clothes, camping equipment and a sailing rig. We did this for at least twelve hours the first day, and then some more the next. My trousers were shredded from the serrated sawgrass, as were my wrists and any other exposed skin the sawgrass could find. Actually, it is surprising where sawgrass can find itself.

On day one of what was to become a most memorable adventure, I found myself suffering from chaffing in my buttocks due to sweat, heat and friction, as we pushed inch after inch through the unforgiving serrated grass. During one of the breaks, I reached for my first-aid kit and got some sudocrem (nappy rash cream) to apply to the chaffed area. I applied it generously for instant and soothing relief, at least for a short time anyway. After about twenty minutes, we decided to carry on, and though initially it felt quite nice, as the cream helped the sore skin glide together, it was short lived as it soon started to sting again. This time it was a lot more intense and after ten minutes or so, I just couldn't take it anymore.

We stopped and I went to apply some more cream, but there was now blood everywhere. What had actually happened was that during the initial application, I had managed to get a small piece of sawgrass stuck on my creamy fingers, and then put it between my buttocks. This stray sawgrass fragment had then rubbed up and down against both sides as I had walked, shredding my skin. I still clench tightly at that memory.

We had started during sunrise in early October, 2003, at a place called Frog Pond. Frog Pond was a couple of miles north of the park road, and then we made our way through Taylor Slough, into the heavily tourist populated area of the Anhinga Trail. We entered into the Anhinga trail area to shouts from onlookers who were warning us:

"There are alligators in there!" they screamed, as they must have thought we were all crazy.

We then made our way through some real backcountry, and into the mangrove areas. We hacked our way through with machetes, as we weren't following a marked trail, and then finally out into the saltwater of Florida Bay. Once in the open we could set up our sails and sail down to the Florida Keys.

Actually, during our last night in Florida Bay, before heading to the Keys, we had a wonderful night paddle, where we got to experience illuminating the waters with our paddle strokes, as we disturbed bioluminescent dinoflagellates, often just referred to as bioluminescence. These are marine plankton that illuminates the water like a radioactive leak. If you can imagine holding a fluorescent lamp under the water, then this is what it looks like, and it is amazing to paddle through.

During day one, we had just made our way through the busy Anhinga Trail area, where we then disappeared through the other side into the backcountry. Once we had made our way through, there was some more pushing and then a welcome interlude, as we made our way onto an old airboat trail, once used regularly by the park service. We now had a chance to put the sails up. I was in the front (stern), and my good friend Rustin was in the rear (bow) of the canoe, and we were now making some headway.

I had decided that I needed to take a bathroom break and not the pee in a bottle kind. Without informing my co-pilot, I just stood up and squatted over the side (starboard). All of a sudden, we found ourselves in chest deep water, surrounded by alligators. The sail was soaking wet, all the equipment including the contents of the cooler was now floating all around us, and the canoe filled with water. Rustin's expression was a picture, and he just looked at me, dripping with water and algae and simply said:

"What the F***" and then we both started laughing.

The other boats were sailing away ahead of us with no idea of what had happened, as we struggled to right the boat. We then had to bail out the water, gather up the food, including some lovely marinated steaks floating away in Ziploc baggies, and then get back to the trip. It was all good fun, and a great laugh.

The first night was also interesting as most of our equipment was still wet from the unexpected dip, and as we were out in the middle of nowhere we had to sleep in the canoes, so the sleeping bags and Thermarest pads were a little damp. The mosquitoes that night were some of the worst I had ever experienced. The water levels were high and it was the tail end of the summer. We were sleeping out in the open amongst the dwarf mangroves at the head of the brackish waters, and all we had were some mozzie nets and some repellent. Rustin was again swearing aloud, as he became victim to the mosquitoes, frustrated that I would not pass him the repellent, as I thought it was funny listening to him whine.

We all had a great trip though and we went through some stunning areas of outstanding natural beauty, and yes, Rustin and I are still good mates, though he is a real reactionary. He is, however, one of the best and most knowledgeable outdoors people and guides that I have ever met, along with a fantastic photographer.

Let us now head back to the park road and on with our journey to Royal Palm and the Anhinga trail.

If you remember before I went off on a tangent about my trip, we were in the middle of Taylor Slough, driving along the road, at the entrance to the park. As you drive along, I suspect you will see plenty of egrets, herons, hawks, and the fabulously entertaining black vulture (*Coragyps atratus*).

I would usually make one or two small stops, the first being at the side of the road in a small layby. There is an information board here telling you about Taylor Slough, and a little overview of the park. I would stop here and give a short overview of the Everglades, and the tour itself, mainly covering what I did in the first two chapters here in the book. I would talk about the history, geology, weather and the wildlife, along with a rough itinerary for the day ahead.

It is worth taking the chance to get out here, if for nothing else than to get your first feel for the air of the Everglades, hear the silence (aside from passing cars), and see what you can see. Typically, at this point I would introduce people early on to the infamous sawgrass. I would demonstrate why you shouldn't touch it, or what it can do to the skin and clothing, usually by cutting my skin or shorts to demonstrate its small paper like cuts.

Sawgrass (*Cladium jamaicense*) is the bane of exploration in the Everglades. Forget the alligators, snakes and mozzies, sawgrass is a constant pain in the butt (literally if you remember my earlier story) when exploring the Everglades. Sawgrass has spiny serrated leaf blades that resemble a saw, and technically, it is sedge and not a grass.

Sawgrass will only cut one way due to the position of its teeth. When it does, it in itself is not too bad, but combined with sweat or mozzie repellent it can be irritating. The cuts are easily infected, and so they can become a real irksome first aid situation if prolonged exposure is experienced. However, not that many people spend much time walking through it, and those that do usually wear some type of protective clothing to help them.

Sawgrass can grow up to around nine feet, and can be real thick and sturdy enough to cut quite deeply, so it is an important consideration for backcountry travel in the Everglades.

Savory Sawgrass

A quick backcountry survival tip for you though. The young shoots of sawgrass are edible. Best plucked from the base, while being careful of the serrated edges, and then peeling away the outer white to reveal the inner. It is nice either raw or cooked. It is tasty fried in some garlic butter with salt and pepper, or added to a wilderness stew.

Something you will discover about the Everglades if you spend a lot of time there is that most of its flora and fauna is venomous, poisonous, edible or medicinal. Venomous and poisonous are different things, which I will go over when we talk about some of the snakes.

Moving on a little from the layby you will head towards the turn off which leads you to the Royal Palm Visitor Center, and Anhinga Trail. Before you get to the turn though, there will be two large culverts on either side of the road, just before the buildup of vegetation. These are great in the spring months to spot alligators. These culverts in particular are almost guaranteed to have some babies in them during springtime, along with the mother, so don't go trying to pick one up. Technically, picking up a baby alligator is harassment, and carries hefty fines.

You could spend hours at these culverts, alone, and taking photographs, watching in awe. This would typically be the first real chance to see an alligator up close for people on my tours, if we had not seen one previously. There is no guarantee that there will be one here though, so stop where you like.

I will now, like on the tour use this opportunity to explain a little about alligators, before we get to the hustle and bustle of the next major stop.

The American alligator has many myths associated with it, one of which of course is that it will eat you. Though getting too close is unwise, as it is to any wild animal, for an alligator to eat you, it would need to be large, very hungry, and you would need to be very small and unlucky. However, this does not detract from their obvious raw predatory power and awe. People do suffer injury from alligators in Florida each year, as they do with venomous snakes, though most are likely the result of alcohol or stupidity, and not a hungry reptile.

American alligator. Courtesy of Rustin Gooden

The American alligator has one of the most powerful, if not the most powerful bite in the animal kingdom, or at least its family does, and its family is the crocodilians. Their jaws can crush bone at an average of fifteen-hundred pounds per square inch, and even more in large alligators. Possibly, up to around five-thousand in a crocodile, either way it is strong. To put it in perspective the average lion is around seven-hundred psi.

Crocodilians are a species that comprises of twenty-three distinct varieties. The Everglades are home to two, the American alligator and the American crocodile (*Crocodylus acutus*). If you are lucky, you may spot the odd common caiman (*Caiman crocodilus*), though you probably won't be able to tell the difference from an alligator, though I think they resemble a crocodile more than an alligator. There is only one other family of alligator in the world, and that is the Chinese alligator (*Alligator sinensis*).

During the tours, one of the first questions asked is:

"What is the difference between an alligator and a crocodile, especially as they are part of the same family?"

Well, they are actually extremely different visually, and it does not take long to be able to spot the differences. The obvious distinction is that they are a different color, but also amongst the two species in Florida, then it is usually straight forward as the American crocodile is saltwater and the American alligator is a freshwater reptile.

The vast majority of crocodilians you encounter in the Everglades would be the American alligator, as we know that the Everglades is predominantly freshwater. In fact, the alligator is everywhere, and not just in the Everglades, it is throughout the whole of South Florida, and all the way up as far as North Carolina, and west towards Texas. Some are even a little further out than that. However, the Everglades are their real home, and you will see hundreds during a typical day during the low water months.

The alligator is a dark obsidian olive, and some appear jet black. This is due to the higher levels of melanin in the skin, making them darker than the American crocodiles that are typically a grey to light olive green color. The different levels of melanin are quite important, because the darker you are, the more heat you will attract. Crocodilians are reptiles (or herptiles, depending on whom you speak too, which is a contraction from the study of both amphibians and reptiles), and they are cold blooded, which means they need to heat up their own blood, unlike us mammals.

Reptiles are ectothermic, so they rely on their surroundings to regulate their body temperature, which is why you see snakes curled up in the sun, or alligators and crocodiles sat around all day doing nothing but sunbathing. Their blood has also found to be antibacterial, and so wounds heal rather quickly. Scars, chunks, and holes are common markings on alligators and crocodiles from fighting and attacks. Alligator blood has been studied, and found to combat over twenty strains of infection and bacteria including HIV.

Alligators are temperate reptiles so can endure colder temperatures than crocodiles, which are tropical reptiles. This endurance comes from the darker skin and explains them being found in the more northern states of the USA, which are a lot colder than South Florida.

The obvious differences are the different colors, and different locations, as the American crocodile prefers the saltwater areas, which are quite a ways from the entrance to the park (around 40 miles) with the exception of a rare few.

Croczilla is one of the rare few, residing at Nine Mile Pond. Croczilla is a behemoth of a reptile who lives at this popular canoe trail, which is only very slightly brackish (brackish is a mix of salt and freshwater), and here it is almost fresh. Yet he dominates the waters here amongst the alligators. He is a spectacular site when found sunbathing on a bank somewhere.

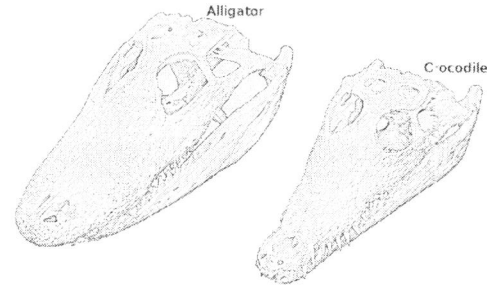

An alligators head is short and rounded near the snout, whereas a crocodiles is long and thin with a much longer and narrower mouth and jawline. Alligator eyes protrude higher from the water, whereas crocodile's eyes sit shallower. With an alligator when its mouth is closed, you can typically only see the upper teeth, which point downwards, unless it has some type of deformity, which a few do. A crocodile displays both the upper and some lower teeth, making it look a little more sinister.

Though it may look ferocious, both American species of crocodilians are typical Floridians, and would rather laze around in the sun all day, taking a dip when it suits them. They have little interest in any major activity, least of all trying to eat you. There are plenty of fish and turtles and an abundance of other food sources available to them.

Going back to the color one more time, have you ever noticed that when an alligator appears in some form of artwork, such as in a children's book, or perhaps as a toy, they always seem to be green? If you have ever seen an alligator, you will know they are nowhere near such a color, dark olive at best. This is a historical thing.

When the Spanish landed in Florida back in the 1500's, it must have appeared to be a very strange land indeed. What they thought about alligators I have no idea, except that when they saw them they probably were green a lot of the time. This wasn't their color, but a layer of algae laying on them, and it is still not uncommon to see them peeking just above a thin film of light green algae laying on top of a still pond. To the Spanish they probably appeared to be green, but this is just nature's own camouflage. The alga is sparser these days due to the nature of the water flow, which differs greatly from the historical Everglades.

Talking of the Spanish, the term alligator is an anglicized version of *el lagarto*, which means 'the lizard'. Many of Florida's names are Spanish in origin, including Florida itself, named by Juan Ponce de Leon, who upon discovery referred to it as *La Florida*, which translates to Flowery land, or Land of Flowers.

We now know alligators color and habitats, which differs from its cousin the American crocodile that I will go over a little later, when we get to the saltwater areas. Before we move on though, here are some additional facts about alligators.

Alligators have around eighty teeth, and they are hollow with another one growing ready to replace it, should it fall out when chomping through a turtle shell for dinner. They will go through upwards of two-thousand or more teeth during a typical lifespan of around thirty to forty years in the wild. I have a large bag of them on my shelf that I collected over the years from rotting corpses or skeletons. The various birds and insects make very short work of any dead animals in the Everglades, from flesh to bone in just a few days.

They can hold their breath for long periods, depending on what you read, for maybe up to eight hours or more. I cannot validate that, but I have definitely seen them just sitting at the bottom in the mud underwater for up to an hour at least. They hold their breath and do not breathe under water, as they do not have gills, which is a common misconception. They also have an extra eyelid. This eyelid is translucent, allowing the alligator to see underwater without damaging the eye. Out of the water, the alligator uses its regular eyelid like humans.

They also have an interesting feature allowing you to estimate their size when under the water, with only the snout and eyes sticking out. When you can only see the small bumps of its nostrils and the mounds of its eyes, if you guess the distance between them in inches, then that distance in feet is the relative size of the alligator. For example, if the distance between the eyes and nostrils is about six inches, then the alligator is approximately 6-feet in length. This can be surprising, as an alligator often looks much smaller in the water than it is out of the water.

By far the most amusing fact you will often hear about alligators is the speed at which they can run. Some of the rangers in the park (most of whom are seasonal, except for the local experts such as Frankie or Larry and a few others), will repeatedly spout that alligators can run at up to 35mph. Now personally I think this is a tad of an exaggeration. The fastest man on the planet can reach around an average of 24mph. I would love to see some 1000lb. dumpy lizard with webbed feet and stumpy legs extending a foot long, outrun him. If you ever see one walk, it is like watching a fat drunk sausage zigzag awkwardly and lethargically for about ten seconds, before they need to stop and rest. The fact is though, they are very quick in terms of reaction, and can move on land quicker than you think but only in short bursts, but you will not see one in the Olympics anytime soon.

If you are close enough and it is annoyed enough, it will be able to grab you. I always made sure that I was faster than my tourists who were behind me. Do not worry if you can outrun the animal, only worry that you can outrun the person or people behind you.

I think I read somewhere (don't quote me) that the fastest ever recorded time was about 11mph for prolonged movement, but due to their stature, they are not built for endurance, and are more anaerobically than aerobically suited. This brings me to how they breathe.

Crocodilians breathe the same way as avian species. Their breathing is a unidirectional flow, as oppose to air coming in and out of the lungs, and this helps with the ability to be able to hold their breath for very long periods. This helps when staying underwater, where their metabolism and heart rate also slows down considerably.

I mention this for good reason on my tours, to demonstrate that just because you can't see an alligator; it doesn't mean there isn't one there. I will repeatedly emphasize this fact with sadistic glee, when they are chest deep in the middle of the water, with no clue as to what is with them. This is especially more exciting under moonlight, though I never lost a tourist to a gator. There were a few narrow escapes, but all limbs as far as I know remain intact.

Getting back to traveling down the road, and heading towards the

Royal Palm Visitor Center. You will see the sign to take a left off from the main road and head to Royal Palm. As you take this turn, you yet again see another panther sign. There is a Florida panther known to frequent this area, so keep your eyes peeled, but don't hold your breath.

The Florida panther (*Puma concolor*) also known as (*Felis concolor*), is sadly an endangered species numbering one-hundred to two-hundred in the wild. Panther, puma, cougar, mountain lion are all different names for the same type of cat, in Florida it is called the Florida panther, and it is dying out due to being hunted ferociously during the 1800's and 1900's. It was one of the first endangered species in the USA, listed as endangered in the 1970's, and remains one of the most endangered mammals on the planet. The ones that remain are tagged and tracked constantly, but due to losses in their habitat and disease, it seems unlikely that they will recover with so few remaining. You might see their footprints from time to time in the mud, or remains of their kill, but actually seeing one is unlikely, though remember they are probably looking at you.

As you head now in a southwesterly direction towards the main visitor trails, which tourists frequent all through the busy season, you will be driving through what is a hardwood hammock area on the edge of the pinelands. Shortly you will come across a right turn, but you will head straight past that to reach the Royal Palm Visitor Center.

If you were to take this turn, you could either go straight on towards Old Ingraham Highway, or follow the main road around, through the pinelands forest, along to where the park scientists are based, out in the Daniel Beard Research Center. This road also terminates at a derelict missile base that once had its missiles trained towards Cuba during the Cuban missile crisis. These days it is deserted, and is a great place to find deer, pythons and other wildlife. There are sometimes tours of the missile base conducted weekly by the park service rangers. However, outside of these tours it remains closed to the public.

The Old Ingraham Highway is what is left of the historic highway (dirt track) which back in the 1920's was the first thoroughfare to Flamingo. In those days, you would have seen the old Model-T Fords trundling precariously along its raised limestone embankment, to make their way to the old fishing village that is now the terminus of the main park road. Today all that remains is an 11-mile or so straight track running through the wild backcountry of the Everglades, and you will rarely see any other people down here, as it is not well signposted and most people do not know it exists. It is marked on the map and does have a designated backcountry campsite available though.

In fact, over the twelve years or so, that I was in and out of the area, I never actually saw another soul ever around here. I used to frequent it regularly during the summer months, so I could run the 22-mile round trip back to my car. It does get extremely hot out there, and is a great place to see python, but the direct heat can be blistering.

This area and the pineland forest near it are a great place to explore if you are a keen adventurer, as there are a few hidden gems dotted all around. One such oddity, unexpected in Florida, is a cave (or sink hole that is large enough to get into, if you fancy a spot of spelunking). However, you should be careful, as it is home to a large alligator that likes to hang out in there. So make sure you have a flashlight and spare pair of underwear (as you are likely to soil the ones you are wearing). If you ask nicely at the hostel, they might give you the coordinates or organize an ad hoc trip to explore it. I will refrain from releasing the exact location to prevent an inundated mass of explorers trampling down the hammock where it is located. There are also a few hidden ponds and just some generally unexplored areas rich in wildlife. This area doesn't encounter people very often, so have a good forage, but be careful, if for no other reason than to avoid poisonwood, and poison ivy, which are common throughout the Everglades.

Continuing in our original direction towards the Royal Palm Visitor Center, you will drive once again through an open expanse of sawgrass, which is to your left. This area is one of my favorite locations for viewing the sunrise in early to mid-spring time. If you can make it out here for sunrise then I fully recommend you do so.

Sunrise is amazing here. The mist rising from the slough, the sawgrass prairie draped in thousands of tiny cobwebs weighted by droplets of water, glistening like tiny light bulbs in the early morning sun, as the wilderness begins yet another day. Maybe you will catch a whitetail deer bounding like Bambi through this fairy-tale land covered in cobwebs, as the new day comes into light. Whatever you see it will be yours and yours alone.

Finally, you will arrive at the end of the road into the car park for the Royal Palm Visitor Center, which comprises two major and famous trails: the Anhinga Trail and the Gumbo Limbo Trail. Both of which are incomparable, yet they are right next to each other.

CHAPTER FIVE – Royal Palm

"Adopt the pace of nature, her secret is patience" - Ralph Waldo Emerson

Royal Palm

Envisage a zoo filled with jungle plants and beautiful flowers, flowing waters and liquid mud pits. Fill that landscape with weird and wonderful creatures like alligators, snakes, skinks, butterflies, dragonflies, lizards, birds, fish, and turtles. Remove all the staff, all the fences, all the boundaries and cages, and let them roam freely. Now you must walk amongst them.

Royal Palm Visitor Center and the name Anhinga Trail are often names used interchangeably to refer to the same location. This is because the two are located together. Royal Palm Visitor Center is the name usually used for the whole area where you park and the buildings, and then there are two trails: the infamous Anhinga Trail and the Gumbo Limbo Trail.

The Anhinga Trail is famous the world over for its abundance of wildlife and opportunities for amazing photographs, whatever the camera. During a typical day here, you will see at least two or three professional photographers, taking hundreds of shots for various publications across the globe.

As an introduction to the Everglades, you could do much worse than to only visit here, and then just be done with it. However, you would be missing lots more adventures available further on in the park. This area does definitely provide plenty of wildlife for you to encounter up close, and in a natural wilderness setting, aside from the boardwalk of course.

I'm not a fan of observing wildlife amongst large amounts of people, but I would often visit here on the tours, allowing my group to take some photographs, and to introduce them to some Everglades science, such as facts about the alligators. This was so that during the rest of the tour they could focus on what was going on at that point in time. Although everything here is wild, it does feel a little contained or controlled, though it is not in anyway. However, at the end of visiting here, back in the van I would then clap my hands, rub them together and say:

'Right now we have done the tourist stuff, we can get on with the fun stuff', which after being so close to so many alligators would often leave them wondering what in the hell was coming next.

It may sound that I am not too keen on this location, though that is not true at all. In fact, it is one of my favorite places within the park. I just prefer it when it is less busy.

Sunrise is a great time here, as is night. Both will be absent from visitors and you have it all to yourself, apart from the company of alligators, snakes and hundreds of birds, fish and turtles. At nighttime, it is amazing, illuminated by the Milky Way or the moon, and a flashlight kept handy to scan across the water for the eerily red reflection of alligator eyes, which will accompany you all the way around the trail. It is peaceful and orchestral at the same time during the night here. There are splashes from fish, the odd sudden slap of water from a diving alligator, buzzing mosquitoes, and the grunt of pig frogs. The hostel night walk that comes here is a great opportunity to experience this place at night, along with an interpretive guide.

Depending on the time of year and time of day that you arrive here at the Royal Palm Visitor Center, you may find either an empty car park, or one that is overflowing with cars, camper vans, tour buses, and coaches. No matter when you arrive though, it is extremely likely that you will encounter the turkey vultures (*Cathartes aura*) and the black vultures that I mentioned previously. These are foul smelling, corpse eating, gothic looking creatures, and are everywhere throughout the Everglades. They are the parks undertakers, eating everything as soon as it dies. You will often meet them tucking into some rotting carcass somewhere in the park, especially in the mornings, as they sit down for a tasty breakfast of snake road kill. The black vultures tend to be the larger groups, with the odd turkey vulture in amongst them, differentiated by its red turkey like head, and with a browner hue to its feathers.

There is a warning about the vultures when you enter the National Park, and again with a sign as you enter the car park to this area. The reason for the warning is that they will land on your car in droves, picking at the rubber around your door seals and windows, including your windscreen wipers, causing quite a lot of damage in a very short time. Why they do this nobody seems to understand. My own personal opinion is that when rubber gets hot from the Florida sun, it gives off a fishy smell, though it's not as if I go around sniffing hot rubber. Rubber also has the texture and tactile feedback of flesh and tendons when pulled, similar to that of a rotting carcass, which is why I think they enjoy it so much. They certainly do enjoy it though, so beware.

There are a couple of preventative measures you can take, such as tying plastic bags to your windscreen wipers that seems to occasionally have some effect. There are also more drastic measures that the park itself has taken in recent years, where they have started to hang dead vultures (road kill) from trees in areas such as this, as a sort of scarecrow for the vultures. I personally doubt its effectiveness though, as I have seen vultures lining the tree branch from where the dead vulture is hanging.

Car Club

The car park had around twenty cars or so parked in it when we arrived, so we parked up and then headed off to the trails. We had been gone about an hour or so, when we started to near the end, which is when we saw a bunch of people starting to walk the trail. They were all wearing t-shirts with various car insignia such as Ferrari and Lamborghini etc. They were obviously in some type of car club on an afternoon jaunt out together. Fancy sports cars are very common in South Florida. Ten minutes in the ostentatious and affluent Miami and it is likely that you will see a Lamborghini, Bugatti or a Ferrari somewhere.

They headed off around the trail, and we headed back to the car park. There were thirty or so, beautiful Italian cars, in showy flame red, pearl white and glossy black, all lined up together. The vultures only seemed interested in these new flashy vehicles. On every one of them there was at least ten vultures scratching their talons over the paintwork, and pulling and clawing away at what rubber they could find. I guess the owners didn't like the idea of carrier bags on their cars. I wonder if they liked the vultures though.

As an ironic and amusing twist to this, was that at either end of where the cars had parked, there was a dead vulture hanging from a tree, meant to scare the vultures away.

In the car park as you arrive, aside from the populace of vultures and scavenging crows, one of the things that may strike you, is the large trees on the island in the middle. These are mahogany trees, or West Indies mahogany (*Swietenia mahagoni*), and the reason people tend to ask about them is that one in particular looks different to the rest, and so people wonder what type of tree it is. In fact, they are all the same, it is just this particular tree is draped with Spanish moss (*Tillandsia usneoides*).

Spanish moss is also known as Spanish beard moss, because of its likeness to the beards of the Spanish conquistadors. However, it is neither Spanish nor a moss. This prolific air plant is in high quantities throughout the Everglades and the Southern states in general, and when draped through the trees it adds a real ancient and Tolkeinesque beauty to the landscape.

An air plant or epiphyte is a plant that grows upon another host such as in this case, a mahogany tree. Air plants gather their nutrients from the sun, rain and the air around them. They take nothing from the host itself, which if it did would make it a parasite. An epiphyte however, does no intentional harm to its host, but sometimes it will inadvertently.

Birds drop the epiphytic seeds, or the wind carries them, and that is how they find their host. Probably one of the most famous epiphytes would be that of the orchid family (of which there are many, and some extremely rare like the cowhorn orchid). Epiphytes also include lichens and mosses (of which Spanish moss does not belong to), and bromeliads, which we will encounter shortly. This Spanish moss is growing all over, and hangs down like a weeping willow from this mahogany tree, making it appear to be something different than it is.

Spanish moss is a popular home for chiggers (*Trombiculidae*), which are small red biting mites. This is unfortunate, as over the years it has become useful for all sorts of stuffing and padding applications, including the first Model-T Ford cars, which allegedly had it as stuffing in the seats, according to some legend.

The rare swallow tailed kite (*Elanoides forficatus*) also uses it extensively for nesting. It is a wonderful sight to see a kite flying around, with clumps of Spanish moss trailing behind them; they seem to perform for the hordes of photographers with huge camera lenses, which have come from all over the world, often specifically to catch a rare glimpse of these birds. If the photographers only took a drive down to the Nine Mile Pond area, there are a couple of nesting pairs there each year, and always seem to be keen to put on an aerial show of some type, yet I have never seen a photographer there.

Swallow tailed kite. Courtesy of Rustin Gooden

In addition to the Spanish moss, you will also find this particular tree to be hosting a ton of other epiphytes such as bromeliads. Now, you may think you have never heard of them before, but there is one bromeliad that everyone is familiar with, which is the pineapple. If you see a bromeliad, you will understand, as it looks just like the top of a pineapple, but growing on the branch of a tree. Of course, pineapples do not grow on trees, although most people assume that they do. They grow on the ground, as they are a terrestrial herbaceous perennial that happens to belong to the *Bromeliaceae* family. The most common bromeliad in the Everglades has to be the cardinal air plant, which you can identify by its red spear like tip, similar to a *Heliconia*, and you can see some huge ones at regular intervals throughout the park.

They are probably the most abundant or at least most noticeable plant (aside from sawgrass) within the Everglades. They are in almost every tree from the hardwood hammocks, to the pineland, and down to the mangroves, where there is actually a carnivorous epiphyte, which we will discover later.

Okay then, that is the main attractions of the car park covered and we have not even joined the trails yet, though there is still some more to see in the car park itself, but nothing you will not see around the trails or elsewhere. However, before we hit the Anhinga Trail, it might be useful to know a little history of this particular area.

The Royal Palm Visitor Center gets its name due to the towering royal palm (*Roystonea regia*) trees you can see standing proud for miles around, as it is the tallest of the palm tree species. There is also one in the hostel garden, next to the waterfall. As an ecosystem, this area is a hardwood hammock. Mahogany is prolific here amongst many others, such as gumbo-limbo (*Bursera simaruba*), and pigeon plum (*Coccoloba diversifolia*), to mention a few. In fact, the hostel garden is just a small hardwood hammock, similar to this area.

The Royal Palm Visitor Center is on Paradise Key Hammock, which is the name for this particularly large hammock. Discovered in 1893, it was actually the first part of today's Everglades to come under federal protection, before the Everglades National Park ever existed, thanks to its diversity. This area became a State Park in 1916, then later consumed into the National Park, established in 1947.

Remember that the term hammock when referring to the landscape implies slightly higher elevation that tends to resist flooding, and will populate with hard wooded trees and jungle like undergrowth. Hammocks appear topographically or from aerial photographs of the Everglades as tree islands dotted amongst the sawgrass and pinelands.

The key to the hammocks diversity is as with all elements of the Everglades; is water and elevation. Perfectly situated in Taylor Slough, Paradise Key Hammock enjoys a lavish flow of water, and so retains a good portion of it through the dry season, thus lots of wildlife congregates here, and that today attracts plenty of tourists, and with good reason, as it is stunning and jostling with activity.

The water retention is thanks to its deeply excavated pond areas known as 'borrow pits', which is a term given to an area in the Everglades where they have dug up the limestone to use for construction. These pits which are also known as 'gator holes' have a depth that will hold enough water through winter, and thus will retain fish, which then attracts lots of birds. This leads to a wildlife extravaganza during the dry season, as it becomes an aviary during the winter months, except that nothing is confined. However, during a real 'dry' season this area can just be a mud bath, as all the water can evaporate, leaving an alligator filled chocolate pudding. The gators lay unperturbed in the moist sludge or dragging their bodies through, leaving tracks and trails all over. Including mud trails all across the path like a school kids dirty footprints across the kitchen floor, but with a large powerful tail and four webbed feet.

Remember that you are in their territory, and not the other way round. The minute you enter the park everything is wild and it can go anywhere it pleases and at any time. Pythons and alligators can be crossing the road, relaxing next to it or even on it, across or on pathways and boardwalks, venomous snakes in trees, snapping turtles, spitting vultures, and anything else you can imagine, can be anywhere. It is up to you to avoid it, and let it be. Do not harass anything, if you do not get a fine for harassment then you will probably at least get bitten or worse.

Anhinga Trail

Anhinga Trail is essentially a boardwalk that makes its way round a 0.8-mile loop of easy flat walking, which is accessible by wheelchairs. You can take pushchairs and prams around here too. These boardwalks offer easy tourist access, and are common in the park at easy to access areas near to the main road. However, having the facility to take pushchairs or prams around is not always a good idea.

Baby Food

It is not wise to place your pram or child close to an alligator sat on the path to take a photo. You would think that would be common sense, but apparently not for some.

There was this one time when a woman had actually put her young child (one or two years of age) sat on the grass about 6-feet away from a sunbathing alligator, and then stepped back from her baby about 10-feet to take a photo. People never cease to amaze me.

The recommendation is that you stay at least 15-feet away from alligators at any given time, though at Anhinga trail this is often impossible. Certainly, on the tours, you will always be well under 15-feet away, perhaps even touching them with your paddle, canoe, or feet when walking in the water.

The trail is short in distance, although during the winter months you should allow at least an hour to get around here. You will be stopping to take photographs every two minutes, aside from having to navigate through all the other visitors. It is for good reason that I refer to this trail as the 'Disney Trail', due to the surreal amount of visual entertainment and the vast number of onlookers.

At the trailhead, just on other side of the buildings that hold the restrooms and small store, you will notice a myriad of different birds speckled amongst the trees, or perched on the limestone rock walls that surround the pond area. If you glance into the water, you will notice copious amounts of fish, including gambusia, Florida gar, bass, Oscars and many more. There will be alligators basking on the banks and on the paths, vultures and crows everywhere. Anhinga will be diving in and out of the water, cormorants perched on the bird-poop stained rails, and egrets and herons fishing, and even the endangered wood stork can often be quite plentiful here.

Alligator walking across Anhinga Trail

This whole trail is just one large creature-fest. It is an aviary, aquarium, terrarium and a botanical abundance that is hard to see anywhere in the wild at such close quarters. If you were to visit this trail during the summer months, it is unlikely that you will see even one alligator here, and perhaps not even one person. The mosquitoes can be quite bad here during that time too, but during dry season, it is pretty much the standard for wildlife viewing in the Everglades.

Before we carry on, let us go over one thing, the name of the trail. The Anhinga Trail takes its name from one of its most entertaining and abundant bird inhabitants, the anhinga (*Anhinga anhinga*). The snakebird in its colloquial, due to its long slender s-shaped neck, is a water bird, yet unlike some water birds, it has poorly developed oil glands. The anhinga is classified as a darter, as you will often see it

Anhinga with catfish. Courtesy of Rustin Gooden

darting into and through the water like a torpedo hunting for fish with its long, slender, and sharp beak acting like a spear. This is very entertaining, as you will see them diving down or darting into the water, then you can see them swim around and pop up moments later with a fish stuck on the end of the beak. This of course then keeps their beak closed and they need to get the fish off, so they will shake their heads violently, or find a rock to do it for them. Once they have removed the fish or readjusted, in one fell swoop it is gone, swallowed. They will often catch and attempt to swallow fish that are far too big for them, which can be amusing, but you will be surprised at the size of the meals that their thin and slender neck can swallow.

Anhinga perch regally upon branches and rocks with their wings spread, drying them in the sun. Spending time here in the spring, you can get to watch them nesting. Over a few weeks, the chicks will hatch and then wait for the caring parent to feed them. Eventually these chicks will take their first flights and grow into adults. When the chicks are hatched, it looks like bundles of cotton wool are peppered amongst the trees all around the ponds, as they are fluffy and white and of course extremely cute.

As a guide, I would get to see them grow up and take flight by visiting daily. The adult female can be distinguished from the male by the creamy tan neck, whereas the male tends to be black, though they both have black bodies with a silver upper surface on the wings.

The anhinga is often confused with the cormorant, but only from a distance, as up close they are easily distinguishable. The double-crested cormorant (*Phalacrocorax auritus*) is very common in South Florida and certainly the Everglades. Its name refers to the double crest of white and black feathers that it displays during mating season. Adults are black, and the immature tend to be browner. Unlike the anhinga though, the cormorant does not display sexual dimorphism, so it can be difficult to spot a male or female, as there are no real obvious differences to the casual observer.

Unlike the anhinga, which has a straight beak, the cormorant has a hooked beak and a short neck with an orange-skinned face. During mating season, you can also observe a beautiful luminescent blue exhibited around, and in the mouths, as they regulate the body temperature with the beaks open, taking in air. The anhinga will also exhibit this blue around its eyes during mating season.

Birds, as with most wildlife at this trail, are quite comfortable with the human presence. They will happily sit while tourists put their heads right up close to them to take photographs. You can literally stroke their feathers as you walk next to them.

Let us now take a trip around the trail and see some of what it has to offer. It is a good idea when in the Everglades, to have a bird-spotting guide with you, and some binoculars for observing things in the distance. There have been over three-hundred and fifty species of bird spotted in the Everglades, from wading birds, birds of prey and land birds. I am merely introducing you to some of the common and more interesting species in context.

At the head of the trail there is a sign informing you that there is no smoking, no bikes, no food and no feeding of the animals. There are also two trashcans here, and as with most trash cans in the park they are raccoon proof, to prevent the raccoons from scavenging. It is kind of like a childproof lid where ironically no one can actually open it apart from the child. The handle has a lever inside it, for those wondering.

Damn Trashcans

A tourist was having trouble getting the lid open on one of these trashcans, as do most visitors. However, what was funny was that they were ranting and raving, as I was talking to rest of the group about a turtle we could see perched on a rock. I was just about to head over to give her a hand when she finally figured it out, and all of sudden as she opened it a raccoon jumped out, scaring the bejesus out of her. She stumbled backwards as the raccoon ran off into the brush behind. She fell right onto her bum, and then a bird flew over and pooped right onto her denim skirt landing on her lap. She sat bedazzled on the pavement, as we all looked on in hysterics. I went to help her up, trying not to laugh too much, but she did see the funny side moments later. We then all fell into laughter as she tried to remove the poop stain from her skirt.

I think those trashcans have now been removed, but nonetheless a funny story.

As you walk around the trail, on one side is vegetation and on the other will be the pond areas. Any of the wildlife here can be anywhere along the trail on either side, so keep your eyes peeled. They pulled a 13-foot python from the bushes at the side here a few years ago, and there was once a world famous wrestling bout between an alligator and a python filmed here back in 2003. The bout was between an alligator and python that fought it out in the water for twenty-four hours, until finally, a larger alligator got involved and the snake escaped. This wildlife-wrestling bout attracted hordes of people from all around, along with helicopters filming from above for the news. So always remember you are in the wild, and anything can come from anywhere at any time, something I like to reiterate repeatedly.

One of my favorite snakes that I have only ever seen in the wild twice, I first saw here, just on the grass to the right of the path at the beginning of the trail; the eastern coral snake (*Micrurus fulvius*). The coral snake is a highly venomous elapid snake from the *Elapidae* family, and is one of the four species of native venomous snakes found in South Florida and the Everglades. The other three are the eastern diamondback rattlesnake (*Crotalus adamanteus*), the water moccasin or more commonly known as cottonmouth (*Agkistrodon piscivorus*), and the dusky pygmy rattlesnake (*Sistrurus miliarius barbouri*), which are all from the *Crotalinae* family.

The coral snake has very small fixed fangs and round eyes, the remaining three venomous snake species found in the Everglades are all pit vipers with collapsible fangs and slanted eyes, with a heat-sensing pit between the eye and nostril. Two of these *Crotaline* snakes are also rattlesnakes that exhibit a trembling in the keratin rattle at the end of the tails. This usually signifies the snake is distraught and is sending out a warning sign.

The eastern coral snake is a beautiful snake and stands out a mile in any vegetation due to its bright coloring of red and yellow bands combined with black. There is another species of snake, which looks similar, the harmless scarlet kingsnake (*Lampropeltis elapsoides*).

The eastern coral snake has neurotoxic venom, which can lead to respiratory problems, nervous system failure and potentially death. If you happen to mix your color bands up and pick up an eastern coral snake, you might be in for some trouble. I would say here, that of course you shouldn't go around picking up snakes in the first place, especially not in the Everglades, as it is classed as harassment. The coral snake has a very small head and mouth, with fixed fangs, so does find it difficult to bite and envenomate a human. However, its venom can be deadly.

Coral snakes are quite rare, I was very lucky, especially to see it where I did, and then a few years later I was lucky enough again to see one close up in the grass in the cypress forest area.

The way to remember the difference between the harmless scarlet kingsnake and the venomous eastern coral snake is with the short rhyme and ditty:

'Red on yellow, dangerous fellow, Red on black, friend of Jack", which also comes in some other variations.

The rhyme pertains to the way the bands of color meet, where on a coral snake, the red touches the yellow, and on a scarlet kingsnake, it does not. Confusingly, this only applies to coral snakes found north of the Florida Keys though, as there are some color morphs in the Keys and South America, which do not follow those identification rules.

You will notice I said venomous and not poisonous, when referring to the snakes, whereas many people will call them poisonous snakes. This difference I found difficult to convey to international tourists, as the two terms do not translate well, and poisonous seems to be the only word understood internationally. Technically there are no poisonous snakes (aside from a few which when eaten could be considered poisonous) but there are venomous snakes. Venom is a collection of proteins that an animal produces, and is stored in glands usually delivered or envenomated through hypodermic type fangs, such as in snakes and spiders. For venom to be effective, it needs to arrive in your blood or lymphatic system.

Snakes, spiders, or any other venomous creatures don't want to waste their valuable venom on a human. They much prefer to deliver it to their prey, so that they can subdue it and break down the muscle tissue through necrosis, making it easier to digest. A snake will typically only bite a human accidentally, or when defending itself, and the vast majority of bites from venomous snakes are dry bites, which mean they do not deliver the venom at all. Snakes only bite as a cautionary reaction, though most juveniles will deliver venom with every bite due to their lack of control over its release. Snakes have a bad reputation, and seen as aggressive animals, when in fact they are largely passive creatures.

Poison, as oppose to venom, affects us through ingestion or from contact with the skin. If you touch or eat a poison then it takes effect, such as a plant or berry, or some animals. In theory, you could drink snake venom and it will not harm you, though it is not a good idea. I will stick with my Guinness and fine single malt.

Mind the Rope Don't Bite You

I was driving down the park road one day with a van full of tourists. I was keeping a keen eye out on the road, and the grass at the sides. I was always screeching to a halt or making sudden turns in the road to stop and see something that looked interesting.

Turning in the park road with a tour van and a canoe trailer with eight canoes on the back is not an easy feat, but I got extremely adept at it after a while. As I was driving, I saw a red, black, and yellow s-shaped object in the road. I brought the van to a sudden stop with all the canoe paddles coming flying forward on the floor of the van, along with a few of the tourists who all wondered what had happened. I was so excited. I built everyone up verbally, and then explained the importance of moving slowly and staying behind me. I then proceeded to get everyone out of the van.

I walked slowly over to the coiled snake with the tourists all following quietly with anticipation behind me. I then showed them a beautiful piece of black rope, that someone had taken the time to paint red and yellow bands around, exactly matching that of the morph of the eastern coral snake. They even took the time to melt the end of the rope, and shaped it like the rounded elapid style head of these snakes.

I was gutted, but laughing at the same time, more so at the effort someone had gone to just to play a trick on someone. It was a funny five minutes though, and the tourists were extremely amused.

Keeping an eye out not only for snakes, but also for anything interesting, we would walk around the Anhinga Trail admiring all the alligators everywhere, often with turtle's right next to them or even on top of them. The birds diving and fishing or perhaps the large soft-shell turtles with pig-like noses will be swimming around or upon the bank laid quietly in the sun, though surrounded by inquisitive onlookers.

You will often see alligators surrounded by birds, fish or turtles. When people see this happening, they often question it:

"Why are the alligators not eating them?" they ask.

My answer was simply that they are not hungry. Which is succinct and to the point. I mean, do you eat every piece of food that you pass by? No! Neither do alligators.

You may remember from earlier that I talked about alligators and the common misconception that they regularly eat people. In fact, since at least the 1970's there has only been around twenty fatal attacks from American alligators, and not one of them was in the Everglades National Park. They can be a nuisance at times, but that is more down to humanity being a nuisance to the wildlife, than the other way around.

The bulk of their diet is fish, turtles and small mammals, though occasionally they will hunker down on a nice joint of venison in the form of a whitetail deer, if it can grab one. Fish and turtles are in plentiful supply, and more accessible in the dry season, however, when water disappears the alligators tend to stay in a spot where water remains or seek out areas of water. This often ends up being people's swimming pools, but eating people is definitely not high on their list of protein requirements.

During the dry season, it can be difficult to source accessible food supplies. Alligators do not actually eat that often, and when they do, depending on the size of the meal relative to the size of the alligator, the meal could last them for several months, and maybe a year or more. People find this hard to believe, but you have to remember that the American alligator and most crocodilians are largely inactive most of the time. They spend their days basking in the sun or taking a slow swim around the Everglades, though they can be playful at times.

It is common to see a turtle resting peacefully next to, or upon an alligator, appearing to be living in perfect harmony. However, this scene can also quickly turn more macabre, as it is also common to see an alligator masticating away on a tasty morsel such as a red-bellied cooter or a more delicate soft-shelled turtle, shell and all, along with any other comestible that comes its way. Blood, shell and bone fragments falling out the sides of the powerful jaws as it consumes its meal, the resonating crunching sound of the turtle's demise will echo around the Anhinga Trail, as the alligator goes about his lunch.

Perhaps the alligator has a more discerning palate and fancies a nice fish dinner, such as a big and bony Florida gar. Maybe even a Burmese python like the great photo my friend Rustin took of an alligator sat with a python in its mouth, and then running underneath him as he sat on top of his delicious meal whilst eating one end of it.

If you visit in around March and April time, it is mating season. They are more active, and you will most likely get to see them eating quite often around this time, to get their energy levels up for the impending reptilian fornication, along with playful antics, fights and general reptilian debauchery.

The American alligator has dominated the Everglades for quite some time, and indeed the planet, as a species. Crocodilians, like birds, are an order of the *Archosauria* family, and so have been around for about two-hundred and fifty million years, and so they predate dinosaurs, which actually make them a 'living fossil'. However, if you ever wanted to see a dinosaur, or at least get close to a real one then you cannot go far wrong with a crocodilian, as they are close in the scheme of things.

Crocodilians have survived for so long due to their innate ability to adapt and evolve, and over millennia have developed various biological and physiological attributes that have helped them to survive.

I mentioned earlier their remarkable respiratory system, along with a four-chambered heart unlike most other reptiles, which have only a three-chambered heart, and so they share a similar cardiac biology as mammals and birds. Crocodilians have a palatal valve, which, when submerged covers the throat, this can be for very long periods, and so they will not drown from the ingestion of water into the lungs. They also have flaps that cover the nostrils and so are very efficient at both static and dynamic apnea.

Of course, another obvious question and observation relates to their sex, age and size, which all tend to correlate. Identifying the sex of an alligator accurately, would involve you sticking your hand inside of it, which is not something I would recommend unless of course you have someone with you who can upload the hilarious video to YouTube. They are sexually dimorphic in terms of size. With adults, the male is generally larger and fuller bodied, but a lot will depend on the diet of the individual. The size across the sexes range from around six inches when hatchlings, and up to around 13-feet (the Florida record being just over 14-feet) for males. The females typically will not exceed 9-feet or so, and they reach sexual maturity around 7-feet after growing typically a foot per year.

As for their age in the wild, it is of course survival of the fittest. Even from hatchlings, where their mother gives them great care, they are not safe as she can also be cannibalistic. That is aside from the danger from hawks, egrets, herons and other prey including some snakes. As they mature, then the survival comes from their ability to hunt, and to avoid the obligatory gator brawl often seen throughout the park, though most often through mating season when the males like to exhibit their manliness to the female. Bearing all this in mind then you can assume the average alligator in the wild to live for around forty years if it is lucky, a bit longer and up to around seventy years or more in captivity. Alligators were once an endangered species, though now they are listed as protected, numbering in the millions. However, you can get a license to hunt them.

A park scientist once estimated there to be around one alligator per half acre. The park is around 1.6 million acres, which explains the amount you tend to see in the dry season as they collect around the local watering holes. Statistical data aside, there are plenty of them around, unlike the American crocodile that we will encounter later, which is a threatened species and number in the low thousands. The alligator is now thriving, and is largely thanks to efforts from the Alligator Farm. There is now no need to hunt for the meat or teeth or any other part for food, ornament or jewelry. However, as I said, there are occasionally licenses given out to hunt them, though not within the Everglades National Park.

During the spring, the alligators begin mating, along with the bizarre, and entertaining courting rituals, such as the water dance. The water dance is when male bull alligators let out a deep bass rumble from within their belly. The vibration will then cause the water upon their back to dance like falling raindrops hitting the concrete, which is an auditory and visual delight for tourists and female alligators alike. These courtship rituals start around April, and mating usually occurs in May. As with humans, the guy who demonstrates the most vehement desire to 'get with a chick', has the dance moves, is not scared to do a little karaoke, and generally outperforms the other males will eventually get the girl. The lucky couple will then slope off to get intimate prehistoric lizard style, usually at night in shallow waters, where the male will circle and then mount the female. The female will later nest, in time for the pending offspring around June and July, which is, as you will notice only a short time later.

Alligators are oviparous and lay eggs, unlike some reptiles that we will encounter later that are ovoviviparous which mean they give birth to live young. These nests can be up to 10-feet in diameter and around a few feet in height, regularly making an appearance in the vegetation close to the paths at Anhinga Trail. The park rangers will cordon off these areas, as pregnant alligators or females guarding their young are especially volatile.

One of the more interesting facts about alligators, is that they are sexually deterministic, in that the female controls the distribution of male or female hatchlings based on temperature, although probably not intentionally. A clutch can vary from thirty to fifty eggs, but can often be more. The mother will cover them over, and after around sixty-five days or so, the eggs will hatch. If the eggs remain at a temperature above 93° F (33.8° C) then it will be male, if it is below 86° F (30° C) then it will be female, anywhere in between and it has a shot of being either sex.

Once they hatch, they make a high-pitched squeal sound, and this is something to listen out for as a tourist. This will signal the mother to remove the vegetation. They will often continue this squeaky sound throughout immaturity, especially when feeling threatened. Be warned that female alligators will aggressively defend and protect their young, even though the mother can be cannibalistic. When baby alligators are around be certain that the mother is close by!

As you walk along the trail, aside from all the wonderful wildlife, there is also a thriving array of both tropical and temperate botanical treats along the way. Probably one of the most prominent here at the trail is the large Florida strangler fig (*Ficus aurea*).

Many arrive here at the strangler fig to use the provided bench that offers a little shaded respite from the hot Florida sun and to rest old or weary bones for those that cannot walk too far at a time. I would stop here to ask the tourists if they know what tree it is that stands so ostentatiously, yet unassumingly at the same time. It is at this point when it looks like I may be a park employee, as I am giving a public speech that tended to attract lots of passers-by, all getting in on the free guide interpretation where they could. The most common response to my question was "a mangrove" or "a banyan".

Mangrove would be the typical response, as the Everglades are famous for them, and most people haven't seen them before. If they had, then they may remember a pretty prop root system, which I suppose does rather resemble the structure of the *Ficus*, but we will get back to mangroves later down in the saltwater. The latter response of banyan is somewhat closer, as the banyan is from the *Ficus* family, but again it would be incorrect, though often used as a term for the strangler fig.

The Florida strangler fig is actually an epiphyte or air plant. At this point, you should remember what an epiphyte and air plant is from when we were in the car park discussing the mahogany trees and the Spanish moss.

You will remember that an epiphyte will find a host to attach too, and then grow, whilst taking its nutrients from the air, sun and rainfall. The strangler fig does exactly that, except that overtime it will metamorphose into a tree in its own right. It does this by sending its taproots to the ground, where it will then thrive like a regular tree or plant, taking water and nutrients from the ground. The strangler fig stands out because of its intricate array of entangled and strangling limbs that slowly envelop their host into a suffocated and rotting inner core. However, it is not a parasite, in that it takes nothing from the host. The host is, however, unable to thrive any longer, and will be shaded from sunlight so no longer able to photosynthesize. This means it will eventually die leaving the beautiful strangler fig as the outer shell, hence the term strangler. They can be found throughout Florida and the Everglades, and really stand out. There is a real beauty in the chaotic pattern that the taproots and enveloping shell creates during its growth.

Shortly after the strangler fig stop, you will cross a small wooden bridge, which is a good stop to look under, to see if there are any baby alligators around, or sometimes an adult lurking underneath in the cool shade. This is also a popular fishing spot for wood storks, egrets, herons and other avian waders.

On the right hand side of this bridge, as you cross there is a little hole in the concrete, which has a black plastic pipe leading into it. If you look in here, you have a good chance of seeing a brown water snake curled up. This reptile cavern has been the home to one since at least 2004. There is no guarantee that it will be home though.

Wood stork. Courtesy of Rustin Gooden

The bridge provides a vista over the sawgrass prairie and Taylor Slough. It is a common to see the endangered wood storks here. The wood stork (*Mycteria americana*) is a beautiful, yet ugly bird, if that makes sense. They stand up to around 4-feet as adults, with a wingspan of up to 6-feet. They have a large body draped in wispy white feathers, but with a baldhead like a vulture, and a big long beak. Their beaks are long and curved similar to an ibis, but not from the ibis family. They are the only wood stork that breeds in the USA, and is an endangered species. It is also, what is termed as an indicator species. This means that its population and ability to thrive indicates the health of the ecosystem in which it lives. It is easier to monitor a single species, than it is to assess the health of a complicated ecosystem.

The long bill is invaluable to a wood stork, as it doesn't use sight like some birds to find its food, such as small fish. Instead of sight, it uses tactolocation, which is the ability to find food by touch. It does this by sweeping its bill from side to side in the shallow water, and snapping at anything that meets its bill. The hydrological conditions of the park have affected the wood storks habitat greatly over the years, leading to the inability to nest and feed successfully, though when I left the Everglades the numbers appeared to be on the rise. This is likely down to the conservation efforts to increase water flow into the park. I hope that one day they will be as abundant as they once were.

The wood stork is easy to spot due to its large body of white amongst the grass and trees. However, there are a few other white birds common to this area and the Everglades in general. One of which is extremely common and historically significant, the great egret.

The great egret (*Casmerodius albus*) is one of the largest wading birds in the Everglades, often mistaken for the white phase of the great blue heron. Historically, the skies here were a canvas to countless silhouettes of different birds, whose sheer amount would darken any light. There were little to no dangers, other than natural selection and the cycle of life and food. It was once said "the skies were black" with the amount of birds here.

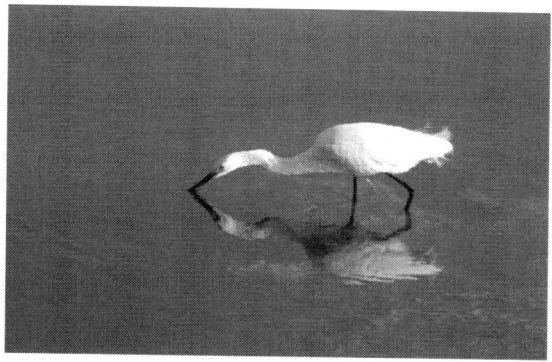

Snowy egret showing the sought after tail feathers.
Courtesy of Rustin Gooden

In the late 1800's, the feather trade boomed. Feathers were sought for fashion, for decorating women's hats. The great egret suffered greatly from the hunters looking to make a buck from these birds by shooting them from the skies. The tail feathers of an egret during mating plumage are beautifully light, soft and wispy, and were attractive to the women of fashion. The name egret comes from the French *aigrette*, referring to the mating plumage of these birds. In the 1900's an ounce of these feathers were worth more than an ounce of gold, all in the name of fashion, and the ignorant stupidity and greed of humanity.

There is a memorial and key named after an Audubon warden called Guy Bradley down in Florida Bay. Guy Bradley was shot and killed, trying to protect roosting birds from the hunters, and this became the end to the 'feather wars' with Federal protection being brought about in 1918.

There are other types of egret in the park aside from the great egret, all of which were victim of the feather trade, but as I said previously, you really need a dedicated bird guidebook. I could talk for pages and pages about the various birds here, but I want to limit it to the most abundant and significant species, especially as most of it is lost without photographs. Any animal or plant that I mention with detail tends to be relevant to the big picture, though everything is relevant in the wild, as it all depends on each other.

The next significant stop I would arrive at would be 'Alligator Beach'. 'Alligator Beach' is a name that I gave to an area where you could see ten or a hundred alligators, all laid in the sun. Here, they all lay on top of each other, yawning, awkwardly and slowly moving around, and all interspersed with egrets, herons, and vultures, all precariously close to the sudden snapping jaws of alligators.

'Alligator Beach' is right at the end of the straight-line boardwalk without taking the left turn, which is where you will exit from, unless of course you decide to walk anti-clockwise if you are the rebellious type. I personally always prefer to go widdershins, as the road less traveled is often more interesting, and the same road traveled in a different way offers a different perspective.

Before you get here, you will pass more of the same repeatedly. Though beautiful, it could take all day to move 10-feet. Especially if an alligator is wrestling with a python, or an anhinga is struggling to get a fish removed from its beak. Perhaps a python is slithering across the path, or coiling up at the side where the rangers will then come along to remove it, as it is an invasive species.

Arriving at 'Alligator Beach' you can then hang out, usually in awe with your camera and happily snap all day long (excuse the pun) at the alligators. Do not however drop your camera, as a member of a tour once did.

Don't Drop Your Camera

We were stood looking at the alligators, and I was sat on up on the rail. There were probably fifty or more alligators laying around, some directly underneath where the tourists were leant over admiring, and yes alligators can jump, but you should be okay. However, like I said before, they can go anywhere they want, and the low knee high rails offer no real protection. The rails are merely to remind people that it's probably not a good idea to cross, but you can if you wish, and the alligators can walk right under them anyway.

A member of my group was happily snapping away, when she suddenly dropped her camera right in between two fat bull alligators, and it was like a $500 camera. In the event that this happens, you should contact a park ranger, and though legal, you shouldn't attempt to recover your camera yourself. The only time you should do this is if it is for a girl that looks like Mila Kunis who has dropped it, and who might buy you dinner afterwards.

I said that I would get it back and not to worry. She and the rest of the tour thought I was joking. Now if this had been mating season, I would not have attempted this, as they are little more volatile. Alligators will lay motionless, often looking dead, but if there are sudden movements, or a sound, then they will move at the speed of a bullet.

I found an area close to the alligators where I could land, but not right in the middle of them. I then jumped right over. As I landed, exactly as I predicted (and hoped), the two big alligators suddenly turned, diving towards the water creating a domino effect, where every other alligator started to run, dive and splash in pandemonium. The tourists above were screaming a high-pitched squeal from phobophobia (being scared of being scared). I casually picked up the camera, nonchalantly climbing back up, while trying to hide the fact that I had hurt my knee during the landing.

Now there was a chance that I could have lost an arm or worse. But, after years encountering these reptiles every day, not only do you get to understand them, you also lose any sense of fear, which if course is what protects you, so there is always luck involved and I don't recommend it.

If the girl had not had been so attractive then I probably wouldn't have bothered. As a *quid pro quo*, she treated me to my favorite Mexican meal and a few beers that evening, so it was a good result. I did spend the rest of the tour trying not to limp though.

Actually, from an alligator wrestling point of view, they are for the most part easy to contain, even with just your hands, unless it is a big one. Anything under 6-feet or so and I have no qualms about sitting on top of and holding its mouth shut. Though they have a crushing jaw, they only have the strength in closing their jaw. They have little strength for opening the jaw. This means that you can hold their powerful jaws together with two fingers, or even under your chin, as you will see some alligator wrestlers do at the Alligator Farm and other places. However, you do need to get your hand there in the first place to keep it shut, which can sometimes be tricky.

Leaving here, you may choose to head back after having your fill of alligators, or continue with the loop. Continuing on the loop, you will enter into the open pond areas where the boardwalk now sits on stilts in the water, so you can look over and admire the flotillas of alligators, turtles and fish swimming beneath. You will notice gators gliding peacefully through the water with no sound, as they wag their powerful muscular tails from side to side with their feet tucked back beside their bodies. If it's a clear day, and the water is clear, then take a close look, as you will often see alligators submerged. Alligators will lie stealthily in the mud below, burrowed under a layer of mud, or lying with a clear outline, as they lay silently and peacefully under the water. I loved to point this out and then remind the tourists of it later on when they were waist deep in the murky waters of the 'swamp' like cypress forests.

Continuing on, you will notice the presence of a new tree. You would have passed it already, except that they were not as large or easily distinguishable as the ones in the areas of open water. The majority of the trees stood in the water here are pond apple (*Annona glabra*), easily spotted when it is bearing its fruit. The pond apple is a large hard looking apple, and bears a beautiful yellow tulip shaped flower. The fruit is edible, but it tastes like turpentine, as my tourists would often discover after I had offered it to them to taste, before I told them how foul it tasted. The pond apple has other names such as the custard apple, monkey apple, and the alligator apple, and alligators seem to enjoy the bitter narcotic taste after chomping on a fallen floater. These pond apple trees will be bustling with nesting anhinga, little green herons, and many others through the springtime, which is the mating, laying, and hatching time for many animals here.

Carrying on around the boardwalk there will be more alligators, bromeliads (keep an eye out for the snakes), birds, fish and turtles. You will then come to a vegetative area as you come back around to join the paved path where you started. Here you will see lots of coastal prairie willow (*Salix caroliniana*), also known as Carolina willow. These willow exhibit some beautiful cotton wool like blossom.

Remember earlier on when I said that most of the plants and animals in the park had some type of usage from medicinal to edible etc. Well the willow is no exception. The Latin for willow is *Salix*, which is where salicylic acid comes from. Salicylic acid is the main ingredient in aspirin, and so the inner bark and the leaves from willow make an excellent wilderness analgesic.

After a short walk through vistas of Taylor Slough and Paradise Key Hammock, you will finally emerge from the boardwalk and back onto the paved path to return towards the trailhead.

Gumbo Limbo Trail

Back where you started at the trailhead, there is another trail that is completely different from the previous boardwalk. The Gumbo Limbo Trail twists and turns its way for 0.4-miles through the inside of a beautiful hammock, and is the remains of the original hammock that once covered the car park and other areas close by. Given the opportunity, it is preferred to enter a hammock that has no paved trail, though this beautiful example will suffice to give you an overview.

This trail takes its name from one of the common trees found here and throughout South Florida, which is the gumbo-limbo (*Bursera simaruba*), which is a beautiful and interesting tree. It has red and brown flaky skin, which gives it its other common name of 'sunburn tree'. Although, I liked to call it the 'European tourist tree', as they were perfect for demonstrating the effect of too much sun upon white pale skin. Like most of the animals or trees that I single out for discussion, it is because they have an interesting feature or history, and the gumbo-limbo is no different. The term gumbo-limbo comes from a westernization of an Afro-American term, referring to the stickiness of the sap that this tree oozes from its wounded flesh. This sap would coat the branches of trees, where birds such as northern cardinals and buntings amongst many others, could then be captured and subsequently traded.

This tree could fill a chapter on its own, as it has many features and stories associated with it. One of its useful traits makes it perfect for growth in South Florida, especially in people's yards. It is an extremely resilient tree and during the hurricanes, the branches may break off, but then start growing again very quickly. This is useful for recovering a destroyed yard, such as in the hostel garden, which Hurricane Wilma almost destroyed in 2005. Only a year later you wouldn't know anything had ever happened, as is the speed of recovery and replenishment of the vegetation down in South Florida.

Historically, people would harvest the sap to make turpentine, candles, and the hardwood that is cheaper than mahogany was also a popular alternative for carnival merry-go-round horses. Some people even smoke the leaves for a mild hallucinogenic. However, I have heard mixed responses to its potency from the various hallucinogen aficionados in the form of the many hostel hippies.

The good thing about this trail is that it rarely has other people walking around it. I think this is because as a natural hammock it is heavily shaded, and thus is a great place for mosquitoes, as shade is their preferred home. There are a few pools and ponds of stagnant water throughout the trail, such as sinkholes, and these are prime breeding grounds for mosquitoes.

You may remember from earlier that I mentioned that mosquitoes do not actually bite. They insert their proboscis, which is like a small syringe into your skin, and inject saliva, which is an anticoagulant to thin your blood. The anticoagulant helps them suck the blood up through their straw like proboscis. This anticoagulant is what produces the irritation and the itch. Once they have your blood, they then use it as protein for egg production, and so the cycle continues. There are close to three-thousand species worldwide with over one-hundred and fifty recognized in the USA. Only the females want your blood, as the males pollinate. They can be annoying, and they can carry disease, but they are part of the ecosystem and everything in nature lives symbiotically, the only thing that doesn't is humankind.

Walking through a hammock is not unlike a jungle. The majority of the vegetation is tropical in origin, and there is jungle like canopy overhead, providing shade, though accompanied by heat and humidity. There is also a wealth of lizards, tree frogs, terrestrial and tree snakes (though all snakes can climb but some are more arboreal than others are), skinks, salamanders, and an ever bustling entomological frenzy of activity in the undergrowth.

You Never Know What's Round the Corner

I was walking a tour around this trail one day with four Chinese girls, which I didn't do too often, as I would usually leave after Anhinga Trail. As we turned a corner, laid diagonally across the path was a 7-foot alligator. This wasn't anything special, as we had just seen like a hundred or so, but it was mating season, and this one was standing his ground. He wouldn't budge at all (I am assuming a male due to the full body, but you never know). I clapped my hands, and stamped my feet, trying to generate enough sudden movements to make him budge, but he didn't even move an inch. I started to think he might be dead, as there was no hissing, or attempts to move, though a dead alligator has an extremely acrid stench once it is dead. I was all for leaving him alone and walking around as best we could, but the girls were petrified.

    I decided to start lightly tapping his tail with my foot. The first few flicks moved his tail from side to side, and once again, the rest of him didn't move. I finally lifted the heavier part of his tail with my foot, to see if he really was dead. Suddenly he let out a resounding hiss, and slammed his jaw shut, which made a clapping sound that echoed around the hammock, and then bolted back towards us. I quickly sidestepped, and the girls ran screaming off into the vegetation at the side. The gator then suddenly stopped and laid down facing the other direction, where the girls had once stood. At least the path was clear, and we could move on. It had a short burst of activity and then slumped grumpily down facing the other direction as if nothing had happened. Asian girls are the funniest to watch when scared.

The hammock environment, like most of the ecosystems in the park, is a flurry of unseen activity, from the micro to the in your face macroscopic level. It is worth spending some time exploring hammocks, to discover wonders such as orchids, like the infamously rare and endangered ghost orchid (*Dendrophylax lindenii*), to the endangered tree snail (*Liguus fasciatus*). Hammocks are unique environments with an exceptionally subtle beauty that you just have to experience, much like a jungle such as the Amazon.

CHAPTER SIX - Pineland

"I went to the woods because I wished to live deliberately, to front only the essential facts of life, and see if I couldn't learn what it had to teach, and not, when I came to die, discover that I had not lived" - Henry David Thoreau

The Pinelands

I love the woods. I understand the woods. I respect the woods. I connect and feel at home in the woods more than anywhere. Since I was a child I have wandered, ran, camped, and built shelters in the forests. I have sat and watched the wildlife go about their daily business, climb, and forage, and immersed myself into their community, becoming one with the woods.

Quoting from Thoreau a little here, and reminiscent of *Into the Wild*:

"Rather than love, than money, than fame, give me [the woods]"

Whether they are lowland, highland, deciduous, coniferous, sparse or dense, the woods comfort and soothe me. Even as an adult, I walk among the inanimate majesties of the forest and I feel their sentience. Trees are magic, and trees are alive.

Trees are living there is no doubt about that, but I imagine them watching me, and when I leave I envisage them uprooting and walking around like a scene from a Disney movie. There is a sense of wisdom about them that I cannot describe. Trees may seem insignificant, but they date back to the Devonian period, around three hundred and sixty million years ago. They know a thing or two about survival, and all they seem to do is sunbathe, drink water, and make and metabolize sugar.

I have slept bare on the forest floor, with nothing but needles and leaves amongst the broken night sky for a ceiling. I have slept in everything from makeshift beds in homemade shelters, tents, sleeping pads, hammocks and tree houses. If I were to spend my last days struggling for survival in a forest, then I would pass peacefully and content.

You may have noticed by now that we are in the woods, the pinelands to be precise. As you leave the Royal Palm Visitor Center and get out back onto the main road, you will take a left to continue west to Flamingo. Almost immediately, pineland forest will appear on one side and sawgrass prairie on the other. The pinelands, when talking of the Everglades National Park, describe both an ecosystem as well as referring to a specific trail, called simply: the Pinelands. As you travel towards Flamingo, the Long Pine Key trail will appear first as a left hand turn shortly before the Pinelands trail. Long Pine Key is a magnificent example of pineland, which we will come too shortly.

When visiting the pinelands I had no problem waxing lyrical, as we would slowly wander, seeking, examining, admiring, and inhaling the sweet and fresh intoxicating aromas that a forest or woodland provides. There is no smell quite as invigorating as the petrichor of sodden canopy and undergrowth after the rain or morning dew has lifted from the fallen leaves and needles.

Did I mention that I love the woods?

The Everglades pineland forests are not like any pine forest you have ever seen before. Most people can identify a pine tree, as they are a prolific conifer the world over, though often considered a temperate tree. Yet here they thrive in a subtropical climate. Not only that, but they are growing straight out of the rock, instead of the nutrient rich peat like soil forest floor that you may be used to.

Historically, as little as five-hundred years ago, Florida looked completely different to what we see today. In North Florida, longleaf pine would have thrived and dominated the landscape. In mid Florida, the vegetation would have varied somewhat with a mix of pines. In South Florida, slash pine would have dominated the inner landscape. There were thick mangrove coastlines, sawgrass prairies, and grassy glades, that all made an historic Florida one large forest and grassland, which has vastly diminished today due to the development, logging and agriculture.

There are seven noticeable species of pine tree in Florida, but within the Everglades the pineland areas are comprised mostly from slash pine (*Pinus elliotti var. densa*), which survives as the remains of a once magnificent ancient lowland forest. The slash pines get their name due to the 'slashes' of swamp like ground covered in trees that defines its habitat. They would also be 'slashed' with a blade to allow the sap to drip out into a container for collection, and then used to make turpentine.

These ridge rock perched forest ecosystems are brimming over with plant and animal life. There is the Florida panther, the bobcat, deer, wild turkey, mice, snakes, owls, woodpeckers, spiders, fox squirrels, fire ants, butterflies, orchids, ferns, and rainbow colored tree snails. The list goes on and on as with every ecosystem in the Everglades.

Rockland habitats refer to an area where the limestone is exposed, providing elevation and covered in little to no soil, though rich in calcium. Rockland areas are either pine rockland, or rockland hammock. Both are lands of exposed limestone, with an overstory of either pine or tropical hardwood such as mahogany, pigeon plum and gumbo-limbo. Pine rockland, or simply pineland is a fire dependent habitat, and within them, you can find rockland hammock habitats where fire does not have such an effect. Pine rocklands now occupy around four-thousand acres in South Florida, and are a threatened environment.

Florida City still has a few small areas where this habitat survives, though it is fenced off and protected. In the park, there is also evidence of this rock ridge, which once extended from Miami down through into the Everglades, where the parks pinelands now survive.

Rockland habitats are extremely hazardous to wander through off trail, although, if you know what you are doing it can be extremely rewarding. Aside from the animal and plant life that can injure you, the underfoot is extremely sharp and ragged. There are many solution holes or 'sink' holes, which can range in depth, from an inch to a few feet deep, or even a cave. You need sturdy shoes and a good sense of balance to negotiate these areas off trail. Some luck is also handy to have on your side, as eastern diamondback rattlesnakes have a strong aversion to wearing feet as a hat.

The eastern diamondback (*Crotalus adamanteus*) is the largest venomous snake in North America, reaching up to 8-feet in length and weighing 10lbs or more. As if rattlesnakes do not strike enough fear, an 8-foot, 10lb snake, rattling at you, is quite something to behold. This pit viper from the *Crotaline* family derives its common name due to the black diamond shapes upon its back, which when upon the floor blend in perfectly with the saw palmetto of the pinelands habitat. It has an aggressive reputation, although like most animals, it is not interested in you, but will defend itself in the event you harass it, or get too close, and can be very hostile when pregnant.

The diamondback is the most venomous snake in North America, and bares the largest fangs. Combined with its size and amazing striking speed, it is a formidable reptile. They can strike at one-third of their body length, and have the ability to strike both ante and postmortem. They are not to be underestimated. Its striking ability after death, is part of its nervous system, so do not pick up a dead rattlesnake.

Eastern diamondback venom is primarily hemotoxic, causing severe pain, and serious tissue damage. A bite from these beauties can easily be fatal, and will often result in at least severe scarring, or the loss of a limb.

The calling card of rattlesnakes is of course its infamous rattle. Its tail maraca, made from keratin (the same material in your skin, nails and hair). The rattlesnake when feeling threatened will vigorously shake its tail, as most snakes do, except with the rattlesnake you get the maraca sound of doom. The tail is shook and combined with its own internal amplification system., the rattle then emits a percussive warning sign, which means you are too close, and you should beware. They can do this for a long time without suffering from fatigue, but will not generally do so, unless it feels threatened.

A journalist on a tour with me wrote the following in a Boston Globe article:

'The thrill of our day: an 8-foot Eastern diamondback coiled and rattling within snapshot distance." - Patricia Borns, *'Ways to the Glades'*, The Boston Globe.

However, rattlesnakes do not have to coil to rattle their tail. They do not need to coil before striking either.

There is also a myth that says if you can count the segments on the rattle you can determine its age. This is not quite accurate. A rattlesnake can shed its skin three or four times a year, and will often lose segments, especially when they are young, as they shed quite regularly, so it is not a good idea to rely on the segments to determine their age. However, if you are close enough to count the segments, then it is unlikely that its age will be important, and only how fast you can seek medical treatment.

As already mentioned there are two significant pineland trails in the park provided at easy to access points, Long Pine Key and the Pinelands.

Long Pine Key

The first trail designed for the visitor to the pinelands, is Long Pine Key. It is located on the left hand side, as you travel the park road, towards Flamingo, about 3-miles after the turning to the Royal Palm Visitor Center. This is also the first major campsite within the park boundary, which also happens to be the most popular aside from Flamingo, although camping in the Everglades should be in the backcountry wilderness where possible. Both Long Pine Key and

Flamingo fill with tents and the infamous American RV, in all their gas guzzling and landscape blotting glory during the tourist season. It can seem at first glance like any other campsite across the USA, with outside grills and picnic benches, a small lake, toilet facilities, and some nature trails through the forest. To be quite honest it is just that when populated, except for the fact that in the lake there is usually a sole alligator who will quite happily amble up from the water towards picnickers, as it has become very use to people. The familiarity that wildlife possesses in these areas is likely due to the illegal feeding, which carries fines and possible jail terms if caught in the act. Many asinine individuals feed the wildlife, usually in an attempt to impress others, or to tempt the animal closer to catch or kill. Remember that when you feed wildlife in areas such as these, you are endangering yourself and others, not to mention sometimes endangering the animal too. The park regularly relocate this alligator, placing it further north due to its familiarity with people. Although it seems to find its way back, and is easily recognizable by the injured snout, giving it a sort of cleft palate.

There are also many rattlesnakes in this habitat, easily camouflaged amongst the foliage, blending in to resemble the ground bark of the saw palmetto. Many other beautiful and non-venomous snakes also enjoy this habitat.

One of the things that makes this area popular, is the diversity of habitat, though it is predominantly peppered with pine, there are also various hardwood hammocks, and the infamous 'glades' themselves, which makes reference to the "opening in the forest" definition of a glade. There are various trails in and around the pinelands. Some are great for walking, running, or even a bicycle. If I was to visit this area with tourists, it would be to walk what we called the 'three-in-one trail', as it is a trail that happens to encounter three various habitats.

The 'three-in-one trail' starts in pineland, along the edge of the small lake, and then meanders into the dark jungle world of the hardwood hammock, and then out into a glade. During the summer, the headwaters flow from the slough, filling the woods with its glittering and replenishing glory. The trail then comes back out into the pinelands, returning to the picnic area. This also happens to be one of the few places in the park to see the rare ground (terrestrial) orchid *Spurred neotia*, which is hard to find but beautiful to see in bloom, but I will leave that as a prize for discovery.

The countless creatures encountered here could fill a book of their own. However, there are a few worthy of note, as they are common and easily seen without too much of a foray into the unknown. Such as the golden orb spider and their glistening silk webs, various snakes, salamanders and other lizards, and not forgetting the Florida tree snails (*Liguus fasciatus*), which I will cover shortly at the Pinelands trail, as they are heavily concentrated in the hammock found there.

The Long Pine Key area and its trails are fun, and as most areas of the park will be weather dependent, changing daily throughout the year. However, it is always a great place to go with the kids, as it offers public bathrooms and picnic areas. It is relatively safe in the open areas for them to play, where you can keep your eye on them.

Exploring the pinelands can be much like any other wooded area anywhere in the world to the untrained or unobservant, but there is always more going on than meets the eye, and will require multiple trips over the various seasons to allow it to reveal its true secrets. Long Pine Key will go from a RV filled trailer park during some months, to a peaceful and often eerie asphalt blot on the pristine landscape of the glades during the other. It is beautiful here during a downpour of rain, with no one but you, the trees, the animals, and the open sky.

The Pinelands Trail

Whether you choose to visit Long Pine Key or drive straight on down the main park road, you will find shortly on the right hand side another trail in the pinelands, simply called "The Pinelands", and is my favorite public trail in this ecosystem. It is a short, yet diverse trail, and I would bring visitors here more often than to Long Pine Key.

The trail is around half a mile loop. I always chose to go anticlockwise where possible, because I abhor convention, and either way it has no bearing on anything, and there is no right or wrong.

I would typically start the trail at the first right turn next to the small information kiosk, which has information on wild fire, and what plant and wildlife you may encounter. Upon emerging out into the open part of the path, through some palmetto brush, I would stop to explain the environment. The path then makes its way through the open ridge rock forest.

Next to the path, you can see examples of sinkholes, which if there has been recent rain, they will contain water, or if dry then may be home to some salamanders, snakes, toads or other wildlife. This trail was for a few years home to a large speckled kingsnake (*Lampropeltis getula holbrooki*), which is a beautiful non-venomous snake in the king family, which refers to species of snakes that eat other snakes. However, a snake does not need to be a king to be a cannibal. It could often be found sunbathing somewhere along this first part of the trail, and wasn't at all shy.

It is rare in Florida to experience any incline or decline due to its lack of elevation. However, here on this trail you can see, and experience, an ever so gentle ascension towards the end of the open pineland scrub, as you approach the large hardwood tropical hammock, which is at the center of this trail. It is due to this elevation that the hammock is able to grow. Instantly the trail will go from open pineland into the beautifully dense and microscopically active world of the hammock. Every hammock is similar yet so different. This particular hammock is great for tourists, as it is home to many beautiful tree snails.

The Florida tree snail (*Liguus fasciatus*), although arboreal in its habitat, is an air breathing land snail, or gastropod mollusk. These rare beauties are a malacology and conchology Mona Lisa. What make them stand out are there unique colorings, numbering around fifty or more distinct combinations from oranges, yellows, greens, pinks and many more. The colorings give them their other name, 'living jewels'. They are around two to three inches in length, and you can find them on the side of a tree, on top of a branch, or hanging upside down from one. You can also often find them in pairs atop each other mating, precariously combating gravity as they cling to the bark, engaged in conch coitus. During the dry season they estivate (a kind of hibernation) where they use their mucus to seal themselves to the bark, and await the summer rains. If removed during their estivation they will unfortunately die.

The predominant trees along the edge of this trail, through the hammock, are the pigeon plum and gumbo-limbo, and tree snails seem to love these, so you don't need to leave the trail to find any. They mate during late summer, and you can find small pearlescent egg clusters around the base of the trees, until the rains come. They are a threatened species, and only found in South Florida. Due to habitat changes, and years of hunting, their numbers are dwindling, so please do not remove any if you see them. Legend has it that many years ago, hunters would burn down the hammocks after discovering a unique color, the hunter would then sell the snail to collectors. The motive being, that it would increase the value of the snail to a collector, and reducing the chance of a similar color combination reappearing.

There is another common inhabitant of hammocks, and certainly in this hammock, which is the amazing golden orb spider, which is also known as the golden silk orb-weaver (*Nephila clavipes*), which is from the family *Nephila*, and is known as the banana spider in some parts of the world. This amazing

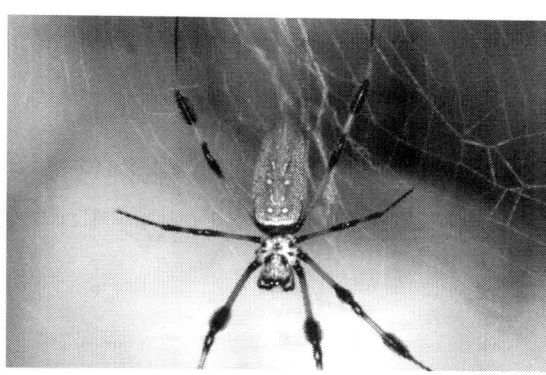

Golden Orb Spider. Courtesy of Rustin Gooden

arachnid beauty produces a golden web or orb. The silk when hit by sunlight glistens like gold thread in the canopy, like sunbeams that you could reach out and touch. This web is also stronger than steel with a tensile strength of around 4x109 N/m2 (that is four-billion newton per meter squared). If you find one, just place your fingers lightly upon it and gently press, you can really feel the webs strength. Be careful not to damage it though.

Part of my sadistic nature often comes out with wildlife such as this, especially when accompanied by phobophobiacs or arachnophobiacs. If I could judge that it would be more comedic than induce apoplexy, I would often purposely avoid a web by walking a certain way, knowing that those behind me may not see it. They would then get a face full of high tensile spider web, which never got old for me. I myself came home a few times with webs and spiders entangled up in my Jeremiah Johnson beard, after a long day slogging through the backcountry

The golden orb is a large orange/yellow and brown/black spider, with furry bands on their legs like a dancers leg warmers. As with most spiders, the female is the largest and the males are rather small. The adult female grows to around five centimeters in body length, but with a large leg sprawl, making a large one around the size of a hand palm, or face if you are unlucky.

They are the largest non-tarantula species of spider in North America. Though it can bite, it is rare, and not particularly painful, possibly a little redness and some swelling. One of their favorite delicacies is dragonflies. You can often see them en-snared, and wrapped up in their golden tomb within the webs throughout the hammock, awaiting their impending demise.

There is one particular spot along this trail, where a wall of a golden silk hangs like wallpaper, and within its Midas threads, you can find four or five large adult females, like a sight from an Indiana Jones movie.

Golden orb spiders are beautiful, but there are also many other species of spider in the Everglades, including the infamous black widow and the brown recluse, and I found one of them in my beard once. So be careful of spiders, and do not touch any unless you are following a guide who makes sure you get a face full of them.

As you leave the hammock you will emerge back out into the pine rockland, the temperature will subtly change, as will the aroma and vista. The path begins to make its way back to the kiosk from where the trail starts. This is a good chance to find some fire stubs.

Fire stubs are a term given to the charred remains of a pine tree standing often at nothing more than a few feet high, a lonesome charcoal stump. This is evidence of fire obviously, and fire is essential for the pinelands survival. Fire in the wilderness is a cleanser, clearing out the old and ushering in the new, *tabula rasa*.

Fire will come naturally, either through lightning, excessive heat, or as a controlled or prescribed burn. Prescribed burning is a term that is exactly as it sounds. An area deemed sick, or in need of cleansing, will be prescribed by the park service, a controlled or intentional burn, that is kept within a boundary, and burnt at a given rate. This fire clears out excessive growth, preventing one habitat encroaching on another. An important result of the heat is that the pinecones will open up, dispersing seeds, and thus the new pineland is born.

You can see in many areas where there is a clearing, the fresh saplings reaching for the sun, surrounded by the odd burnt out or charred remains of its ancestors. You may also notice stray, single fire stubs, with no evidence of mass fire. This is usually the result of lightning, which only struck that particular timber. This can lead to devastation if a stray ember from the burning tree hits the dry undergrowth. The fire service will then need to fight and take control of a fire, which could potentially devastate a habitat.

During the dry months, there will be regular fire warnings along the road reminding you not to park on the grass due to the high risk of fire. When these fires take place you can see the wildlife escaping from every exit they can find, but it's interesting to comb through the remains a few days after the fire, to see what skeletal or charred bodies remain. It is sad but essential. It is nature, and the process has happened naturally for millions of years.

Remember, these fires do not destroy the pine tree necessarily. Their bark protects them. The controlled burns are to remove the understory, which may take over if left to its own devices. The pines wear their bark like Kevlar, scarred black, a few feet high from the ground, yet still alive.

Tourist enjoying being close to a playful alligator

Some tourists in a shallow tunnel with an alligator for company

A tourist enjoying some mangrove limbo on the Noble Hammock trail

Tourists escaping the water after spotting an alligator in with them

Croczilla leading the author on a sunrise guided tour at Nine Mile Pond

Tourists entering the Movie-Dome, and wondering why they paid for this?

Tourists enjoying a free Everglades mud cleanse

The classic Everglades cypress dome facial expression

A Valentine's Day mud bath. Better than flowers and chocolates

Tourists enjoying some mangrove swimming

Osprey feeding on some freshly caught fish

The Everglades after a storm. Courtesy of the Everglades National Park

Alligator Beach

Alligator eating a soft-shell turtle. Courtesy of Rustin Gooden

Alligator affection. Courtesy of Rustin Gooden

Cottonmouth/Water moccasin

Fantastic photo of a cottonmouth with a dragonfly. Courtesy of Rustin Gooden

Turtle and alligator living in perfect harmony. Courtesy of Rustin Gooden

Eastern diamondback rattlesnake. Courtesy of Rustin Gooden

Alligator obstructing the path on the Gumbo Limbo Trail.

An aerial view of the Everglades. Courtesy of the Everglades National Park

Alligator performing the 'water-dance'. Courtesy of Rustin Gooden

Croczilla smiling and sunbathing

Black Vulture at Anhinga trail

CHAPTER SEVEN - Cypress

"There is an ecstasy that marks the summit of life, and beyond which life cannot rise. And such is the paradox of living, this ecstasy comes when one is most alive, and it comes as a complete forgetfulness that one is alive" - Jack London

Cypress Forest

Swamp filled wooden amphitheaters, stray tussocks of sawgrass, trees laden with beautiful pineapple tops. All illuminated by disco ball style lighting, and guarded by alligators and venomous snakes, with the odd python for good measure.

The cypress forest habitats of South Florida, and in particular the Everglades, stand out in memory for many reasons. I could write a book of anecdotal stories from this ecosystem alone. They have a rare quality about them, which is their ability to summon every profanity available, from terror-stricken tourists, and I have heard every one of them, in every language from around the globe. The facial expressions I have seen in this environment, from people who are scared literally out of their wits, contorted at every angle, are countless. Their own shock that not only are they doing it, but also paid to do it, and signed a death waiver releasing the guide from any responsibility, should they die during the adventure. The cypress habitat really is a "Never Safe, Always Fun' environment.

After leaving the pineland forest, you will head almost due west, and after about 5-miles or so, you will see the vegetation begin to change. If it is during the winter months, you will enter an almost barren wasteland of pitiful forest as far as the eye can see. At both sides of the road are frail looking, grey and white limbs, that look like the remains of an apocalypse. A common question asked was:

"Why are all these pine trees dead?"

Well they aren't dead, nor are they pine trees, these are cypress trees, which initially along the road is part of a dwarf cypress forest. The reason they look so forlorn and straggly is that they are deciduous conifers, which shed their needles during the winter, and then become a thick and plush emerald green again during the summer months, in almost what seems to be overnight. They are also heavily laden with huge bromeliads, which during the winter can often look as disheveled as their host.

Cypress trees (*Taxodium distitchum*) come in two varieties, bald and pond cypress. Some believe that both are variants of the same species. Regardless, they are very similar, and not noticeably different. The dwarf cypress however, are just that, they are considerably smaller with less stature, and appear like young saplings, but can be as old as the non-dwarf variety.

Cypress Domes

One of the most spectacular aspects of the cypress forest areas are the cypress domes. As their name suggests, they are a gathering of cypress trees that form the shape of a dome. These domes are clearly visible in the distance as you head down the park road, and through the cypress forest areas. There are two domes very close to the park road, both of which are great fun to explore: the Movie-Dome and the Cottonmouth Dome (Triple-Dome).

The domes themselves are essentially a cypress pond that have taller trees around the ponds immediate edge, and then as they spread out further away from the pond, they become much shorter, likely a result of nutrient deficiency. This geodesic gathering is not noticeable when in amongst them, but are certainly easy to spot from a distance or when approaching. Cypress forests and domes are natures TARDIS. Domes transport you to another time and another world. An almost primordial swamp littered with ferns, orchids, bromeliads, snapping turtles, owls, alligators, venomous snakes, pythons, lizards and a multitude of strange looking insects and the infamous mozzie are abound.

The ambience of a cypress dome lends itself well to the imagination. If you were to see a pterodactyl or a stegosaurus, you would not be shocked. In fact, you are almost shocked not to see them. However, when a great blue heron (*Ardea Herodias*) takes off suddenly from the canopy above, its screech and branch entangled panicked wing flaps often seems like pterodactyls are indeed there with you.

The reason such domes exist are for two reasons. They are either a product of an alligator seeking an extension to the wet season, or from a solution hole. People see the first reason as fanciful, but in the Everglades, there is a lot of magic, and I prefer to believe and imagine this happening throughout the years.

Alligators of course love and need the water, and as the dry season approaches, and the water levels deplete, alligators seek out areas that hold onto water for longer periods. At times they will thrash their tails vigorously around in the mud, uprooting vegetation with their mouth and patagium clawed feet, which over time creates a depression where the water collects.

Over many years, this becomes much larger, maintaining its receipt of water for much longer periods after the rainy season has subsided, and it becomes known as a 'gator hole'. This gator hole will trap fish, turtles, crustaceans, and insects, which will in turn attract birds that bring seeds, and eventually a thriving backcountry pond habitat has evolved, allowing the alligator to survive the dry season. If the vegetation around the gator hole becomes cypress trees then it is likely a cypress dome will appear over time.

If there is no alligator to carry out the manual labor, then these domes appear where limestone is weak or eroded, resulting in a solution hole where the limestone gives way. The result is much the same, thus providing a ready built home for an alligator or a reptilian couple to survive through the dry season. The large solid base of the cypress tree, allows it to stand fast in its watery home, and the height will shorten the further away from the center of the dome, as the nutrients decrease.

Exploring the cypress forest in the Everglades National Park, for the casual visitor, is limited to a short jetty style boardwalk, which enters from the side of road, a small way into the dwarf cypress forest, almost as soon as you enter the area. Alternatively, visitors can experience the cypress forest from Pa-Hay-Okee Overlook.

However, there are much better ways to explore this habitat which is what this chapter is really about, and mainly concerns the aforementioned domes; the Movie-Dome and Cottonmouth Dome (Triple-Dome), but first a short foray around Pa-Hay-Okee Overlook.

Pa-Hay-Okee

Pa-hay-okee or "grassy waters", was the term given to the Everglades from the native Seminole Indians, but also the name given by the park service to a particular attraction and vista within the park, just off the main park road. This is a good place to stop for sunset, or to come for sunrise. It is a short boardwalk and observation tower overlooking the dwarf cypress forest and out across the freshwater marl prairies toward Shark River Slough.

You can find the stop to the right, just after the 'Dwarf Cypress' forest, as you travel towards Flamingo on the main park road. I would not always visit here, and when I did, it would depend on the time of day, and the group dynamic, along with the time of year. The sunset is amazing here. After a long day in the glades, you can relax and look out across the wetlands, watching the sun turn from orange to red as it sinks towards slumber, leaving the skies tinged with a seductive blend of romantic hues. It is very peaceful here, and the stuff of poetry and art.

The overlook becomes lit up by the sunset as it beams through the branches and twigs of the cypress skeletons, standing eerily in the slow moving freshwater of this glorious river. The volume of babbling tourists gradually soften, and any movement becomes still. Expressions of contemplation and satisfaction fill the air as the day ends.

Sunset Supper

I was here with a tour one day, and the sunset was on its way. A few of the group and I were looking out over the prairie, near one of the information boards, and I spotted a white tail deer in amongst the sawgrass. Deer are mainly diurnal, with a crepuscular bias, and so twilight is the best time to see these cotton tailed beauties.

I called the remainder of the group over to look, and as we stood quietly taking in the peaceful view, there was an erumpent splash, as an alligator launched itself at the deer out of nowhere. The alligator appeared to catch the hindquarter of the deer, but it managed to bounce away from the powerful jaws of its attacker, and continued to make frantic haste through the tall sawgrass, and at the time what was probably 2-feet of water. The alligator just carried on sitting where it landed after its failed attempt at supper, and I muttered:

"Another day in the Everglades", then turned and walked over to watch the sun sizzle into the horizon.

Though there is a boardwalk and observation tower, it is a wonderful area to get off the reservation as it were. It is wonderful to climb down in amongst the grass, and explore the dense hammock and cypress forest surrounding the base of the tower, and beyond.

A little hint, but not encouraged though, is to climb on the roof of the observation tower, as you will gain an unencumbered view of the sunset out of others reach, although you need to be careful, and I in no way endorse it. However, it is wonderful to picnic up here during the sunset or sunrise.

This particular area also happens to be a regular hunting ground for a Florida panther. Regular paw prints appear in the mud here during the dry season, so keep a close eye out above in the branches of the hammock and cypress forest, and a listen carefully for a soft purr.

Ignorance & Priapism

I was at Pa-hay-okee with a small group once, and one of the members was a volunteer from the hostel. He was a late fifty year old from Miami, called Mike. We had actually started out as friends, but overtime, for some reason he developed some kind of jealousy for me, as being a guide comes with its own natural demigod status, and he didn't seem to like that.

I had already had words with him that day, as when we were paddling, I had caught him smoking, which is an obvious no-no on a tour, as it is unsociable, and we were in a protected area. Upon mentioning it, he then stubbed the cigarette out in the bottom of the canoe, melting a cigarette burn permanently into the hull.

I was stood quietly with the group looking out over through the cypress, watching the sky turn blood red from the sunset, when the volunteer approached from behind. He edged his way forward, saying:

"What you all watching?" he said ignorantly:

"The Sunset" I replied:

"Oh, is that it!" he said lacking interest. Then from his cupped hand, he brazenly flicked a cigarette butt out into the trees.

We were all gob smacked, and if I didn't have tourists with me he would have ended up as gator bait.

As he was a volunteer, he got a reprimanding back at the hostel, but he was very apologetic and allowed to stay, although he was later required to leave the hostel, never to return and with a lifelong ban.

Over the weeks I played various tricks on him, including changing his Hotmail password, subscribing him to a porn magazine, throwing soil over the outside shower just has he turned the taps off, and a few more. My favorite for him though was the Viagra.

He took to sleeping in the TV room, and when he did, he wore boxer shorts. I ordered some Viagra online, and crumbled up two of the one-hundred gram little blue pills, and put them in his dinner that night, as I had made him and some others some pasta sauce.

That night some German girls and I had been down the local bar, and had come back around midnight to a closed up kitchen house, and TV room. When we went in, he was asleep on the sofa with a raging erection sticking out of his shorts, and all the girls took a photo and had a laugh.

The next day, he was complaining of headaches, feeling flushed, and that he couldn't get his erection to go down, worried he had priapism. I think he spent most of the day in a cold shower. I didn't like to ask him what was up.

The Movie-Dome

Probably the most famous of the domes in the park is the Movie-Dome. Documentaries and park footage is often filmed in here. It also gets its name from its amphitheatrical quality. The Movie-Dome is not marked on the map, or with signs, and it is not an official park attraction. Although you can arrange a ranger led walk within it during season, so check with the park for more information on this, if not on a tour.

As I mentioned previously, it is permissible to go anywhere within the park, whether it be designated an attraction or not, except for those areas explicitly labelled as private or out of bounds. If not on a tour then the Movie-Dome is located on the right, shortly after passing the Pa-hay-okee turning. You will see not too far away from the road, a large dome of cypress trees with a noticeable path that leads straight into it.

The path is not actually a path at all. It is in fact, an alligator slide, trampled through by many thousands of tourists over the years. An alligator slide is much like a rabbit trail, where the animal creates a visible trail through the vegetation, as they habitually travel the same old route. In the case of an alligator, they leave a trail behind them as they slide their weighty adipose belly, and large heavy tail through the mud or sawgrass. During the summer months this only presents itself as a passage through the sawgrass resembling a river within a river, as the water levels will likely range from ankle to chest in places, or even deeper if you are unlucky, which happens regularly.

During the dry season, this will slowly become a rock hard undulating mud path. Although prior to this, there are a few months of awesome pudding like knee deep mud soup for tourists to precariously negotiate, before entering the dome.

Unless there is a fire warning, it is fine to park your vehicle on the grass at the side of the road anywhere along the park road. The Everglades hostel tour van with its large canoe trailer attached to the back is a common sight at some point through most days parked here, with a cheekily grinned tour guide leading some nervous tourists back in time. I would pull up here, and instruct everyone to wear whatever they were comfortable getting wet and possibly muddy in, and to apply mosquito repellent, but most importantly to bring cameras.

Once everyone is out of the van, wearing everything from bikinis to military camouflage (both male and female), I would then give everyone a pole to aid in their balance. I would give a short talk on the cypress environment, and sometimes a warning that an alligator regularly resides within this dome and is likely going to be somewhere along the route, although I would sometimes leave this as a surprise. This may mean being in the water with the alligator, which is what you paid for, and signed a 'death' waiver for.

Up until this point the tour and Everglades has largely been safe, for want of a better word. Psychologically, the act of being in a van with a guide, and walking asphalt or boardwalk paths, where there are other tourists, abstracts the wild nature from this rugged and untamed place. It really is not real until faced with the reality that something really could go wrong at any moment.

Walking in chest deep water with the eyes of an alligator looking at you, or a cottonmouth venomous snake only a few inches from your hand, as you unknowingly reach out for support, bring the reality of the Everglades right up close. I also found the question about an alligator being in the water with us rather strange, as I repeatedly during the day reminded them that the park was wild and that any creature was wild and could roam freely. At any point in time and in any place, there could be an alligator or congregations thereof. Pythons, non-venomous or venomous snakes, a rat, rabbits, squirrels or a Florida panther, anything, anywhere and at any time. It is quite common not to be able to negotiate a footpath due to a large seemingly insipid alligator, soaking up the heat from below. Recalcitrant reptilians are abounding in the Everglades, step over, or around, or go home.

Regardless of the time of year, the same rules apply, once you get out of the vehicle you are in the wild. You have to be careful what you touch, and where you tread, and keep your eyes peeled at all time, and always have a camera ready.

Negotiating the alligator slide into the Movie-Dome will be wet, muddy, or bone dry. If it is wet, then it will range from ankle to chest deep. If it is muddy, then it is likely at some point that you may end up face down in mud. If it is dry, it is possible to trip and break your ankle on the hard terrain. Either way you should be very careful.

Walking in the water is a unique experience for the tourist, they kind of expect it, and maybe even specifically request it, but still do not know quite what to expect. From December onwards the water can be freezing, which is often a shock to the system, but during summer it is delightfully tepid on the sweat soaked skin. If there is naked skin involved, then there will be fish and crawdaddies (crayfish), to remind you it is not a swimming pool. There will also be various snake species such as brown or green water snakes, swimming past your calves or thigh muscles, which people often find alarming. One thing to try to remember, whatever the time of year, is the grass all around can and will cut you, do not grab onto it as it will cut, and though not deep, it will become irritating as the day goes on.

Regardless of how you choose to enter the dome, do not be in too much of a rush. Take your time and take it all in. There will be the odd screech from a red-shouldered hawk (*Buteo lineatus*), along with plenty of ibis, egrets, great blue herons, vortices of vultures circling in the rising heat, and various other bird species perched on the dwarf cypress limbs around you.

Keep an eye out for tiny clusters of pearlescent pink, green, red or white eggs on the sawgrass. These belong to apple snails (*Pomacea*). There are four species of apple snail in Florida, and only the Florida apple snail (*Pomacea paludosa*) is native, any others are a non-native or invasive species. The Florida apple snail is important, as it is the primary staple of the snail kite (*Rostrhamus sociabilis*). The importance of the Florida apple snail is that the snail kite is an endangered species, remove the snail and you wipe out a beautiful bird species. Chemical pollutants in the water table, rising water levels, tourists, decreased ambient temperature from rapidly and unexpected cold fronts, are all some of the many ways you would not normally consider that can decimate a species.

Once you manage to reach the perimeter of the dome itself, there is a clear entrance, made mostly by tours over the years. To get to it though, requires negotiation of a rather deep solution hole in the mud or water. I would always step over this and then get my camera ready for whoever was behind. If this were wet season, then the unsuspecting tourist behind would go from knee-deep water, straight to chest or even higher, depending on their height. I have a wonderful collection of photos, all of different people, yet all seem to sport the same expression, and it never got old.

Guarding Hades

Alice, which is the name I gave the resident alligator in the Movie-Dome, would often like to hang out just on the domes edge near the solution hole, where I would lead tourists into the dome. I am not in the habit of anthropomorphizing animals. I just like to give some of them names, mostly from familiarity or affection.

I would often not let my tourists know about Alice ahead of time. Alice could have been anywhere. I always liked the challenge of spotting her or turning a corner and bumping right into her. I should point out, that though I named the alligator Alice; I had no proof that she was female. You cannot tell without sticking your fingers inside, and I like my fingers. However, there were often babies around her so the assumption was that she was female.

On one occasion in around October time, the water levels were still very high, and I was leading a small group into the Movie-Dome. There were three Asian girls (Korean I think), an old couple, and a Canadian girl traveling on her own.

As we approached the ingress into the dome, I knew we were approaching the solution hole, so I stepped over, leaving the lone Canadian girl to approach it, albeit unknowingly. The Canadian girl was making her way through the knee-deep water approaching the hole, grabbing onto the cypress limbs for support, with the others close behind her. I told everyone to be quiet and approach slowly, and not scare any wildlife away from the dome. The girl stepped forward looking right at me, and as she did, she plummeted into the sinkhole right up to her chest. She let out a surprisingly soft but pronounced whimper, likely due to the shock, and then froze while she accepted her lot. I was in hysterics and said:

"Watch out, there's a hole there" she laughed and awkwardly recovered herself onto the higher ground on the other side of the hole.

However, the best was yet to come. The instant she recovered to the higher ground, and only knee high water, Alice (the alligator) suddenly erupted out of the water behind her from the other sinkhole. Her body was prehensile, with about 4-feet of raw reptilian power sticking out of the water, which then came slapping down onto the water like a killer whale at an aquarium.

The Canadian jumped out of her skin and lost her footing, face planting her back into the murky sinkhole from whence she just came. Alice scurried off into the dome leaving my tourists in a state of comatose and awe. The Canadian girl, with little to no dignity left, splashed about like a dead fish in the bottom of a boat, as she struggled to get equal footing, and figure out what just happened.

I was still in hysterics as I watched her stand and look down at herself soaked to the skin, covered in mud. The other tourists started to move forwards to assist her, and after a short while, everyone was composed and ready to move on, though Alice was sitting in the water just a few feet into the dome. She was facing towards us, daring us to approach like *Cerberus*, so of course we did.

The tourists actually loved it, they felt a sense of camaraderie now I suspect, which often happens with shared moments of comedic disaster in the wilderness.

That was just one of so many different, yet same stories. Just change the people and the date, and it repeated every day, not verbatim, but the Everglades tours were a collection of such events, almost as if I had staged them before arriving. A little experience and familiarity though, and you could have a good bet as to what may happen at any given moment, although it was never any less funny to watch and experience.

Once you enter the Movie-Dome, if it is the dry season, then it is easy to follow a well-trodden loop. If it is underwater, there is no visible track to follow, and it is easy to get lost, as in any cypress dome. As you enter deeper into the dome, it really comes alive and you experience an untamed atmosphere. In the Movie-Dome, almost every cypress tree wears thick bromeliads, and hanging air plants, like a snipers ghillie suit. Some bromeliads are sky reaching bright red cardinal blooms, or some that look just like the top of a pineapple. Speckled with orchids, lichens, alert anole lizards, frogs, toads, and insects, the dome sits peacefully and timeless as you enter into its intricate world.

Smack bang in the middle of the Movie-Dome is a large pond. Tips of draping *Tillandsia* (Spanish moss), sit afloat the water and white feathers drift down like snowflakes from the trees above; the remains of startled ibis and egrets that made haste no matter how quiet you tried to be. Fallen tree limbs, sticking out of the water like shipwreck remains, tattooed in bird pooh like Nelsons column.

As you move carefully and quietly through the water using every sense, and relying on your direct and peripheral vision like never before, you will come to an opening that looks right into the middle of the pond. Stand still, and take stock whilst you stand in knee to waist high water. If you keep an eye out for a few minutes, after a short time the eerie appearance of a small pair of eyes will emerge like a submarine periscope from the ponds depths.

The alligator, (Alice), pops out to see what is going on. Usually as you enter the dome, if Alice is around, she will submerge to get away or hide away from people. However, if you are patient, it is great to stand quietly, and watch her appear like that. It must be a real treat to see for the first time. I know the majority of my tourists, whether scared or not, loved this. Then the realization that they were stood in the same water as an alligator, which is now only a few feet away, an adrenaline rush for sure. The feeling exacerbated by the sudden disappearance of the eyes, which now means you are still in the water with an alligator, except that now you cannot see where it is. Although you are sure, the guide knows what they are doing, so the best thing is to cling like mosquitoes to him, usually literally.

All in A Day's Work

I once had a German couple and their son on a tour, who was about twelve years of age, and a few others. I remember the German family because the mother was smoking hot, but also because I had to carry the son on my back, all the way around the Movie-Dome.

We had been approaching the dome when a small python (around 5-feet) had emerged from the sawgrass and slithered off into the murky water. The son who was on my heels anyway, had literally jumped into my arms with fright. He was clinging tightly onto me, and nothing was going to make him let go. I repositioned him around and onto my back, and he clasped his arms around my throat, and his legs around my waist. His father had told him to get down, but I said it was fine, and the son didn't want to get down. It was funny and cute, but hard work. I had one hand on a pole for balance as it was high water season, and the other supporting him to stop him from strangling me with his tight grip.

He was glad he had decided to take the ride, as Alice was soon accompanying us in the water. If I had not seen her, I still would have known, as my speech slurred and I gasped for air, as the boy constricted himself around my body. Yet another day in the life of a wilderness guide.

The father took a great photo, which we later used for tour promotions and my business card, and used on the front cover of this book. I also got a generous tip at the end of the tour, which was never expected, but always welcomed, and often came in large amounts. Like the one tourist who flew in on his private jet from Washington D.C, for a private tour, and who tipped me a thousand bucks ($1000).

The center of the dome is awesome to watch. There can be literally nothing going on but you can watch it for hours, just from anticipation or wonder. The pond itself during a wet season, if the water levels are high, is about 5-feet deep, if you take into account sinking into the mud. I know this because some hostel volunteers and I were exploring the dome once, and I thought that it was good opportunity to take my dive mask and snorkel. I have a great video of me coming out of the middle of the dome, slowly like Martin Sheen from the scene in the movie *Apocalypse Now*. However, when swimming underwater in the Everglades, your movement brings all the detritus from below, whirling around like a washing machine spin cycle. You don't need to see an alligator underwater though, as it is easy to tell if you swim into one.

You move around the edge of the pond amongst the cypress trees, keeping an eye out in the middle and around you for signs of any life, or just watching Alice. Making sure that you know where she is at all times. This does not mean you won't be confronted with another reptilian log floating somewhere in the dome though. As you wander nervously around, taking photos at every step, you will walk through cobwebs, brush by bromeliads, and become terrified as twigs and logs move under your feet in the water below, with your movement clouding your vision. It is hard to cover all your bases in an environment like this, there are so many opportunities to miss something, and all the time there is something somewhere that you will miss. One of the most likely is some sun-tanning snake coiled within a fern or tree stump, or entwined in a spiked bromeliad.

The deciduous conifers shed their needles, and when they do, they fall below, atop the waist hugging bromeliads, creating a comfortable bed for snakes of all shapes and sizes. The heavier collections form like a hive around the air plants, allowing snakes to burrow inside to make nests. It is always a good idea to take a good look around to see what you can find. Though it was often fifty-fifty as to whether the tourists wanted me to find a snake, they seemed to be safe in the knowledge there were some, and they didn't need physical evidence.

The thing about the Movie-Dome, for whatever reason, is that I never encountered a venomous species of snake in there, though there will be plenty to come when I discuss the Cottonmouth Dome. The Movie-Dome is home to many water snakes though, such as the brown, banded, and green water snake. The brown water snake (*Lycodonomorphus rufulus*) is often confused with the water moccasin (cottonmouth), and unnecessarily feared and killed, which of course the actual cottonmouth is also, yet there is no need to kill either of them. You can often see water snakes coiled up on top of a comfortable cypress needle bed, taking in the day, unperturbed by its visitors, but likely would prefer complete peace.

The younger members of tour groups love to find shed snakeskins. If there were only one among the group, I would often give it to them. If there were more than one younger person in the group, I would just let them admire it, or maybe give them all an alligator tooth from my collection. Seeing a snakeskin is also a wakeup call to the rest of the group who now realize that what I was saying about snakes being all around was actually true, and that I wasn't just exaggerating for dramatic effect. In addition to skins, it was also common to find snake skeletons, bird skeletons, lizard remains, all remnants of some prey, or just natural death and demise. Owl pellets filled with shell and other remains are all over. If the water levels are low and there is some naked earth, then alligator scat is always a treat to prod and poke through with the tourists, to see what it had been eating of late. A nice soft fresh one has a specific odor to it as well, always nice before taking a lunch break.

Another repeat visitor to this dome is a rather large soft-shelled turtle (*Apalone ferox*), although it may not always be the same one, but I would see a rather large one here quite often.

Florida soft shell turtles are strange creatures. They have a large pig like proboscis that sticks out of the water upon the end of their long leathery necks, allowing them to breathe. They are almost always in the water, apart from when they seek *terra firma* to lay their eggs, a recurring sight in the grass at the edge of the main park road around March time, and then will hatch a few months later. You will often see the turtle laid at the edge of the road, or at the Anhinga trail in the grass digging the mud up behind itself with its clawed flippers, like a dog burying a bone. The thing about Florida soft shell turtles is their leather like carapace, which is flimsy at the edges if you try to pick one up. As I mentioned before, it is not uncommon to see alligators chomping down on one of these or any other turtle, the bloody shelled remains falling from its jaws all around it, accompanied by a loud crunching sound, and a look of satiated glee on the alligator.

If you become familiar with some of the locals, you may get to try soft shell turtle soup too, it is lovely and a wonderful traditional Southern dish.

Not So Tough

I had a group of six once, and three of which were young French military lads, and the whole group were a good bunch. The three military lads were really loud and cocksure of themselves, as most young soldiers are, but I am down with that.

At the beginning of the tour, they kept saying that they were up for anything, and to make it as wild as possible. We were moving through the Movie-Dome and the three lads were directly behind. The water was waist deep, and we had worked our way around the back of the pond to an area close to the edge of the deeper pond, to look in to try to find the alligator. As we stood in silence, one of the lads suddenly jumped, splashed, and screamed, as something had brushed his leg, and then one of the other lads shouted:

"WTF is that!" and tried climbing up into the tree as it too brushed past his leg.

The rest of the group began to panic, and I looked down into the murky depths, and saw the outline of what I knew was a soft shell turtle. I bent down and pulled out of the water this whopping, alien like dripping turtle, for all to see. I said:

"It's only a soft shell, it won't harm you."

The looks on the lads faces was epic, a mixture of extreme fear and panic tinged with relief.

It is funny how the simple unknown or lack of familiarity with ones surroundings can bring grown men to tears. The woman in the group thought it was hilarious. They were decidedly quieter throughout the rest of the day.

If you walk around the dome anti-clockwise, which was my favorite direction, then around the back of the pond if you look up, there is and always has been since I first explored it, a large nest. This is home to a pair of red-shouldered hawks, which use this nest season after season. There is a high-pitched screech, as they circle the dome from above, or perch out in the sun at shoulder height, making wonderful photographs.

Red-shouldered hawks are beautiful birds and the most abundant hawk in the Everglades. There are many others though, from broad-winged, sharp-shinned, Cooper's, red-tailed and short-tailed. Although, unless you are an ornithologist, or a keen twitcher (birder), then every hawk you see will result in being a red-shouldered hawk, as it is hard to tell the difference from a distance.

One of the more interesting things about red-shouldered hawks though, is they seem to be more sociable and accepting of humans. They will often be around Anhinga Trail, close to the path, to see quite easily. More often than not, they will have some unlucky species of reptilian prey hanging from their talons or beak. They are quite the show off.

There have been numerous occasions and photos taken on tours of red-shouldered hawks perched proudly, and flaunting an Everglades racer, or dusky pygmy rattlesnake, for its soon to be consumed main course.

We are far from done with cypress domes, but the Movie-Dome has been a great appetizer, offering some wonderful wildlife up close and personal, as well as excitement, and a wonderful feeling of accomplishment and an overcoming of fear. At times, it can appear lifeless in there, and you will struggle to see any movement at all. If it is a real dry season then the pond will be nothing but a damp muddy pit crisscrossed with alligator slides like sled marks through the snow. Every month is different in the Everglades.

You will eventually come back to the entrance, and then the slog back to the vehicle. For the soaking wet or muddy tourist, it is a huge relief to reach dry land. They can remove the mud and limestone filled shoes from their pruned feet. Discover the sawgrass cuts all over their bare skinned legs, which they didn't even realize had cut them, yet are now stinging. Finally, they take a hand on hip breather, and look back towards the dome. A sight that is worlds away from what they just saw inside the dome.

A short drive onwards and you will see on the left hand side, a very large dome approaching ahead. The Triple-Dome or Cottonmouth Dome is the next adventure.

The Cottonmouth Dome

As is probably apparent, the Cottonmouth Dome gets its name due to the high population of venomous cottonmouth snakes (*Agkistrodon piscivorus*) that seem to frequent it. Though this name is my own pet name for it, the more traditional name for this dome is the Triple-Dome or Double Dome, depending on whom you speak too, so called due to the belief that the dome is actually two or three domes forming one large one. It is a large dome, and very easy to get lost in. I have guided people into here during the day, and only been five minutes in from the road, asking them where we came in, yet no one was able to tell me, and seem completely lost. This is perfectly understandable though, as it is very disorientating.

So once again pulling to the side of the road, which usually happens to be next to a culvert, you can get out of the vehicle and prepare for another dome, the same, yet so different. The culvert here is a regular haunt to one of the two alligators that tend to frequent this dome; a female and large bull male alligator. The female often accompanied by some babies or yearlings, at the right time of year. The culvert is also a great opportunity to wash your feet or shoes after the dome, until you hear an alligator hiss resounding from within the concrete tunnel, which makes people move very fast.

One of the most prevalent species of poisonous plants in the Everglades is abundant along the side of the road here. Poisonwood (*Metopium toxiferum*), is actually in the cashew family (*Anacardiaceae*), but there is nothing on the tree that you would want to eat or touch. However, the fruits are a favorite among the white crown pigeon (*Patagioenas leucocephala*), amongst a few others. Poisonwood contains urishiol, which is an organic allergen, which can produce a nasty rash ranging from mild to painful blistering. There are many others within the park, such as poison ivy, and poison oak, that have a similar effect when in contact with the skin. Poisonwood is quite easy to identify however, with its five to seven compound pinnate leaves, often with dark spots on them like inkblots.

Historically, the poisonwood leaves and sap were ingredients for a tea. Some people would add bleach to the tea, and then drink it to assist with abortions. Luckily, for me, for whatever reason, I am immune to the allergen and can quite happily rub leaves and twigs all over me with no effect, which is quite useful, though annoying to some who have recently encountered it with ill effect.

Now, though it wasn't at this particular spot, I have to recount a short anecdote about poisonwood, which happened a little further on at Nine Mile Pond. I have plenty of stories to wax lyrical about later from that area, so I will mention it now in context to the mention of poisonwood.

Toxic Toilet Paper

When touring the park, one of the difficulties for such a long journey is finding toilet facilities. Aside from a few stops that are many miles apart, the only option is to go alfresco.

We stopped once at Nine Mile Pond, where there are no facilities. We had lunch first before canoeing, and once lunch was finished, I began loading the lunch gear back into the van. I then began unloading the canoes and gear, ready for the canoe trip.

I happened to see through the rear van door window, that a member of the group was emerging from the trees, over to the left. I asked him where he had been, to which he replied:

"A quick toilet break" he said, relieved.

"Hope you watched out for the poisonwood in there!" I warned him.

"What does it look like?" he replied, dumbfounded.

I wandered over and showed him, and how much of it was in there. He was concerned, and rightly so. He had unfortunately needed to take a poop. In doing so, he had not taken any toilet roll with him, and had used poisonwood leaves to wipe his behind.

I couldn't help but laugh. The reaction can often take hours to appear, or even the next day, often after a shower or bath. I had reiterated throughout the day the importance of not touching anything, but people often don't listen.

That night he was in a bad way, and I imagine it was awkward and uncomfortable for some time. Previously, I had applied on many an occasion, soothing creams to hot girls with sunburn or poisonous plant encounters. However, on this occasion I would decline though, as the thought wasn't as appealing as it had been with the female travelers.

So be careful along the edges of the road, poisonwood like the wildlife, can be anywhere. Even if you think you know what a plant is, do not touch it, it could be something very similar, but different to what you think you recognize.

Aside from poisonwood, there is also poison ivy and manchineel to name a few. Manchineel (*Hippomane mancinella*) is one of the most poisonous plants on the planet, so it is not wise to eat its tiny apples or ingest the sap, or indeed any part of the tree. The apples look like crab apples, so they are easily confused. The word Manchineel comes from the Spanish *Manzanilla,* which means little apple, and is commonly known as *Manzanilla de la muerte,* which means 'little apple of death.'

It is however native and not an invasive, and due to high elimination it is now classed as endangered, so the numbers are not great, and there are none to be found around the Cottonmouth Dome.

Aside from the poisonous plants, another thing you need look out for everywhere in the park, are the fire ants (*Solenopsis*) aka RIFA, or red imported fire ant. These annoying tiny critters love to bite toes and the soft flesh webbing between them. I would be standing there one minute talking to a group, the next thing I knew I had an army of fire ants in my sandal, or on my bare feet. They secrete a pheromone signaling to all to bite *en masse*, and then tiny burning needles pierce your skin. The bites are very uncomfortable, and end up as tiny pustules all over your feet and lower limbs, or wherever else their pincers find you.

Before entering the Cottonmouth Dome, although I would have mentioned snakes previously throughout the day, I would usually go into more detail here, as it was very likely we would encounter some, and with a high chance of them being venomous. Once everyone was ready, we would gather around. With the aid of some photos, I would go into a bit more detail about venomous snakes in general, specifically the cottonmouth, and mention the non-venomous but potentially dangerous, and often large and invasive; Burmese python (*Python bivittatus*). Now, though I would have talked about venom, and its difference to poison, I would go over it again here, but a little more in depth, in relation to the cottonmouth itself.

In the Cottonmouth Dome, year round there are cottonmouths all over the place. They are great swimmers, so when the water levels are high they glide across the top of the water with no problem. Although not arboreal in nature, they are great climbers. Though not a kingsnake, they will, and can eat other snakes, including eastern diamondback rattlesnakes, which there is a great video of on YouTube uploaded by Ojatro.

When swimming, they are easy to spot, as they will swim with almost their whole body out of the water, and their head stretched upwards, though they have been known to dive down to catch fish. However, they do not swim underwater as often as the water snake, which will swim and live happily submerged for long periods, which is a good method of identification. If you see a snake coiled up beneath the water, it is unlikely to be a cottonmouth.

During the drier season, this dome is teeming with them, from the ground to the bromeliads, on tree stumps, on cypress knees, and aside the water in the mud. When asked as to where to look to find them, I would reply with my little ditty:

"Anywhere is their home, inside a cypress dome."

Cottonmouth. Courtesy of Rustin Gooden

The cottonmouth has a hemotoxic venom, which means it attacks the muscle tissue and blood and rather rapidly too, with almost instant pain. The localized pain of a cottonmouth bite can be quite severe compared to other snakes; the chances of fatality though are very slim these days. The bite can lead to a loss of limbs though, or a requirement for a skin graft. The edema and discoloration is likely to last for quite a few weeks, with that being said, as with every snake bite, there are so many factors to take into account, such as the victims age, medical conditions, bite area, amount of venom and of course some luck.

Regardless of any of these factors, if a snake bites you, then you should stay calm and get yourself to medical help as soon as possible. You would be ill advised to attempt any type of medical procedures. Treatments such as tourniquets, snakebite kits, and sucking the venom out are generally a bad idea.

The fact is, if you use a tourniquet, you increase the risk of losing a limb. If you use a snakebite kit, you increase the chance of additional infection. If you attempt to suck the venom out then you risk ingesting the venom into a mouth cut or ulcer, or even a weak and bleeding gingiva, which would create two victims. The primary care for a snakebite victim in the wild, if help is on its way or sought shortly, is to keep the victim calm, keep them hydrated, and keep the limb still, and below the heart where possible.

However, if you must do something else then instantly squeeze the area of the bite, to get the surface venom out as much as possible, and wash away with clean water. Do not attempt to capture the snake, and even if the snake is dead somehow, then do not attempt to pick it up. However, you should try to get a positive ID of the snake to assist the medical team.

If you are on your own in the backcountry and unable to reach medical assistance, then you should still take the same precautions. However, the situation may force you to apply some of the other techniques, but only as a last resort. If you are using a snakebite kit, then be sure you know how to use it. Really disinfect the area well with the supplied iodine, or similar, before making any incisions, and keep the incisions small. Only use the plunger supplied to suck on the bite, and not a mouth. If you do have to use a tourniquet to prevent further venom from spreading in the event of a medical emergency, then do not over tighten, and release at regular intervals.

The best treatment though is prevention, so do not pick up snakes, whether you are familiar with them or not. Watch every footstep, and be careful where you sit or place your hands. More importantly though, is to listen to, and follow the guide if you are on a tour. If you are on your own, then educate yourself before entering areas known to be potentially dangerous.

If a snake unfortunately bites you, or in particular, a cottonmouth, then the pain that you will feel, though excruciating, will in no way be as painful as when you receive the medical bill. Snakebite treatment is with Anti-venom serum, or Antivenin. In the USA, the antivenin administered to treat the majority of bites is Crofab (Crotalidae Polyvalent Immune Fab). This can be expensive per vial, and depending on how many vials the patient may need, along with additional treatment needed, might result in a hefty bill. We are talking in the range of $20,000 to $50,000, as vials are, or were around $2000 per vial. It is neither practical nor cheap enough to carry antivenin around with you, and treatment should be within a medical and sterile environment only. Antivenin comes from venom, so it could result in an adverse effect from the administration itself. Only trained professionals should carry out treatment.

The limit to the medical treatment that I would administer on a tour, if medical help were soon to be available, would not extend beyond the stabbing of an epinephrine pen to avoid anaphylactic shock. If the injury were a bite from a snake, then I would seek medical assistance only, and as soon as possible. I would of course do more if on an overnight trip, or far removed from medical assistance. However, on a day tour, the hospital is an hour away, and the medical team for snakebites would meet you half way or closer, if already in the park.

Venomous Babies

A friend of mine, who shall remain nameless, once had the unfortunate experience of snake envenomation from a cottonmouth. Now most bites are a result of surprising a snake, or unwittingly treading on one. My friend deserved his bite, in that he picked it up.

My friend and a few others had gone out on a private trip to the Cottonmouth Dome, while I was out conducting a tour. When I had returned from the tour, about an hour after, there was a phone call to the hostel. My friend was on the way to the hospital after a cottonmouth had bitten him on his finger.

Of course, a little panic set in around the hostel. It transpired that the reason the snake had bitten him, was that he had picked up a cottonmouth because it was a juvenile, and so he didn't recognize it. It may just be me, but the fact he didn't know what it was, was more of a reason to leave it alone.

The bite was in the end of his finger which was quite badly damaged, which resulted in around a $20,000 medical bill from what I recall, and a about a week's stay in hospital. He was very lucky.

The paramedics and emergency teams that deal with such bites are exceptional in South Florida. Chief Al Cruz from the Miami-Dade's Fire & Rescue is one of the most knowledgeable snakebite and reptilian bite specialists out there, and heads up Venom One, which is the Venom response team.

One of the interesting facts about pit vipers is that unlike most reptiles, they are ovoviviparous, and so give birth to live young. Most reptiles are oviparous, which means they lay eggs. Pit vipers such as the cottonmouth give birth to live young, which are ready to deliver a destructive bite almost instantly. Most mammals are viviparous. However, two mammals lay eggs; the duck billed platypus, and the echidna. Neither of these lives in South Florida though. I just mentioned them for extra information.

With the cottonmouths live young, their venom is ready to go from birth, so it is not a good idea to pick them up. Cottonmouth colorings will change over their lifespan, with the majority of mature ones in the dome, are a blackish grey, and the younger have black bands and a light brown color, which leads to the confusion with the various non-venomous water snakes. If you get close enough, cottonmouths are easy to identify though, from its bright white mouth, which if you can see is its way of telling you to step back. If you are close, you may see them baring their solenoglyphous fangs, which are hollow fangs that act like a hypodermic needle to envenomate their prey. The fangs fold back up into the mouth when closed, but when ready to bite will spring forward like a mousetrap. Venoms are modified saliva, containing proteins and polypeptides, designed to immobilize its prey. The snake will seek out the victim through its heat sensing pits, forked sensory tongue, and devour it by opening its mouth to around 180°. The snake will then swallow its prey, thanks in part to the venom that makes it easier, as it would have started to break down the muscle tissue.

I have read that cottonmouths are usually more inquisitive than most snakes, which can result in them approaching you, as oppose to trying to avoid you. In my experience, this is true, but not very often. It can be quite unnerving though to spot a snake, and think to yourself to be careful and go around it, only to discover it making a beeline in your direction. For the most part though, they are not interested in biting you, or interested in you at all. They want to laze in the Florida sun, as do most creatures. They do not want to waste their valuable venom on you, as it is required for their natural prey. If they do bite, it will often be a dry bite, which means there will be no venom delivery, which is a very welcome result. I know this all too well.

An eastern diamondback rattlesnake in the hammock area of mahogany hammock once bit me. I was terrified but was later to discover it had been a dry bite, and only ended up in a very small infection, with no serious damage. When it came to the Everglades, I was always fortuitous, from no reaction to poisonwood or poison ivy, to a dry bite from a rattlesnake. However, a cottonmouth also bit me many years ago, in the foot. It was only a very small amount of envenomation, only resulting in a $1500 medical bill. It could have been much worse, so thank you Everglades, I appreciate it. I would like to point out that on both occasions I didn't pick either of the snakes up; they were both the result of accidentally treading on them.

Walking in the Cottonmouth Dome has a few inherent dangers. The most likely though is that of stepping on a cottonmouth. It never happened on a tour but was always possible. If a snake bite was to occur, it would highly likely be a result of stepping on them, as they often blend in very well, or appear almost out of nowhere on the other side of a cypress tree, or under a limb that you have to climb over.

The Cottonmouth Dome requires a very keen eye, and attention to detail, be it with a guide, or on your own. Everyone has to be alert and on the lookout out for potential dangers. At the beginning of a tour, after going into some detail about the cottonmouth and its venom, treatment, and avoidance, I would then instruct everyone to make sure they only followed in the footsteps of the person in front of them. They had already said they were prepared to accept death because of the tour, so I was always pretty relaxed, and armed with my camera and a good sense of humor, in the event of unfortunate incidents. The death waiver would release me from any responsibility in the event of any problems. It was an essential document in the litigious USA.

There are a few obvious entry points into the dome from the grass verge. These apparent trails have been made by private tours over the years, but the hostel was the first to start exploring this dome in the capacity of a guided tour. However, others soon followed suit, but the dome still does not attract too many people. Much like the Movie-Dome, the Cottonmouth Dome is not marked on the map, and nor is it considered a main park attraction.

Unless you know where it is, you probably will not find it even though it meets the grass verge, unlike the Movie-Dome. If you do find it, then it is unlikely you will explore on your own. If you do, you will probably end up being lost for a few hours, before waiting patiently to hear the distant sounds of the road, and then make your precarious way slowly back towards safety.

There is also another snake to consider here, and one that I would cover in addition to the cottonmouth speech before entering the dome, the Burmese python.

The Burmese python (*Python bivittatu*s) is one of the largest snakes in the world, and certainly one of the most powerful. It is not venomous. However, it can easily kill a human through constriction, and though not venomous, they can still deliver a nasty bite with their sharp backward facing teeth, that usually becomes infected. The backward facing teeth allow the python to get a good grip, while wrapping itself around its prey, and help to move the prey into its mouth when devouring it. They average around 12-feet long, but can grow much larger. Every few months there seems to be a new record for the largest found in the Everglades, the record currently standing at the time of writing at 18.2-feet and around 150lbs, caught in February 2014. They are often riparian, and this one was no different, found on a levee near the Tamiami Trail in the water management district.

Regardless of their size, unless you are used to snakes, then anything over about 5-feet will be appear overly massive, especially if in the water with you, or on a tree branch above your head.

The Burmese python does not belong in the Everglades, or in North America. Burmese pythons are invasive, and eating the prey of other native animals, and they can eat alligators. They are one of, if not the most significant invasive species; aside from man, to ever appear in the Everglades. There are a few theories as to how they have arrived, or become so dominant here. The environment is of course perfect for them to thrive though, and with an abundance of food sources and hiding places.

In terms of introduction, South Florida and Miami is a global hub of exotic species import, with its close proximity to South America and the Islands. With the widespread exotic species collection and distribution, it is common sense to realize that eventually something will escape or be let go. A young python may seem cute initially, but suddenly having a 12-foot, or larger, snake slithering around the house becomes a bit of a bind, so what do people do? They just let it go in the Everglades, a home from home, where they can thrive and start to number in the thousands, or hundreds of thousands rather rapidly.

There are other theories also, such as a result of Hurricane Andrew in 1992, which devastated South Florida and may have resulted in pets or research animals becoming loose. Certainly, over the last fifteen years they have become a real problem, and one that is hard to combat. To the casual observer, the existence of a snake in a wilderness, such as the Everglades, may not appear to be a big deal. Having a snake such as the Burmese python become prevalent here though, is a major concern, as they eat the food sources required by other animals that rely on those sources for survival. They also endanger the native animals, such as the Florida panther, which is already on the verge of extinction. There have been many necropsies (animal autopsy), that have turned up panther claws. Alligators are not immune to the constrictive power of the Burmese python either, and there have been a few famous battles in public, and resulting in headlines around the globe.

Python easily consume white tail deer, as they do most animals. They will pretty much eat anything in their path, if they are hungry. Pythons like most snakes and other reptiles, certainly like the alligator, only eat when they are hungry, and can survive quite some time after a sufficient meal. A python can go without food for months on end if it needs to, or if satiated from a recent mammalian feast.

The way a python kills and devours its prey is fascinating, and certainly fascinating to watch. Using their powerful bite and rear facing teeth, it will clasp onto its prey, then start wrapping itself around the prey, and slowly begin to constrict. It does not crush though. It constricts, slowly tightening every time the prey exhales, making it harder and harder for the prey to breathe, and resulting in the prey losing consciousness. Once the victim is out cold, the python releases it from its grip, and then at an appropriate point, will start to swallow the prey whole. They have an amazing jaw, assisted by quadrate bones on either side of the upper and lower jaw that stretches. The jaw stays connected via elastic ligaments, and with the upper and lower jaw moving independently, allowing the snake to stretch its mouth over enormously large prey you would think was impossible.

An average white tail deer would be around 150lbs or more. Imagine trying to swallow an alligator whole, and that has happened a few times. The teeth assist the snake in pulling the prey into the mouth and into the murky and acidic depths of the stomach. Snakes also have some inverted vertebrae that pull prey inwards when the snake moves, to help pull the prey down into the acidic digestive juices that will dissolve its prey, like Walter White from *Breaking Bad* with a body in an oil drum.

Remember that the prey wasn't necessarily dead when devoured, only unconscious. I imagine awakening inside a Burmese python to be quite traumatic. I have woken up in some pretty strange and horrific places, but a Burmese pythons belly is not on my bucket list.

Swallowing large prey is risky for python though, they can sometimes have eyes that are too big for their bellies. In 2005, a famous photo went viral on the Internet. It depicted a large Burmese python, which had attempted to swallow an alligator, but then literally exploded, leaving the alligator dead, but also the snake split in two, jack-knifed and floating in the slough.

To sum these bad boys up, they are big, powerful, will eat anything, can climb, swim and move fast. Though are largely nocturnal, the majority of Burmese pythons I have encountered and caught, have been during the day. Yes I said caught! Invasive species need to be eradicated, and python, if found are usually shot. In the early days before tighter regulations came into effect regarding their capture, I would catch them when possible, much like the guides before me, and drop them off at the research center for Skip Snow to deal with. Skip Snow is the head herpetologist dealing with the invasive python problem.

I wasn't the only one dropping them off either, there would usually already be a few when I got there. The captured pythons are euthanized and necropsied. This process is for research into the contents of their stomach to give insight to diet and range. Sometimes the scientists electronically tag the python and release them back into the wild. Releasing them with electronic tags through the Judas snake program, allows the park scientists to track them, and discover their preferred habitats, that ultimately will help the park to eradicate them. Although eradication is unlikely now, as they have secured a strong foothold, but I imagine that suppression is an achievable goal. I would never attempt to capture a python more than say 6-feet long on my own, and certainly never on a tour where I can endanger others under my care.

Capturing a python can take some effort, and you shouldn't attempt to capture a python or indeed any snake without experience. You should try to approach it from behind if possible, whilst remaining alert, as they can turn extremely quickly and can strike from further than you think. Snakes do not need to be coiled to strike either, which is a popular myth.

You should quickly place your hand behind and around its neck and head. The process is easier if you have a hook or snake tongs (animal grabber). When you have the head, you control the snake, and it will become calmer after a short while. Initially though, as it loses control of its head, it will begin to wrap its tail and body around the closest object it can get hold of, usually its captor, and a Burmese python wrapped around a limb is not particularly comfortable. After a short time it will loosen its constriction a little, which will make it easier to direct into a bag (the mesh laundry bags are perfect). Capturing one in the water is a different matter though. They are quite at home in the water, and could easily take you down and under, so on land is certainly easier. The largest I ever caught was about seven feet, but thin, and I had a friend to help me. I had spotted it underneath the saw palmetto at the edge of the Cottonmouth Dome, near the grass verge. I would always point that fact out to the tourists before entering the dome, to make sure they were awake and alert.

After my boring lecture about snakes, and dying to get into it, I would now lead the tour into the dome. The direction I would go would depend on the time of year, as with most things due to water levels. If you head in near the culvert at the wrong time of year and are not alert there will be a large alligator right there with you. At other times of the year, when the water levels were low, then this would just be damp underfoot, but leading into some waist deep mud. I would often go this way because it is hilarious to watch people panic as if in quicksand, as they sink into waist deep ooze, and onto a sharp limestone base. This makes for great photo opportunities, and there are probably many people around the world that have a picture of themselves either framed, or maybe a desktop wallpaper of themselves covered in mud and grimacing at me in the distance, with looks of complete disdain on their faces.

Quoting again, from another journalist who wrote the following in the UK Sunday Times Travel Magazine, March 2014:

'Follow me, said graham (and probably nobody in history has ever followed anyone more closely). We were to enter one of the many dense copses of cypress trees. They grow up from slivers of water between the giant plains of sawgrass that stretch away under blue skies for miles. He took a sturdy walking pole and strode, instantly knee-deep, into the watery woods. I took a deep breath and steeped into the cool, glassy water behind him – both of us under a thin canopy of greenery through which sunlight made shadows on tree trunks and vines. I suddenly felt completely sealed off from the noise and chaos of the modern, mechanized world – transported to a tiny, primordial eco-bubble of steamy stillness" - Joanna Walters, *'The really wild show'*, Sunday Times Travel Magazine.

As a frame of reference for the purposes of the text, I will enter on the right hand side of the dome, where there is a clear and obvious ingress just to the right of a small group of saw palmetto. You will meander slowly through the cypress in mud, water, or a bed of cypress needles. A little way in, any path becomes less prominent, and so it is down to experience and a sense of adventure, as you could spend hours in here. Right in the middle of the dome is a large depression, where the water gathers and retains depth through the dry season, much like any other dome, and as others is home to an alligator; two adult alligators in fact.

Dotted all around this dome are cypress knees, or pneumatophores. The pneumatophores are somewhat of an enigma as to their real purpose. Some scientists believe them to be cypress snorkels. They are growing like stalagmites from the ground upwards, and allowing oxygenation, much like the pneumatophores on the red mangrove, and some believe them to be nothing more than a type of anchor.

Regardless of their nature, the woody cone protrusions that are the cypress knees are short stumps, which do not grow much higher than around 4-feet in the Everglades. They can reach as high as fourteen feet further north though. They also provide a magical quality to the cypress forests. Their appearance in all their differing shapes and sizes, adds further mystique to this amazing place, along with being a popular sunspot for our venomous friends, the cottonmouth.

Much like the Movie-Dome or any other cypress dome or forest, it is dense with bromeliads, clumps of stray sawgrass, rotting tree limbs, skeletons, and various forms of scat. There are two large ponds in the center, which though obvious when you find them, are not always easy to find if you are not used to the area. You will also need to be careful due to the presence of poison ivy (*Toxicodendron radicans*), that if you are not familiar, contains an allergen called urishiol, much like the poisonwood I mentioned earlier. Though its name indicates it is ivy, it is not, it is actually a weed. It is not particularly easy to identify if you are not familiar with it, as it can be confused with Virginia creeper, hoptree, blackberry and more. However, a good ditty to remember is as follows:

"Leaves of three let it be, berries of white, run in fright" which is an indication that if it has groups of three leaves and white berries, then it is likely to be poison-ivy, so if unsure then do not touch it.

Another reason to be careful around here, aside from the obvious snakes, alligators, and poisonous plants, is that there is a small mound next to a large cypress knee on the edge. This mound gives an elevated view. If you slip on this mound, which happens quite easily, you will end up in the pond, and right under the mound, one of the alligators enjoys hanging out. There is a large cypress knee here too, which is a recurring home for a couple of water snakes that like to chill in the sun here.

It is difficult to continue to explain a course through this dome as it is so large, and there is no visible path. Even when dry, there is no real path once inside, though there is obvious ingress and egress points at the edge of the dome. Once you are in, it becomes a lot less navigable than the Movie-Dome, so rather than attempt to explain a direction I will go over some of the attractions of this dome instead.

As I already said, whether it be waist high water or dry forest floor, you should stay alert as much as possible to your footing. If it is wet then I thoroughly recommend some kind of walking pole to assist with balance, for those unnerving times when you come across a solution hole, which you will, without a doubt. When it has become somewhat drier, around what would be February and onwards into summer, the cottonmouths will be all over the place, some easily spotted and others less visible. On one tour of this dome at night, I counted twenty-three, and I suspect I missed many.

If you are alert, then during daytime, if you know where to look, you will probably see five or ten. Some of the favorite spots are on lower tree limbs, cypress knees, atop fallen tree roots, next to water, within the ferns, and inside cavities of cypress knees, or rotten stumps, to name a few. These places also cover all the various other snake species too, including pythons. Cottonmouths do not tend to go very high, like some of the species of snakes in the Everglades, such as the rat snake (*Elaphe obsoleta rossalleni*), or the beautiful rough green snake (*Opheodrys aestivus*), which are often seen quite high in the trees.

A Snake Dinner

Cottonmouths do not tend to go that high into trees, but it doesn't mean that they can't. Most snakes are agile climbers, using a concertina motion to ascend trees and such like. On one of my tours, we were heading further in, after exploring the pond areas, and having already seen four cottonmouths up close, my group was alert and filled with adrenaline. As I moved forward between the trees, I spotted another cottonmouth ahead. I stopped the group and turned towards them. As I was talking, my peripheral vision alerted me to look up, and as I did I could see a hawk heading down towards what I thought was straight at me. Within what seemed like only a nanosecond the hawk had landed on top of a bromeliad, about 8-foot up on the tree behind me, and fluttered a little as it seemed to be caught. It was however adjusting for the new weight, before taking off. It suddenly flew back over me and my group, with a 3-foot cottonmouth in its talons, almost brushing our heads with the serpent. The whole group stood with gaping mouths, and all their heads were turning in unison following its flight path. It was truly amazing and a real value-add moment.

I hate to think what would have happened if the hawk had lost its grip, which happens so often with captured prey in flight. A tourist with a cottonmouth wrapped around its head would have made a great photo advert for the website though.

I had seen some amazing things take place in the Everglades and in the domes in particular, but this moment goes down as one of the best yet. I had seen hawks eating many snakes before, red-shouldered hawks love the dusky pygmy rattlesnakes, but I had never seen one capture a cottonmouth, and certainly not in this manner either.

So be aware, snakes as with everything else can be anywhere, and at any time in the Everglades.

One of the most awesome features of this dome is it is home to the rare cowhorn orchid (*Cyrtopodium punctatum*), which is also known as the cigar orchid and bee-swarm orchid. The cowhorn orchid is an endangered epiphyte, that is not that common within the Everglades anymore, but it still grows in cypress swamps, and in hammocks in South Florida, and down to South America. Sadly, during the years when Florida was a haven for hunters and collectors, this orchid met its demise due to mass collection. It is even believed among some, that it is less common in numbers than the infamous ghost orchid (*Dendrophylax lindenii*), which was the inspiration for the Nicolas Cage movie *Adaptation,* filmed in and around Homestead.

The cowhorn orchid is easy to spot, even when not in bloom, due to the Cuban cigar like pseudobulbs that protrude like cows horns, hence the name. It is a deciduous orchid, so during winter the flowers will disappear, leaving paper like encased cowhorns for identification, almost resembling corn on the cob. The Cottonmouth Dome is home to seven of these beauties on various trees towards the rear of the dome, but all within the same vicinity. The flower is wonderfully intricate, with golden yellow tri-lobed petals, tattooed with purple and brown fleck. They also emit a wonderfully fresh aroma like a plug in air freshener that attracts bees, which gives it its other common name, the bee-swarm orchid. When in full bloom (around March and April) they are truly magnificent. I personally enjoy them the most in this dome, when the sun is behind them shining through the petals, adding to their golden hue and bringing out the purple. Though I have indicated times of year, aside from the water levels, which follow the wet and dry season rules, most of Florida's plants do not really obey the same rules as other places in the world. Due to the weather conditions, many plants can bloom year round, or over extended periods to their northern counterparts, so my suggestions are flexible.

Much like the Movie-Dome, the Cottonmouth Dome has some regular inhabitants. We already know about the venomous snakes and the alligators, but there is another wonderful creature that frequents this dome, an alligator snapping turtle. The alligator snapping turtle (*Macrochelys temminckii*) is a real powerhouse of a turtle, and can easily snip your toe or fingers off. The Florida or common snapping turtle (*Chelydra serpentine*), is the most frequent snapping turtle species in the Everglades, and as far as I know the alligator snapping turtle is not that common. This dome is the only place I ever saw one in the Everglades National Park, and I would see it here regularly. The reason it's called an alligator snapping turtle, is due to its armored carapace, that makes it look somewhat like an alligators back, and they can eat small alligators. These aquatic tanks are short and stocky, Kevlar covered turtles, with a mouth that you do not want to get your little tootsies or pinkies caught in, or any other part of your body for that matter.

They are, like most turtles, edible and tasty. They can grow up to 400lbs according to unverified record; though the average would be 50-150lbs, the one in the dome who I gave the pet name of 'Arnie' (after Arnold Schwarzenegger), was around 80lbs. I know that because I picked him up a few times to show my group. This military hummer of a turtle is so primitive to look at, a real dinosaur. I am sure he was once a pet, but I couldn't bring myself to remove him. I am all for the protection of the Everglades, and the removal of non-native and invasive species, however, Arnie is too cool a creature to come across when conducting the tours, so I let him be.

Probably the greatest time to explore this dome is at night with the full moon for added effect, and the full moon tours were something I came up with to offer visitors something really unique and different. Wading through the murky moonlit waters, accompanied by various reptiles and other nocturnal wonders, and a moonlit canoe paddle, is a truly special experience, not had by many. I had many people do a day tour and then a full moon tour, or the other way round. They all commented on how completely different the two were, even if they were conducted in the same areas.

Imagine a forest, and then fill it with chest deep water. Throw in some alligators, cottonmouths, pythons, toads, frogs, lizards, water snakes and loads of other nocturnal loving reptiles and creatures. Then get in the water with them. Add some eerie owl hoots, sudden wing flaps, splashes, and a few other unidentified sounds, all amplified by the darkness and nervousness, and you will have a little idea what it is like.

The first time I explored the Cottonmouth Dome at night, was in October and the water levels were still very high. I was on my own, and we were not yet conducting tours at night. I had decided late in the day that I wanted to camp out, but just for the night, and not an extended trip. I grabbed my Hennessey hammock (a hammock tent that extends between trees, which are great for sleeping above the water), some food and overnight gear. I then headed out to the park, originally planning to set up in the pinelands for the night.

On my way into the park, I pulled over at one of the culverts, and it was, as always, beautiful. It was so peaceful, aside from the odd pig frog chorus, and the buzzing drone of mozzies. The sky blanketed with stars, though not as much as usual, due to the full moon rising behind me. It for whatever reason struck me, that instead of the pinelands, I should go to the Movie-Dome, and set up there, so off I went. I pulled up on the grass verge next to the dome, but before I switched the engine off, I decided to head on a little further, and go in the Cottonmouth Dome.

After parking, I got my gear together (about 5lbs of kit), and I walked off into the dome barefoot. Barefoot is how I preferred to walk through the water, as no shoe will protect you from alligators or snapping turtles anyway, and cottonmouths do not sit underwater. The bare feet allowed me to maintain better balance, aside from the odd sharp limestone or sharp twig, but you get used to it. The tactile feedback is also nice, and gives you a better idea of what's going on underneath you.

I ended up setting up my hammock tent, about halfway in, a little ways to the rear of the ponds, in the middle. The water was around navel deep, so I used a fallen limb that was out of the water to climb up above water level. I then slung my tent between the trees. It was a bit of a nightmare to get in and out, but once I was in, I laid there and looked up at the moonlight through the mesh roof, relaxing to the sounds of the Everglades at night.

The trip inspired me. The effects of the moonlight, the peace and the unknown, all added a completely different feel to the dome, and I knew it would make a great trip for tourists. Walking through the water obviously gives it movement. This movement creates a kaleidoscopic effect, as the shadows bounce upon the cypress bark, and the lichen, that is truly beautiful. Walking through the water and seeing an alligator in the water with you during daylight is quite invigorating. The effect however, of a pair of spooky orange to red eyes, reflecting the moon or headlamp light, sticking unnervingly out of the water, really does get the adrenal glands working overtime. Especially if you then watch them submerge with no idea as to where it vanished to, other than into the dark water where you walk.

Areegay-tor!

The full moon trips have so many stories. One in particular that stands out is one where I had eight Japanese girls in their early 20's.

As I mentioned before, I do speak a tiny bit of Japanese, however it was of little to no use on this occasion. The tours were always very popular with Asians. We had many Japanese tourists through the hostel and on tours, so I was familiar with their reactions in the face of danger. There is something extremely risible about a Japanese female every time they spot an alligator or *"areegay-tor!"* as they pronounce it. There is this stance and combined facial expression that they all seem to know instinctively. They will stand frozen still, mouth open wide, saying: *"areegay-tor!"*, and then remain open-mouthed, and pointing in complete shock, while putting their hand over their open mouth. In itself, it is funny to watch and hear, but they continue to do it even if they have seen a hundred alligators already that day. Japanese males tend to not say much, but will take three-hundred photos of the same alligator, then continue to do so for each alligator they encounter. This of course applies to snakes and other creatures too.

I had tried desperately to explain the fact that they would be getting wet, and in getting wet, would be in the water with *"areegay-tors"*, and snakes. I know it didn't sink in, due to their reactions when we reached the Cottonmouth Dome. We had already walked around the Anhinga Trail, and so they had a chance to see quite a few alligators already, enjoying shining their flashlights across the water to find the eyes, and had seen a few very close up. The trouble with the Anhinga Trail is that due to its nature, it does not give you that wilderness feeling.

When we arrived at the Cottonmouth Dome, they were all shocked at the complete darkness as we arrived. There was only the light from the full moon, which at this time was behind the dome. I tried to give my usual speech about the snakes and safety, and they stared back at me and politely nodded their heads. However, when I asked questions, they just carried on nodding, so I knew they had not understood me. I decided in the end, that I would just let them follow me, and let the Everglades do the talking.

As I entered, with what I thought was a single file behind me, I realized after a few short steps that no one was actually following. They were all standing in single file, waiting at the entrance. I shined my flashlight over, and ushered them towards me whilst saying:

"Kochira e douzo" which means, "follow me", or "this way please".

The girls started gaping and chattering fast, discussing something that I had no concept of, but I am sure that one of them said *'Ramen'*, but I may have just been hungry.

They eventually started working their way in, and as soon as the first drop of water hit skin, it just became a complete nightmare. Screaming, giggling, and shocked whimpers, with lots of Japanese babbling, bombarded the peace in rapid succession. All eight girls were making some kind of sound, all at the same time. Screaming and shouting every time a cypress branch brushed past them, and the scream or shock of the one in front would then in turn make the one behind hysterical. At this point, the water was only knee deep. I knew it was going to become deeper, and I had already resigned myself to expecting little to no wildlife due to the noise.

As I guided the chuckling, whimpering, female Asian train through the moonlit cypress dome, the ground started to soften, as the space between the trees opens up, and the water began to become deeper. We were now at thigh level. Now though it was thigh level on me, Asians are usually a little shorter than average, and this group of girls were all around 5-feet. To them, the water was now around their waists. The sudden rise of water level brought an instance of complete silence instead of sound. I think due to shock as the genital areas became soaked, and they were now really taking stock of where they were. Though they were now quiet, and had actually began whispering, I still had a few solution holes up my sleeve, along with a few other tricks to scare the bejesus out of them.

We continued to move, now silently through the water. We were using only the moonlight, which adds to the effect, although using flashlights is perfectly acceptable and of course safer, and we had them with us.

We got to where the middle ponds are, though during this time of year they are indistinguishable from the rest of the water, as they become one. I would recognize the area from the canopy, as there is a gap in the forest ceiling above the ponds, usually filled with white ibis and egrets. The screaming had made most of them depart though, their feathers still falling to the water.

I walked up onto the mound underneath the water, and then directed them towards me, signifying with my finger on mouth to stay quiet. We all stood there for a while, and took in the peace. The moonlight was reflecting off the pond with small ripples from our movement, birds, and other activity. It was beautiful. I then took my flashlight, and started to scout the surface for beady red LED like eyes glowing back at us. As my light struck a pair of eyes, there was a sudden sequence of gasps, and two or three of the girls all repeated at the same time:

"Areegay-tor!" followed again by more gasps.

They were scared and shocked, but having such a great time. It was always a good feeling to know that your group was experiencing something unique, amazing, and the stuff of memories and fireside tales.

After a while of watching the alligator, we moved on under the poison ivy, which I didn't even bother trying to explain, so maybe they got it, and maybe they didn't. I was now guiding them towards the rear of the dome. There wasn't much point heading to the cowhorn orchid though, as it wasn't in bloom, and they would not understand my enthusiasm for the plain old pseudobulbs. I did want them to see a cottonmouth though, although, when the water levels are high, this often proves difficult. I also wanted to get them to a particular spot for a little laughter, or hysteria, but usually both.

Over the years, I had learnt the Cottonmouth Dome inside and out. I could walk around it blindfolded. I knew every nook and cranny, every fallen tree, upturned root, and solution hole. You name it, and I could find it in the dark or underwater.

Some fallen trees are just the right size and shape, so that they will have buoyancy to them when the water levels are right. They also sit perfectly, just under the water so that when you apply pressure at one end, it then pops up at the other, causing a splash, and mild to major cardiac arrhythmia to those stood next to, or near it. I of course knew of such trees, and had the perfect one in mind for my group.

What turned out to be even more spectacular, and which added to the palpitations, was the fact that I managed to spot a cottonmouth laying concertinaed along a fallen tree stump. Its head was raised skyward, picking up our particles from the air with its forked tongue that then transfer to the Jacobson's organ (vomeronasal organ) in the roof of its mouth, which gives the snake a sense of smell. From where we stood, we all had a great view with my flashlight beamed upon him. However, we needed to a move a few feet so that I could add the final treat, so we moved a long a little.

Once I found the end of the fallen tree under the water with my foot, I directed their attention back to the snake, and let them ogle in fascination and fear. It was completely silent, and so I pressed down suddenly on the end of the sunken tree with my foot, and the other end sprung out of the water in front of them, right in front of the middle two, so they were all able to appreciate it. There was complete bedlam. I had never heard so many high-pitched screams all in unison before. One of the girls had turned to run, and caught her sleeve on a branch, ripping it right up to her shoulder. As she pulled it free, it continued to rip and she fell, face first, into the water. I was in complete hysterics, they were all running around with nowhere to go, screaming and panicking, whilst I stood there laughing, trying to show them it was only a tree, which they still didn't yet seem to realize.

They did of course calm down, but it was one of the funniest moments, that month at least. They were so relieved to reach dry land, when we eventually emerged back out onto the grass verge at the edge of the road. The poor girl who had fallen over was dripping wet, looking like a drowned rat. What was funny was that as soon as I opened the van, one of the girls reached for their camera, and started to take tons of photos of her sodden and muddy companion. They then asked me to take a group photo, which I of course did, and they chuckled and babbled to themselves all the way to the canoeing.

I should make clear, that though I sound extremely sadistic when it came to the tourist experience, I wasn't really. I developed over the years a good sense for what a group dynamic was like, and whether they would appreciate my sense of humor. I usually kept it as anodyne as possible. There were a few upsets over the years of course, but nothing major and they soon snapped out of it when we reached some other activity.

I could go on and on, with tales of tours in the cypress domes, but there is a lot more to cover. The next major stop on a full day tour would be the canoeing, which takes place in the brackish to saltwater areas, in amongst the mangroves. The first boat worthy trail, along the park road is Nine Mile Pond. It is located around thirty-eight miles from the main park entrance.

CHAPTER EIGHT - Paddling

"Believe me, my young friend; there is nothing – Absolutely nothing – half so much worth doing as simply messing about in boats." - Kenneth Grahame

Brackish & Paddling

Slow flowing sheens of freshwater, weaving their way between tree islands and the thousands of supporting prop roots from halophytic mangroves. The North meets the South, colliding with billions of sodium crystals, gradually becoming one. Building and nurturing unique habitats, and supporting scads of new creatures and meadows of plants that thrive amongst the shallow marshes and tangled forests. This is the brackish water, where alligators and crocodiles co-exist, osprey plummet, tiny carnivorous water plants ornament the surface, and where large slabs of spongy periphyton float like icebergs through the sawgrass.

As I already mentioned, when heading along the main park road, the scenery will change both dramatically and instantly. The change is a result of the elevation, and the amount of water flow, and of course, the nutrient levels. All of which will affect the vegetation that grows here. The further south you travel, the saltwater intrusion increases, as the sweet waters (freshwater) from the north flow out into Florida bay, but where the tides bring in the saltwater. When the two combine, you get brackish water. It is in these areas where the temperate freshwater alligator that dominates the park, also cohabitates alongside the tropical saltwater American crocodile (*Crocodylus acutus*).

It is easy to tell when you start to enter the brackish areas of the park, as the scenery will lose any tall trees, and both sides of the road will open up to large expanses of halophytic prairies, that are filled with dwarf red mangroves.

Halophytic refers to the presence of halophytes, which is a

biological term for any plant that can tolerate salt, as oppose to the most common; glycophytes, which are plants that do not tolerate salt. These dwarf red mangroves resemble bonsai trees, though they soon get larger the further you travel.

There are fifty or so species of mangrove around the world, but in Florida, only four: the red mangrove, black, white, and the buttonwood.

The most dominant mangrove in Florida and the Everglades is the red mangrove (*Rhizophora mangle*). The so-called red referring not to its appearance, but to the hue behind the bark, often seen as your canoe paddle takes a chunk from them as you attempt to negotiate a tight mangrove tunnel. The buttonwood is also a mangrove, and enjoys higher elevation inland, though is still amongst red and black, such as those found at the West Lake boardwalk. The white mangrove is also less of a coastal tree than the red or black species. The black mangrove is numerous around the same areas as the red, except that it looks more like a tree than the red mangrove. The red mangrove resembles a bush, and the black mangrove looks more like a regular tree, and has thousands of tiny pneumatophores around its base, and the ground near it, though I will talk a little more about that later.

Florida's mangrove coastline is the largest contiguous mangrove coastline in the Northern hemisphere and one of the largest in the world. The mangroves are essential for the various marine and aquatic life forms from crustaceans and various invertebrates, to fish and both feeding and nesting birds. They also provide a first line of defense against the tidal and storm surges from hurricanes and tropical cyclones during the summer months.

They are also termed 'nature's nursery', due to the various forms of life that are supported by them. The coastline is close to half a million acres, and you will be hard pushed to visit the ocean in South Florida without seeing some evidence of mangroves somewhere, unless it is an overly developed or man-made area such as Miami Beach.

The red mangrove is easy to spot, as it is the dominant coastline halophyte, and it resembles a bush, sitting atop an intricate prop and drop root support system, covered in respiring pores. The leaves are a light to dark green with a glossy appearance, and that appear waxy to the touch, with a yellow underbelly. The red mangrove takes in some salt through the prop roots, but then expels that salt through what it is termed the 'suicide leaf'. You will often see a few yellow leaves amongst the mangrove bush, which have died due to that salt intake.

Tourists often mentioned that the red mangroves resembled rhododendrons, which meant they either had bad eyesight, or had never actually seen a rhododendron. I personally do not see the resemblance.

Large areas of mangroves are a mangrove forest, or simply just mangrove. However, the correct term would be a mangal. The red mangrove mangals line the park boundary on the ocean side like a castles defenses, with their walking root systems, often standing alone or in small groups out in Florida bay. They provide excellent lone nesting spots for various birds.

I will talk a little more about mangroves a little later on, but want to get back to the changing scenery and the approach to the first paddling area.

It is now the brackish water areas, and though sawgrass is still abundant, hardwood hammocks are still in view, and water is everywhere, the cypress and pinelands are pretty much gone from this area for the most part. As you travel the road, the small bonsai like mangroves will become somewhat taller and thicker. You begin to enter the areas where the marked canoe trails begin, and you have the chance to encounter crocodiles, as well as alligators.

The park has many popular canoe trails, and though you can go almost anywhere, and put a watercraft in at any point as we did in Taylor Slough, the marked canoe trails are further south, beginning at

Nine Mile Pond.

Though the vast majority of visitors to the park see the Everglades from the comfort of their air-conditioned vehicle, or from a braved boardwalk, the only true way to see the Everglade is on foot or by some type of watercraft. This would typically be a canoe or kayak, and of course, in a canoe or kayak you can cover much greater distance, and reach parts of the park you would not usually be able to see.

I would like to take this opportunity to point out the difference between a canoe and a kayak. I will also mainly refer to canoes only as I continue, as that would be the most common watercraft that tourists would use, aside from my personal kayak, which I would often lead the tours with.

There seems to be a lot of confusion the world over about the difference between a canoe and kayak.

A canoe is the open topped style boat, which usually has some type of yoke bracing the sides together. They will have one or more seats front and back. A canoe is steered and controlled, with the aid of a single bladed paddle. The etymology behind the word canoe traces back to the Carib people, and means 'dugout'.

Kayaks are much narrower than a canoe, and though some can accommodate more than one person, a single paddler would typically use them. A kayak is not open like a canoe. There is a small entrance to place your legs into, and you then sit upon a seat on the bottom of the hull. A kayak is propelled and steered with the use of a bi-blade paddle, and can be traced back to Inuit and Eskimo origin.

There is of course some crossover, especially with the recent advent of the sit on top style, which people use for recreational and relaxing short distance trips. We actually had these available for the tours, but I stopped using them, as I was sick of rescuing people who couldn't maintain their balance, and ended up on a pre-emptive swim. This is fine, except that I would rather be in control of when and where my groups would take a swim.

For leading groups I found that canoes offered a much more efficient and pleasurable Everglades experience. They give an upright view, are easier to negotiate with the single paddles through the tight mangroves, and are somewhat harder to tip, although people would always prove me wrong.

The choice will always come down to personal preference. Personally, when leading a group, I found it easier to manage people in canoes rather than kayaks, and found that they tipped less, and could get in and out of a canoe much easier than a kayak.

Nine Mile Pond

This is probably the most famous canoe trail in the Everglades National Park. It is located 38 miles from the main park entrance. The name however, is nothing to do with its distance from the main gate, or the distance of the trail itself, which happens to be a 5-mile loop. Rumor has it that originally there was another visitor center, which was nine or so miles from this pond, hence its name.

Pulling up here you will arrive in a small car park, with a grass verge that meets the water's edge. Be prepared to get out of your car next to, or close to alligators, and definitely vultures, as they love this spot. There are some large trashcans for rubbish, picnic tables, and in one corner, you will see some canoe racks. The canoe racks are for canoes that you can rent via the concession located at Flamingo. They are padlocked and not for public use without the key. This is one of the advantages of bringing your own canoe, either from home or rented from the hostel, as otherwise you would need to drive all the way to Flamingo and back to be able to use the ones at the trailhead. There are no bathroom facilities here, so go where you have to, but avoid using poisonwood as toilet paper.

However, people do tend to need toilet breaks here. Either there is a long paddle coming up, or there has just been one. You just need to be careful where you go and what you touch.

I can recall two funny stories from just the car park. I already mentioned the poisonwood toilet incident, but there is always more entertainment waiting in the wings when you have people from all across the globe.

Lost for Words

We were sitting having lunch at the tables here one day, and with me were a large group. I would always make sure that people had a bag for any trash that they may have, so that I could dispose of it in one of the trashcans, or take it along in the van until we came across one.

We had lunch, and then one member of the group took the large trash bag and started to walk off. He was heading in the direction of the large mobile trashcans that are in the car park, and so I thought nothing of it. I was just about to lift the cooler in the van when I saw him throw the bag into the trees at the side. I couldn't believe it. When asked why he had done so, he had thought that the rangers go around picking it up. I was lost for words!

When you have to go, you have to go!

When pulling up at any spot, I would always remind the group not to touch any plants, and let them know if there were toilet facilities. Nine Mile Pond is always a difficult one, as it as usually already been a long day, and is usually about to be even longer until they had the use of a toilet.

Once again, we had been having lunch here. I was passing the food around, and as I was doing so, a German woman stood up and nonchalantly pulled down her shorts. She squatted next to the picnic table, and without a care in the world, and with little dignity, she just started to pee, right in front of everyone. Nobody said a word, although it was obvious that a few were shocked. I didn't know what to say, so I just let everyone get on with making the sandwiches.

It was shortly after this, that I started to stop at West Lake for lunch, where there were toilet facilities and some shelter.

The car park is a staging area for paddling, and popular for picnics, or hanging out and enjoying the view. There are three large ponds here, and are joined together via the trail itself. Whether you go clockwise or anticlockwise you will head through all three ponds. There is no requirement to complete the marked trail however. In fact, most people don't, as there is a shortcut.

On my tours, I rarely completed the whole trail. I stayed off any trail as much as possible. The Nine Mile Pond trail has plenty of shortcuts, off-trail wonders, and they are great for building a custom canoe trip to tailor different needs and time constraints.

If you plan to tour the marked trail in its entirety, it will take around four or five hours to complete at a gentle pace. This assumes a gentle paddling pace, and plenty of time to stop and take it all in, as there is plenty to see here.

The ponds are considerably deeper than most bodies of water within the park, and as with the Royal Palm Visitor Center, they are borrow pits. The limestone has been dugout from here or 'borrowed' for construction, such as for the road. This has left behind very large pond areas, which lead the boater into the backcountry marshes and mangals that fill a large portion of the park.

The advantage to these ponds is that if you don't fancy trying to navigate the trail, then you can float around these for hours. There are always lots to see, and it is very nice and open in the sun, unless there is a storm. It can be extremely pleasurable, often filled to the brim with alligators, so much so, that from when you get out of your car, you could walk across the tops of them like logs to the other side of the pond. Lurking somewhere around here, will be Croczilla, probably sunbathing on the banks of one of the three ponds, preferring the deeper waters to bathe and hunt in, as oppose to the shallower waters of the trail. If he is out of the water, he is easy to distinguish from alligators, if from nothing more than his sheer size. He is a huge slab of grey to olive, prehistoric predator, cheekily grinning with his pearly white flesh shredders that twinkle in the sunlight, appearing welcoming yet forewarning.

Tour with Croczilla

Whenever I had the chance, I would head in to the Everglades on my own. Even if I had just conducted tours daily for two weeks back to back, I would still then head out on my own, on my day off. One of my favorite pastimes was to head to Nine Mile Pond for twilight and then float and paddle for a couple of hours. Watch the sunrise, enjoy the wilderness alone, and then head back for breakfast.

Croczilla frequents the large ponds of a morning, skulking slowly around the water, before lazing on a bank in the sun for the day. I would often follow him around, sit next to him as he lay silently in the water not moving, and just enjoy his company.

One sparkling morning, the ponds were silent, there was a light mist sitting atop the quiet waters, and the sun was breaking through in the distance, both bright and rich in color. I took my single kayak, slid into the crystal calm, and floated out into the open amongst the light mist. There was the odd light plop from a jumping fish, and the occasional buzz from a mosquito. I sat quiet in the middle of the pond, as the remainder of the thin mist lifted, and the sky turned orange.

After a short time, a little ways off to my side, a lumpy log made an appearance. Something emerged nose first out of the water, slowly followed by the eyes, a little back, and then some tail. It was Croczilla. Croczilla was easily recognizable from his scutes (osteoderms), the bony armor that crocodilians wear, along with his long slender nose and shallow eyes. He floated still for a time, and then turned ever so slightly, as if to get a better look. He then held his position, and turned back, a sort of acknowledgement that I was there. He then dipped back down into the water, and disappeared, emerging a few minutes later, only a few meters in front of my boat. He then floated, once again quietly and still. I sat for a while admiring him and the landscape around me, and then made a slow movement forward towards him. As I moved forward, he began to slide his tail sideways, propelling him ever so slowly forward, and I followed him across the pond.

It was somewhat surreal. It was as if he was guiding me, leading me around his domain. I had followed behind him many times before, but this was cooperation, an appreciation of where we were, and how beautiful it was. With no word of a lie, he led me across, through the gap, around the second pond along the edges, through the further gap into the third pond, and around once again. He then floated aimlessly for a little, before dipping silently back down into the murky depths and disappearing.

He had taken me on a sunrise tour of his home, led me around, showed me the sights, and then bid me goodbye for the day. Perfect!

If he is not around the banks, then he is probably in the water. His head sits a lot shallower than the alligators, and will be seen paddling his huge motor of a tail back and forth, rippling slowly through the ponds calm waters. His tail is almost square to look at from behind, and if you paddle close to him quickly, he will vanish into the depths in a huge splash of water. The splash will rain down on you, as you hope you don't tip, or that he comes up from beneath like jaws, to devour your boat.

Typically, you would only expect to encounter crocodiles when a little further south, where the salinity increases. In fact, one of the main reasons a tourist would go to Flamingo and Florida Bay is to see the crocodiles that are regular attractions in the marina. The fact that Croczilla resides in the brackish waters of Nine Mile Pond is rare, but a welcome treat for the brackish paddler.

There is a no swimming sign here, though it would seem obvious to most people that it is not a good idea. However, you can guarantee on my tours that you have the opportunity to swim in the mangroves, in the company of alligators. I wouldn't usually let people swim here in the deep open ponds, as it was hard to manage. I preferred to let people swim where I could see the bottom. However, there was always an occasion where I had no choice, such as when people would tip their boats, or the time my kayak floated off from the grass verge when I wasn't watching, and I had to dive in and retrieve it.

My groups were usually shocked when they realized that I would actually let them go swimming. I would mention it repeatedly during the day, but they tended to think I was joking. Then at some point during the canoe trip, I would stop and dive in, or usher them to do so. Swimming here is no more dangerous than walking in the cypress domes. As always though, it is never safe, but it does add to your trip. I never had any major issues, or at least no attacks, just a few scares.

That was lucky

A group and I had stopped off trail, in a waist deep area not too far from the third large pond, towards the end of our paddling. I was swimming around, to the shock of the onlookers, though they soon joined me. Once people had gotten in, or seen someone else get in, they loosened up a little, and always enjoyed it. The water itself is cooling during the hot days. Though clear when paddling through it, once you dive in, the water becomes very murky, as all the marl (mud and limestone mix) churns up from below. In addition, it is dangerous underfoot due to the sharp limestone, but if you keep swimming around you are okay. After all, it is more about the experience than doing laps.

I had returned to my kayak and was taking some photographs of those still swimming, and everyone was having a great time. Eventually the group was back in their boats, refreshed, and ready to get back on the trail, and get back to the van. Around thirty seconds after the last person was in the boat, Croczilla came silently through the mangrove opening into where we had been swimming. Using his huge tail, he powered himself silently, and gracefully, between our boats, and through to the other side without a care in the world.

Croczilla rarely ventures from outside of the deep ponds, so to see him this close, in shallower water, and after swimming, was a heart stopping moment for the group.

I casually said:

"See, they are not interested in you" and paddled onwards thinking to myself, *"Well that was lucky."*

When paddling here, you have the choice of either following the white markers all the way around, which will be around 5-miles, or you could take the traditional shortcut at marker #44. The markers are white poles with fluorescent bands on them. They are easy to follow, though you do need to stay alert, as they are not all equally spaced, and sometimes the mangrove growth can hide one or two, not to mention the pranksters who like to move them.

Like I said, I would rarely follow the marked trail, but would encourage those without knowledge of the area to do so. Once you go off trail it is very hard to get back on, and an hour or five hours can easily turn into ten, or an unplanned overnight trip.

When you are in the mangroves, everything looks the same. I would often ask my group if they knew where they were, or to point in which direction the van was, and very rarely would anyone know.

Starting the trail is easy. You get in your boat and head east across the main pond. As you get about half way across, you will begin to see the white marker on the mangroves edge, which is not very easy to see from the car park. This marks the beginning of the trail, and leads into the first mangrove tunnel, eventually emerging out into the shallow waters of the backcountry. This marker and tunnel, is the 'portal.' Once you emerge into the shallow waters, you will then navigate around tree islands, through tunnels, across expansive halophytic prairies, following the markers all the way. After a few hours, you will arrive at the third pond, which you will paddle through to arrive back at the car park area and the main pond. All the time you are paddling, you could encounter alligators, snakes, various birds, diving osprey, jumping fish and much more.

One of the nice things about this trail is that it sets its own pace. The atmosphere of the trail and its scenery is very relaxing. There are large clearings where it is nice to just lay back and float in the sun, or to tie boats together and crack open a few beers from the cooler. Paddling this trail is usually easy, unless it is shallow, or if you manage to tip.

Country Roads, Take Me Home

Back in early 2000, we had a large group of German travelers from a 'Habitat for Humanity' group. Habitat for Humanity participants pay to go to places around the world, to help on volunteer projects. This group stayed at the hostel for around two weeks, and I had some great times with them, both on and off the tour.

We had decided to paddle at Nine Mile Pond. Most of the boats had gone through the portal where the trail begins, and I was in a canoe at the rear with one of the girls. As we had gone through the portal, a fish had jumped into the boat. The girl had jumped out of her skin, and started to panic, standing up and tipping the boat. We ended up chest deep in the mangroves, with her now panicking even more, due to the high volume of alligators we had already seen.

I managed to help her get back in the boat, but she had taken her handbag with her, which had emptied out into the water. For the next ten minutes I stood in the water searching around for the contents of her bag, along with my $200 Oakley sunglasses which had fallen from my head during the tip. I finally found her hairbrush and a few other items, but couldn't find her camera, our extra paddle, or my sunglasses. I got back into the boat, and we finished the tour.

A memory that will never go away, is the resounding dulcet tones of a van full of Germans all singing John Denver's *"Country Roads"* in German, for the whole hour journey back to the hostel. They were a great group, fun to hang out with, and were all wonderful people. They were a perfect group for an Everglades tour.

As for the sunglasses, paddle, and remains of her bag, well in 2009, ten years later, I found them.

I was taking a small group through the portal, and we had to stop, as there was a large alligator blocking the tunnel ahead. This gator was a frequent blockade here, and quite aggressive. As we pulled over towards the mangroves, to allow me to go ahead to try to bump him out of the way, I noticed in the water below me, the tip of a paddle. It never occurred to me that it was the paddle from nine years previous. I got out the boat to retrieve the paddle, as an extra paddle is always welcome, and I noticed the handle was broken, and the blade had a small chunk out of the side. This meant it was the exact paddle from all those years back. Here I was nine years later, stood waist high this time, in the same spot where we had tipped.

As I stood explaining the story to my group, I noticed a flicker of light around the rear of the roots from the mangrove. I walked around, and there tangled in the roots were my sunglasses. I couldn't believe it. At least two major hurricanes had blown through this area since we had tipped. Here in the same spot, there was the paddle, my sunglasses, and a few minutes later, I found the camera too. It was an awesome find. The funniest part of this story though, was when I returned to the hostel.

I cleaned up my sunglasses and they were as good as new. However, the next day, while sitting in one of the Adirondack chairs in the garden, I broke them. I had got up to go to the kitchen, come back, and then sat on top of them, breaking the lenses and the arms. They had survived the Everglades, hurricanes, and the other elements, but they saw their demise by me carelessly sitting on them.

Even the Guide Tips

During one trip, I myself managed to tip. The problem was that in my small single person kayak, I kept the keys to the van and a few other items. If I went in a canoe, I always put the valuables onto a waterproof Otterbox that attached to the gunwale (the outer top rim of the canoe). I did have a small waterproof dry bag that I used in the Otter, but for whatever reason (Murphy's Law) I didn't have it this time.

We were off trail, and taking a break to go swimming. This particular spot, at this time of year, was around 5-feet deep, due to depressions in the limestone below. We had all been swimming, and everyone had loved it. We were there for a good half hour splashing about, keeping any eye out for alligators, with everyone feeling very brave and accomplished. It was a good time.

It was time to head back, as I had already extended the paddling time for our swim. I climbed back into my single kayak, which was always a trial when in deeper water, and I sorted myself out. As I went to pull away, my paddle had caught in the mangrove beside me, and there I was again, swimming. My kayak was upside down taking in water, and everything had tipped out, including the van keys. I righted the kayak, and then begun what turned out to be an hour of foraging in amongst the marl, limestone sinkholes, and the periphyton. There was no choice but to try to find them, as there was no getting home without them. Everyone helped, but the trouble was that as more people moved around, then the more churned up the water became. We found the camera first, and so I thought the keys would be close to it. They turned out to be about 10-feet away in the end. They had probably floated, and been moved along with all the fuss. We eventually recovered them though, and everyone was fine about it, even though we had spent more time in the sun than I planned.

Although I had tipped and made the guests help me, I was still tipped (as in gratuity) at the end of the tour, and made a fair amount of money which was surprising due to the lengthy paddle, and extra work.

One of the more interesting features along the trail is the large amount of periphyton. Periphyton is an algal mat that floats on top of the surface of the water in large sheets, as well as lining the bottom, which is a strange sensation to walk through. This alien like ooze also clings to the rushes, reeds, and tussocks, creating a sort of sodden breadstick or corndog. Periphyton is an organic community of cyanobacteria, detritus, larvae, hydras, algae and microbes, resembling a moldy mattress when seen floating. If you get out and walk, which you may have to in the dry season to push your canoe, then it is like walking through 3-feet of soggy bread. Periphyton is an essential ingredient to the survival of the Everglades, as it is the primary food source to hundreds of tiny creatures, fish and invertebrates. It is also an indicator, which means that its abundance and appearance is indicative of changes in the surroundings, and is useful for scientists involved in the restoration project.

Amongst, and around the periphyton, and standing on its own throughout the trail, there are tiny carnivorous water plants, known as bladderwort (*Utricularia*), which resembles the butterwort family, and can appear in many colors. The most abundant colors on the trail seem to be white, yellow and purple. These beautiful tiny flowers sit atop the water hiding their carnivorous activities below. They have a tiny trapdoor in the bladder, which sucks in the water from around it, and then traps tiny insects, or mosquito larvae via the trapdoor. They always sound more sinister when described as a carnivorous water plant. Members of my group would envisage a large man-eating triffid launching itself out from the mangroves, only to be disappointed at this unassuming tiny flower, which eats larvae and tiny insects.

Adding to the sinister and the macabre insectivorous plants, there is another around this trail. Although this time it is from the *Bromeliaceae* family, much like the cardinal bromeliads found in the domes, though they too thrive here in the mangroves. This new carnivore is the powdery catopsis (*Catopsis berteroniana*), which much like other bromeliads sit upon branches like pineapple tops. The catopsis has a long lance like yellow flower, which reaches high towards the skies above. A white slippery powder coats the leaves, deflecting the UV rays, and attracting insects. The plant traps the insects in between the natural chalice formed between the leaves, in a fluid where they then rot and die, consumed by the plant for their nutrients.

From the macro to the micro, everything, everywhere, in the Everglades, has an interesting story, or something going on that does not meet the eye.

Tough Mudder

During April/May time, and later before the rains come, the Nine Mile Pond trail can become nothing more than mud. It is deceiving as you pull up and take a glance around the pond. The ponds stay full year round, though there will be signs of recession around the edges, which if you have no frame of reference, will not mean much. I had many tours that experienced the following, but one sticks out in memory.

I had a large group, and they all had canoes (17-foot and heavy). We had a nice paddle around the edges of the main pond, and I could see it was shallow, even more so than the day before. I warned them the trail would be muddy, and they would probably have to get out and push, but everyone seemed up for it, and keen to get muddy.

As we started the official trail, near the portal, there were about ten alligators, that all needed to be negotiated before entering the tunnel, which was fun. Once through and into the tunnel, it was literally a foot deep of water sitting atop about a foot of liquid mud. Smack bang in the middle of the tunnel was a large bull alligator (a bull because if the sheer size), who was there on a regular basis, but this time didn't want to move at all. Due to it being mating season, he was also more playful, or what the park service term as aggressive.

I was leading the tour in a canoe, with a young girl in the front, whose mother was in her own boat, as the girl had wanted to go with the guide. The mother had wanted the daughter to go with the guide too, assuming greater safety. Although it soon became distressful for the mother, who had to watch her daughter crash into a large 12-foot alligator, and thrown around like a fairground dodgem. The girl loved it, she was so excited, and she kept leaning forward, trying to get a better glimpse of the monster blocking our passage.

After some time we got past, and made our way into the backcountry trail. By this time, there was no surface water though, and the whole trail was like melted chocolate, but not quite the same smell or taste. The canoes turned into gondolas as we used the paddles to push through the slime, as paddling was doing nothing. For every 2-foot that we moved forward, there was at least one alligator laid in the mud, mouth open and thermo regulating, splashing and bellowing, flipping mud with their tails. It was a real reptilian funfair ride. Everyone was having great fun as mud splashed over them, gators bellowed, and tiny fish trapped in the mud were flailing around everywhere, trying to find some water.

After a short time, we managed to get onto some open water, though only for a short while, until we hit mud again. This time it was so shallow that I had to decide whether to push on or turn around. We discussed it, everyone seemed keen to get out of the boats and push the canoes through the knee-deep ooze, and have a real Everglades adventure, and so we did. However, they made this judgment when there were no alligators in the mud where they had to push.

The girl stayed in the front of my boat, and I pushed her like a princess through the wilderness, without her having to get wet or dirty. We all pushed our heavy boats through the mud in the heat, yet everyone was having a great time. Some were even having mud fights, throwing and using the paddles to flick mud at each other.

After about ten minutes, seeing no alligators, we then come around a corner into a veritable dinosaur soup. I counted thirty-four alligators all laid, sliding, or playing in the mud. It was time to make another decision, this time they were a little less keen to push on.

I said that I would push on for a bit to see if they moved out of the way, and that everyone could stand, watch, and then move forward. Let's just say that after about 6-feet, and the mother screaming at me to turn around, we ended up not moving forward any further, and having to go back the way we had come. The fun wasn't over yet though.

When we got back to the tunnel, the large alligator was still there, but this time he was waiting for us where we had exited. I pushed the canoe into his side a few times, not to hurt him, but to encourage his movement. All of a sudden, he flipped, rolled, and then disappeared. We started to move forward ever so slightly, then there was an almighty bump and splash, and he emerged right next to our boat, and then went right under us. The girl was screaming with excitement and her mother was screaming with fear. The alligator then slid off beneath us, emerging next to the mangroves, allowing only a small, four-foot wide channel next to him to get through, meaning everyone would have to slide their boats passed him, and with their boats touching him. It took me 45 minutes to get the six boats passed him. Once passed, and back into open water, they all started to breathe again.

Funnily enough, there was another situation the same as this, where a girl was in the front of my boat and the mother in another boat. The same alligator was causing a ruckus in almost exactly the same spot, this time though the water was a little deeper, not too much though. We didn't have to turn around on the trail this time. It was just that in the tunnel the alligator was causing a fracas. Actually, there is a great photo of the girl in the front of my boat peering over the side to a huge reptilian tail sticking out from under us, after he swam underneath the boat. The hostel use it on the website so that people know they may get up close and personal on the tours

This trail has a bit of everything, from large open areas, tunnels, periphyton, mangroves, alligators, crocodiles, birds, sunbathing, picnics, deep waters, shallow waters, carnivorous plants, sawgrass and much more. There are hours to spend here, and always something to see. From March onward, the trail off from the ponds becomes very shallow and you will be paddling, poling, or getting out and pushing through liquid mud like lumpy gravy. All around you will be alligators in their natural spa having a mud bath, and due to the time of year will be very playful for want of a better word. They will be much more active, eating more often, and doing their various mating rituals. They will be a lot less shy, and will often approach your boats, or stand their ground more than throughout the rest of the year. This makes for great photos. There was the odd occasion when the park service would advise paddlers not to visit this trail, as the alligators would become overly hostile. I prefer the word playful, and saw it as an opportunity for adventure, and of course, tourists loved it.

This trail is wonderful, but it is a tourist trail. There are other marked trails in the park, which attract fewer visitors, and in my opinion are a lot more fun. The next one after Nine Mile Pond, is Noble Hammock, and is on the left hand side of the road a little ways after leaving or passing Nine Mile Pond.

Noble Hammock

Noble Hammock is worlds apart from Nine Mile Pond. Without the sign on the road pointing to it, you may struggle to locate it. There is no car park available for this very intimate paddling trail. The trail is a short 2-mile loop. However, the low canopy tunnels, twists, turns, rust colored water stained from tree tannins, and nose tingling pungent aromas from the hydrogen sulfide (rotten egg), creates a unique paddling excursion. Noble Hammock is the antithesis of the tourist filled and open skied trail of Nine Mile Pond.

Although the trail is a loop, the start and end are not the same location. There is a short distance between the start and end on the same side of the road. There is a small parking area on the grass verge, though it is not particularly visible. When you end, you will need to either walk back, or drive your car to where you finished, or portage the boats back to the vehicle, though it is only a short trip. A portage involves carrying your watercraft. Paddling in the Everglades off trail, or in the backcountry will often involve a portage, but the Everglades portage is not the same as a traditional portage elsewhere. In the backcountry, it is an assault course of mud, low branches, alligators, crocodiles, and the will to carry on, and a good sense of humor is a requirement.

The beginning (usually the first stop, though you can do the trail in any direction you wish) is a tiny wooden jetty at the small ingress that marks the start of the trail. You will need to lower your boat into the water, and then you need to attempt to get in the boats without tipping. It is wise to make sure you apply insect repellant here, as not only the mosquitoes, but also biting deer flies (*Chrysops*) can get quite bad around this trail. Deer flies are of course everywhere in the park, but I always found that most of the bites I received were at this trail. Deer flies have vampire like mandibles that puncture the skin, and can be quite painful, especially if repeated around the neck or on your back where you cannot reach.

The trail itself goes from tunnel to tunnel, to open pond and back to tunnel. If you are not an experienced paddler, this trail will certainly introduce you to the mangroves intimately. They will be in your face, along with plenty of cobwebs. You will need to duck down beneath them, to get through the tunnels, and just when you think you have gotten the hang of it, there will be an immediate 90° turn. These turns can be difficult if your chosen vehicle is a large 17-foot canoe. Noble Hammock will really test your "divorce boat" skills, the name derived from a canoes ability to change the nature of a once stable relationship.

The trails name comes from the large hammock about halfway round the trail. Willie Noble was a Gladesman, who hid out here during prohibition, and made illegal moonshine, hence its name. Though the trail is a loop, you can turn off east around marker #60 and #61, heading through Still Creek (it is fairly obvious to the eye), all the way to West Lake, and meander through history down Willie's route from the hammock. Don't try this unless you are an experienced paddler and navigator, as it can be hard to find your way.

The hammock itself is large, and you can get off and explore, though there is only a small inlet allowing you to reach high ground. The mozzies can be bad in this hammock, though it does make a wonderful impromptu overnight, with a sleeping hammock such as a Hennessey, or a plain old rope hammock and a mozzie net.

Water snakes are abundant around this trail, as are alligators. However, the alligators here are shy. You will really need to keep an eye out for them here, and there will be a lot more around than is usually obvious. There is one rather large alligator here, which can be playful during mating season, and he will block the tunnel towards the end of the trail. You have to turn around and complete the 2-mile loop over again, or budge him out of the way, if you dare.

Eventually, if you have gone the traditional clockwise route, you will arrive once again at the side of the road via another small jetty, which marks the end of the trail. Unlike Nine Mile Pond, Noble Hammock does not have as many opportunities for off trail paddling, and so it is likely that most people stick to the marked trail. With little to no people ever frequenting this trail, it feels very wild anyway, so no need to venture off trail. However, if you are adventurous, as I mentioned before, the creek to West Lake is a fun filled excursion for some value add, and some nice backcountry paddling, achievable within the timeframe of a day.

Hells Bay

Hell to get into and hell to get out, just about sums up the next trail down from Noble Hammock, on the right hand side of the road traveling towards Flamingo. Hells Bay canoe trail is an extremely confusing mix of tight waterways, canals, and mangrove tunnels, with intermittent large ponds, and access to the major waterways and campsites of the West Coast backcountry.

Hells Bay is what is termed as a backcountry trail, meaning that it really leads you into the backcountry of the Everglades. People tend to choose this trail for overnight camping, as it gives access to chickees (raised wooden platforms in the water) and Hells Bay Chickee, Pearl Bay Chickee and Lard Can Campground are all accessible from this trail. Actually, you can go from Hells Bay all the way north up the Wilderness Waterway to Everglades City. Paddlers often choose this trail as their start or finish point, mainly to avoid the boat traffic found in Florida Bay.

The Hells Bay canoe trail does not have a set distance so to speak, though it is 5.5-miles to the Hells Bay Chickee. However, as I mentioned the Hells Bay starting point is the launch for many destinations, although you wouldn't normally begin this trail for only a short paddle.

If you are a camper, then the first designated campsite along this trail is Lard Can, found at **GPS Waypoint: N25 14.956, W80 50.827**. It is about 3.5-miles into the trail. I love Lard Can campground, and have spent many a summer night there. Lard Can is a ground campsite, in that it is not on a chickee. The campground lies in a hardwood hammock, and derives its name from the large storage canisters that the Gladesmen once used to store their food and other necessities. They would then stash them in the Everglades, Lard Can being a popular location for this. Camping during the tourist season will need booking, as it can get busy, and official permits are available for up to ten campers. I personally preferred summer, as there will be no one else there or anywhere on the trail for that matter, due to the high mozzie population and summer rains. There is no dock here though, and as I found out when I first arrived there, if you get out of the boat too soon, it is easy to find yourself underwater.

The Hells Bay Chickee is located in Hells Bay itself, at **GPS Waypoint: N25 15.203, W80 52.719**. This is a twin chickee connected by a small walkway and has a portaloo toilet facility. It is very similar to the Pearl Bay Chickee, which is close, and located at **GPS Waypoint:**

N25 15.569, W80 51.375.

Chickee is a word that means "house in the creek" and comes from the Miccosukee and Seminole Indians. They are raised wooden platforms sitting in the water, that offer limited shelter from the elements, but are perfect for hammocks if you are on your own, or for free standing tents, and fires are obviously not allowed. These backcountry wooden platforms are booked heavily during tourist season, but out of season will probably be empty. It is wonderful to rest, dangling your legs over the edge, drinking a cold beer under the moon rise, watching as alligators, crocodiles, manatee, dolphin, bull sharks and other wonderful creatures come by for a quick visit or investigation. Both Hells Bay and Pearl Bay Chickees, have a resident alligator that has become accustomed to people visiting, who have probably fed it over the years, so do not feed the wildlife, which encourages them to approach people.

I have only a mentioned a few of the backcountry sites here, there are many more, and the information is available within the park or on the Internet. Remember that all camping does require a permit, and just because a campsite is official, does not mean it is any less wild or otherwise beautiful. All the official campsites are wonderful places to stay and they range from traditional tourist traps to true deserted wilderness locations reserved only for the adventurous. I did camp in places where camping is not permitted, such as in the cypress domes, but as long as you leave no trace, and respect the environment you will be OK. However, I do not endorse or encourage it, and neither does the park service.

West Lake

West Lake is the next stop in the brackish area. West Lake is located on the left hand side of the road traveling south to Flamingo. This is a popular stop for a welcome interlude, along with some minimal bathroom facilities and some shelter to have lunch. West Lake offers a small slipway for small watercraft, and a limited dock. I would often stop here for lunch, providing the tourists an opportunity to wash their hands and feet after a muddy dome walk. I would roll out the lunch materials and allow everyone to sit around and make their own sandwiches. We would then sit and relax on the docks in the sun and chat, or shelter from the rain. West Lake is, however, another preferred location for deer flies, and scavenging crows, who will snatch anything, so it can at times be annoying here.

Recidivist Crows

West Lake is a popular lunch stop, which subsequently attracts many birds. Over the years, I have seen these annoying critters steal and scavenge allsorts, from sandwiches, keys, scarves and cameras.

Stopping here for lunch one day, we were sitting around the tables trying to eat, and the crows were working their way around the tables, getting closer and closer, trying to see what they could snatch. We eventually moved out into the open, battening down the food box, and sitting down on the docks in the sun.

One young girl from Australia was sitting next to me, when a crow came down and picked up her camera, though it was too heavy and dropped it right into the water next to us. I have seen this happen to cameras more times than you would imagine feasible, but it happens as often as sandwiches and food wrappers.

Luckily, for the girl, she was single and hot, and I had my scuba mask with me. So I grabbed my mask and dove in to retrieve her camera, as it is not overly deep near the dock, you just have to watch out for crocodiles. I was lucky and found it straight away, though she didn't mention it wasn't waterproof, and so it was a waste of time anyway. That evening she did buy me plenty of beers though and the next evening I took her on a full moon paddle of Noble Hammock, which she was very grateful for, but I won't ruin the story with smut.

The moral of this story is that the hotter (not temperature) you are, then the more likely a personal tour is to happen, and a greater chance of recovery of lost items.

Aside from lunch, West Lake has a small boardwalk trail that transports the explorer into the shadowy and tangled world of the mangal, or mangrove forest, and is often guarded by squadrons of saltwater mozzies. Cut right through the mangal, the trail meanders through, and over the swampy world below, and out into the refreshing, or sun scorching overlook to West Lake. As you wander the trail, you get to experience all the main types of mangrove found in the Everglades.

Black mangroves (*Avicennia germinans*) are easy to spot, as they have a black trunk, almost fire charred. All around the ground, under the boardwalk are thousands of tiny pneumatophores reaching out of the swampy gloop like tiny fingers. These are from the black mangrove. These pneumatophores, allow the tree to breathe when submerged under the water, as it does not have prop roots like the omnipresent red mangrove.

The large red mangroves (*Rhizophora mangle*) of this forest have huge solid prop roots, allowing you to clamber through like Tarzan, if you want to climb over the boardwalk that is. Though the ground looks solid in the dry season, it is often still sodden underneath the fallen leaves and pneumatophores. You can suddenly find yourself knee deep in rotten egg like mud here.

An interesting aspect of this small boardwalk, is as you walk along you will see, and maybe have to avoid, the prop roots growing out of the mangroves from all around, and above. The mangrove is constantly reaching out for more support, and the long roots from high above, will reach down to the ground, and then take hold, adding more support to the tree. The cigar like fingers with small black tips point out at you all along the trail. You can easily imagine the trees coming alive at night and using these slender fingers to take hold of prey, maybe even a noctivagant tourist.

Mangroves are viviparous, and so you will see string bean looking seedpods hanging from them. These seeds are propagules. Propagules are all along the trail, on the floor, and on the boardwalk itself, where they have dropped off. You will see them all over the Everglades, along the shorelines, hanging from the mangroves, and even on Miami Beach. The propagule (as in propagate) is a living tree. They will often float for hundreds of miles, usually on its side, but over time its buoyancy can change, and will be then found floating upright. After some time, roots will appear from it its lower end, and a sprout of leaves will take shape from the upper. The roots will take hold in the ground, and the Everglades have yet another mangrove. This propagation is responsible for the lone mangroves or small islands that you see out in Florida Bay.

Once you have walked, or ran (due to mozzies), through the trail, it will come back on itself at an opening that looks over West Lake. Here, you can look out over the large lake, see some crocodiles or manatee, and maybe the odd fisherman. West Lake also gives paddle access out to Florida Bay, and various other interesting spots such as Alligator Creek, which is a wonderful overnight camping trip, and you will see some of the parks largest alligators and crocodiles here.

The boardwalk then returns to the car park and bathroom facilities. The next stop down the road is actually Snake Bight; the term bight refers to the shape, and not an actual snakebite. Snake Bight is a small trail that cuts through the mangroves, and out to a popular birding outlook, where you can get some excellent photos of wading birds such as flamingos and roseate spoonbills.

Snake Bight also happens to be, ironically, the largest concentration of both dusky pygmy rattlesnakes and Burmese pythons that I ever came across. What I mean by that is over the years, my encounters with them here, outnumbered the total in any other one place.

Again, as with most mangrove areas, the mosquitoes can be horrific here, and so can the deer flies. The trail also joins up to another trail called Rowdy Bend, and this circuit makes an enjoyable bike ride.

The next stop along the road for brackish and saltwater access is Coot Bay Pond, which is difficult to miss, as there is a layby and large sign marking its location. The pond gives access to Coot Bay and to the backcountry saltwater's of the West Coast.

Coot Bay and Coot Bay Pond

Coot Bay Pond is a small pond hidden behind a wall of vegetation with a few small openings, allowing you to look across the pond, or to put some small watercraft in. It is named after the vast amounts of coots that float around here, a small water bird similar to a moorhen, but with a white beak and forehead.

Here, like Hells Bay, is another common starting, or ending point for the Wilderness Waterway, along with other backcountry explorations. The pond is often chocker block with floating logs (alligators), and is shallow in the dry season. Though it is not obvious, over in the far left corner on the other side of the pond is a marvelous and large mangrove tunnel giving access to Coot Bay and beyond. The tunnel is a fantastic paddle through tannin rich water, glorious cobwebs and a game of dodgems from branches of fallen trees sticking out along the way. It then emerges out into the saltwater expanse of Coot Bay.

Once out in the open on the other side of the tunnel it can be difficult to know where to go without a map, as it is a large bay with no visible entry or exit points. The bay can also be very choppy if the winds are up, but it is a good opportunity for a paddle during dry season, when the more popular trails become too shallow. You can either hug the coastline, which may be advisable anyway in the wind, or head straight to one of the egress points leading elsewhere. Choosing to head into the backcountry or just down Buttonwood Canal to Flamingo to see crocodiles, manatee and plenty of tourists.

Up S*** Creek without a Paddle

I had headed out into Coot Bay one day, emerging from the tunnel into a rough choppy bay. There were whitecaps and the wind was blowing a real hoolie.

I thought about it for a while, and thought it would be fun to paddle across and into Mud Lake. It wasn't too windy to try and paddle, it was just going to be a real effort. I got about halfway across, and stopped for a short breather, resting my paddle across the front of the kayak, turning behind me to pull my seat forward and reach for my dry bag. As I did this, my paddle fell into the water. Not only did it fall in, but also it disappeared, and didn't float back up. The paddle was probably stuck in the mud, or caught in the meadows of seagrass. I was fuming. I had been in a similar situation in almost the exact same spot before, but I was with others, and I had caught my paddle in vegetation and tipped. This time though, I had not tipped, I was up s*** creek without a paddle, literally.

I rarely took a spare paddle with me in a kayak, though on tours I always made sure everyone had a spare. I tried reaching over and feeling around, but no joy. It was probably at angle, on its side. So there I was in the middle of a bay, white caps hitting my boat, black clouds looming ahead, and no paddle.

For the next seven hours, I battled to move my boat with the use of both hands to the coastline and around, back to the calm of the tunnel. My shoulders were like Johnny Bravo the next day, with deltoids like bowling balls. I was walking like a gorilla, knuckles scraping the floor, with no strength to lift them up.

What a nightmare trip. It had poured with rain, my kayak had filled up, I had to bail it out, and keep crawling my way to the edge. I slept as if I was dead that night, and always carried a spare single paddle in my kayak in the future for emergencies.

To the left upon exit from the tunnel, and across the bay, is

Buttonwood Canal, which leads down to Flamingo. It is a beautiful paddle if you want to get up close and personal with crocodiles and manatee, both of which are quite numerous along here, and so are alligators of course. Remember that the Everglades are the only place on the planet where alligators and crocodiles live together in the wild.

Alternatively, you could head across the bay in a WNW direction to Mud Lake, which is one of my favorite quiet spots. Mud Lake can be difficult to access, especially after the summer winds, as the tunnel that leads to it, can become very narrow or even unpassable, unless you come prepared with a machete and a willingness to climb. The tunnel is marvelous though, very beautiful, and filled with fish and various snakes sitting in the mangroves around you. The tunnel will then lead you into Mud Lake, a large basin filled with what seems like milky coffee, and inaccessible from any watercraft other than that which can make its way through the tunnel.

Technically, there is another point of entry or exit into and from Bear Lake, and along Bear lake Canoe trail, but it is not very popular. Though I don't know why, as it is very pretty and quiet, offering a day trip into backcountry without hordes of others, even during the busy season.

The other exit point from Coot Bay is heading in a NW direction down Tarpon Creek that leads out into Whitewater Bay, and is part of the official Wilderness Waterway. Tarpon Creek lines itself with white and grey tree limbs, offering sunspots for sunbathing crocodiles and another popular manatee spot. The one issue with Coot Bay, Buttonwood Canal and Tarpon Creek into Whitewater Bay is the likelihood of small motor craft, and including the tourist cruise boat that conducts daily sightseeing trips from Flamingo. However, as with everything here in the Everglades, this will be dependent upon time of year and weather.

I have mentioned most of the popular trails for day trips and some overnights in the brackish and saltwater areas. I have not covered any in any great depth, as they are very similar in certain aspects, yet very different also. It is best to grab a kayak, a paddle, a map, and head out and explore.

I fully recommend the following paddling guide to the Everglades:

Molloy, Johnny. *Paddler's Guide to Everglades National Park*, 2nd ed. University Press of Florida, 2009.

CHAPTER NINE – Flamingo & the Bay

"Wildness is a necessity. I am losing precious days. I am degenerating into a machine for making money. I am learning nothing in this trivial world of men. I must break away and get out into the mountains to learn the news." – John Muir

Flamingo

The words above speak of altitude, and in particular the Sierras, although they are equally applicable to humanities need to escape the modernity, and mundanity of life, wherever our wilderness maybe. The wilderness replenishes our depleted souls, recharges our batteries, and when we head to the wilderness, we are heading home.

Flamingo is a staging ground for such an escape. Hundreds of escapees from around South Florida, all flock to the glistening calm waters of Florida Bay. Every weekend and available holiday, you can see them with their gas guzzling trucks, boats and rods in tow, and plenty of beer in the cooler, all heading to the bay.

Flamingo, given its name for the once bountiful Flamingo wading bird (*Phoenicopterus ruber*) that was once rife here, and in Florida Bay, was once a small community of homesteaders, who made a living fishing, hunting, charcoaling and moonshining. Settlers arrived around sixty years prior to the establishment of the National Park, back in the late 1800's. Although Tequesta Indians inhabited the area before that, and still their burial mounds survive at various locations up the coast, and in South Florida in general.

The original Flamingo settlement from where the modern location takes its name was originally about 5-miles away, up the coast from the current Flamingo campground. The remains of which can be found along the Coastal Prairie trail. This trail is a wonderful biking or hiking trail, and makes its way through some beautiful coastal scenery up to Cape Sable. However, the trail can be treacherous in the summer months, and is a haven for wildlife including crocodiles, and plenty of rattlesnakes. It also gets extremely hot along the trail, and it is not very often that you will encounter other visitors, even during the winter months. It makes an excellent running route though, but you will need plenty of fluids. I would occasionally drop my visitors off at Flamingo for an hour, and then head out for a quick midday jog along the trail, losing about 4lbs of water along the way, but invigorating all the same.

The original settlement came about in around 1892, and the name 'Flamingo' came about after the establishment of a small Post Office a year later. Back in those days, Flamingo was no sunny tourist trap. It was both harsh and forbidding. The early settlers here would have been a very tough breed, coping with the heat, black clouds of mosquitoes, fleas, snakes, and the various poisonous plants. It was a very remote and wild place, and still today, remains the southernmost inhabited part of the contiguous continental USA, though it is now a little more enjoyable of course. The early settlers didn't have AC, or a store to buy sunblock and ice cream, or even a decent road in and out either, so it was definitely extreme living.

The survival of Flamingo, like anywhere, was dependent upon its economy. Ironically, however, it turned out to be one of its most profitable sources of income that lead to its demise. The early 1900's was the golden era of plume hunting. Flamingo attracted many hunters, due to the high concentration of wonderfully ornate and beautiful feathers found amongst the immeasurable amount of birds here in South Florida. Unfortunately, there was an Audubon warden murdered by plume hunters here. His murder led to the federal legislation outlawing the plume hunting trade. This loss of income and the legal issues, led to the communities disbanding, and ultimately leaving Flamingo as a ghost town. Buried at Cape Sable, Guy Bradley also has a key named after him called Bradley Key, close to the coast at the current Flamingo. His memorial stone was originally located at the burial site, but is now underneath the Flamingo Visitor Center near the water's edge.

Flamingo did have a short revival during prohibition, as a popular location for moonshiners, like Willie Noble from Noble Hammock, however, in 1947 it became part of the National Park, and thus federally protected.

Today, Flamingo is the southernmost HQ for the Everglades National Park Service. It is a busy marina, campground, staging ground for trips into Florida Bay, the Keys, and the most popular spot for manatee and American crocodile viewing from tourists the world over. It is also a large nesting area for the North American bald eagle (*Haliaeetus leucocephalus*), and the osprey (*Pandion haliaetus*), with both of their nests seen high upon the radio tower, and in various trees around the whole area. Both the bald eagle and osprey thrive here at Flamingo and the surrounding area, however, the osprey is the most abundant. Nine Mile Pond, Mud Lake and Florida Bay, are also popular areas for these kamikaze dive-bombers. They will drop from the sky at great speed, plummeting into a fountain of water, emerging temporarily disheveled, before taking off with grace, with flapping gills, tails, and fins beneath them in their grasp. They will then find somewhere to rest and eviscerate their fish lunch with their sharp beaks.

Osprey and dinner in flight. Courtesy of Rustin Gooden

I may have made it sound like Flamingo is once again a city of inhabitants with a busy supermarket, post office etc. It is not. Flamingo is merely the end of the park road. It offers a small store for boaters and tourists, toilet facilities, canoe rental, a few trails, a visitor center and some accommodation for the park service and concession staff that live here through the season. It is predominantly a marina, giving access to the glistening saltwater of Florida Bay and out into the Gulf, and down to the Florida Keys. The coastline here is also a popular landing spot for the odd oil drum filled with Cubans (humans, not the cigars, as if they can make landfall they get a Green Card).

From a tour perspective, I would either end up here as the last stop before the soporific hour journey home, or I may come here midday and go for a run, or may come here just for a paddle. I would always change the tour itinerary and the paddling locations around, more for my benefit than anything else, as no one was any the wiser unless they had done a tour before. If they had, then they welcomed the change anyways. I did receive a few return tourists, hoping to catch a glimpse of something that eluded them previously, or just to repeat everything they had done, as it was so much fun the first time.

Don't Feed the Wildlife

On a sunny day, it is nice and relaxing to hang out around the tables at the rear of the marina store, which is something we would often do here. Drink a cold beer, eat an ice cream, and admire the wildlife, while chilling and chatting in the sun.

I would often sit here and have an ice cream, while my group took photos of the crocodiles or manatee. Both of which are usually easily visible from this area. One of the issues with this area though, is that there are hundreds of crows, vultures, and gulls, all looking for a tidbit of food at any opportunity.

A group and I were chatting, when a gull swooped down and picked the packet of crisps from the table, which a Canadian girl had been eating. Whilst we all laughed, a crow then swooped to pick up the lanyard attached to a digital camera on the table, which it then subsequently dropped into the canal behind us. Unfortunate, but very funny in retrospect, and even the Japanese couple who had owned the camera, found it amusing after a short while.

Sadly, I didn't have my scuba mask with me this time, nor was the woman my type, she wasn't single, there were too many crocodiles, and the water was too dark from the mangrove tannin for swimming or heroism on this occasion.

Headcount

At the end of a tour one day, I had finished up as I often did at Flamingo. I had been giving a short talk on the bridge, looking over towards the crocodiles, known as the plug. I had obviously attracted a passer-by who subsequently got into the tour van, along with the rest of my group.

I had said to my group:

'Right then, if you need to use the bathrooms or visit the store, then do so now, and I will meet you back at the van, and maybe we can catch sunset, and then head to 'Robert is Here' for a milkshake."

I had gone to get an ice cream and then went back to the van. When I returned, there were four people in the van, and so I got in, let them talk amongst themselves, and ate my ice cream. We waited for everyone else to get in. The last person shut the door. I assumed all was good, and we headed off.

As I was driving up the road, I kept looking in the mirror and seeing a Vietnamese lad looking at me, smiling away innocently. After driving for twenty minutes or so, I realized he had not been on the tour. I pulled over and asked him politely where he had come from, and in broken English he said that he wanted to see the sunset that I had described. I asked the rest of the people in the van why they had not said anything, and it appeared they had thought I had invited him along, and didn't think to question it. I was laughing so much. It had obviously been a long day, and I had not been paying attention. I drove him back to Flamingo, and then returned to watch the sunset with the right people this time.

Funnily enough, a similar thing happened once when I drove off from the same place without one of my tourists, which I had left in the bathroom. The reason it was so funny, was that his wife was in the van, and she had not even noticed I had left him until five minutes later. When I returned, he hadn't noticed we had left either, as he had gone from the bathroom to taking some photographs.

During the summer months, it is barren here. In the winter, it can be difficult to park, with the huge boat trailers jutting out at every angle. Boaters from Miami and other cities come to escape for the day or weekend onto the open water fishing, floating, and sipping on cold beer, but leave the car park full to capacity.

During the quiet periods, I would try to gather up volunteers from around the hostel to come down and do beach clean ups. We would take some black bin bags, comb the beach along the campsite, and clear up trash that was washed up, or left behind by Mexican fisherman that come here in droves to catch their dinner. They have fires and drink beer during the quiet months when there are no tourists, but they also litter heavily, leaving the job of picking up the rubbish to someone else.

There was also opportunity for more organized volunteer trips through the resident park service volunteer coordinator, Jackie. There was usually help needed to do something, like clearing out the invasive plants like Brazilian pepper (*Schinus terebinthifolius*), which at one time was rife at Flamingo. Back in the early 2000's, as you came over the Buttonwood Canal bridge, the whole right hand side of the road to Flamingo was vegetation, with a whole habitat of invasive species. The majority of invasive species found here, have now been either suppressed or eradicated. Clearing out invasive species is always fun. Covered up as much as possible, mozzie repellant, a machete, and some spray cans to kill the plants off, trying to avoid the native species of course, and not forgetting the rattlesnakes.

As you approach Flamingo, you will go over the Buttonwood Canal bridge. This obviously sits over Buttonwood Canal, which runs from Coot Bay down to the concrete barrier at the end, which separates it from the saltwater of Florida Bay. This concrete barrier is the 'Plug', and prevents unnecessary saltwater intrusion.

The plug is a bridge near the marina store, and is the most popular viewing spot for crocodiles, as they tend to sit up on the banks around this area over the other side of the plug. The other side of the bridge is out of bounds to the public, because of the crocodiles, and because it leads to the staff accommodation.

Once you have crossed Buttonwood Canal, you will see the large car park on your left. Find a free space, preferably in the shade of a mahogany tree, but watch out for falling mahogany nuts, though they do less damage than the vultures. Mahogany trees line the car park, filled with Spanish moss and nesting osprey. There are also many palms, gumbo-limbo, pigeon plum and seagrape (*Coccoloba uvifera*), which spawns a delicious grape like fruit, with an ever so slightly furry outer casing, and a large pit. It really is quite delicious.

Once parked, where you go will depend on your needs. There is the marina store that sells souvenirs, water charts, maps, sun and mozzie repellant clothing, basic camping needs, ice creams, basic food stuffs, beer and other cold refreshment, though it can run low pretty quick when it is busy. There is the visitor center offering a small museum, with plenty of information on the saltwater areas, history and animals.

During the busy season, there will be talks by one of the rangers at various locations in and around here too. A small hut outside the store, offers canoe rentals for those wishing to paddle Buttonwood Canal or out into Florida Bay. This concession also holds the keys for those what wish to rent from the park the canoes available at Nine Mile Pond.

In terms of wildlife, there are two main attractions here in the marina and Buttonwood Canal on a regular basis. They are the American crocodile and the Florida manatee, which is a sub-species of the West Indian manatee.

The American crocodile (*Crocodylus acutus*) is a saltwater reptile, with a few exceptions that live happily in freshwater areas such as Croczilla. Although they don't match the infamous Australian saltie in size, aggression, or legend, the American crocodile on average is still a large animal, and crocodilians as a family are the largest reptiles on the planet. The American crocodile is one of the largest in the crocodilian species overall. However, its diet consists mainly of fish, turtles and other reptiles, and occasionally larger prey, such as deer and other mammals. They are not as aggressive as the Australian or African crocs, and are actually rather placid. This doesn't mean that they are safe to approach though. However, you will not hear many tales of large American crocodiles snatching paddlers from their boats, or shore anglers taken as they stand fishing at the water's edge in Florida. Like most Floridians, they enjoy nothing more than a nice sun bathe, a good tasty meal and a refreshing dip. Life has a slow pace in South Florida, for both the people and the animals.

American crocodile. Courtesy of Rustin Gooden

Sadly, unlike the American alligator whose population grows daily, the American crocodile is currently at a vulnerable classification. It was previously an endangered species. There are many reasons for its low numbers, such as mercury poisoning, other chemicals, habitat destruction etc. All of which have made it difficult for the American crocodile to recoup its numbers. Being a tropical reptile it is a lot more susceptible to colder temperatures than the American alligator. Back in 2010, a cold snap came through and Flamingo marina became dead fish chowder, and over a hundred crocodiles died as a result. This was a devastating number to hit such a fragile community.

The American crocodile has a range from Central and South America, Coastal Mexico, and in Cuba and Jamaica. However, Florida is its northernmost point. Any further north and it would not survive due to the colder temperatures, something that the Alligator and their darker skin can handle much better. Though, there have been a few reports over the years of stray crocodiles finding their way north, even to South Carolina, but this and others are extreme cases, and not the norm, nor its preferred habitat or zone.

Crocodiles are often regarded as the most aggressive of the crocodilian species. Although, this is primarily a result of the legends of the Australian and African crocs, though, the American crocodile is still considered by the ill-informed to be aggressive, but this down to its appearance more than physical acts.

Reptilians are cold blooded, and they enjoy sunbathing like most Floridians, during the day seeming sedentary. They are regularly spotted, and admired, as they lay still on the banks, baking away. Crocodilians open their mouths to thermoregulate. The crocodile has a much more snarly appearance than that of an alligator, although no less impressive. It is just that the crocodile and in this case the American crocodile seems to have more sinister teeth, and so looks a lot more aggressive. If a crocodile is seen trying to cool down with its mouth open, it does not mean it wants to eat someone, or anything, it just wants to be cool.

Though reptilians prefer to hunt at night, they still just eat when they feel like it. If it were hungry, it would swim off into the water and hunt for something. This does not mean they are not dangerous though, as there have been attacks, and they are deadly. It is just that the attacks are much rarer than the more infamous species known as the 'Old world crocs'. Like most animals, they don't come looking for humans, but if they are hungry, and you are around, then you might make the main course, or even just dessert.

Danger is relative in the animal kingdom, some more than others are 'potentially' dangerous, but none seeks out humans as prey. Soda, alcohol, and nicotine, are all more dangerous than the animal kingdom. I remember reading an article back in early 2000, from Reuters I think. Based on serious studies, more people every year in the USA are more likely to die from vending machine related deaths than from shark attacks, and sharks are feared the world over as a dangerous animal. Crocodilians, venomous snakes, sharks, and other feared animals are all dangerous predators, but humans are not their prey, unless we make ourselves prey.

Endangered in parts of its range, the American crocodile is suffering. In South Florida, their numbers are approximately twelve-hundred to fifteen-hundred, which was the estimate given the last time I spoke to a park scientist.

They are certainly a beautiful creature, though they sit and do nothing much of the day, it does not stop people taking thousands of photos, or ogling them all day long. I can personally sit for hours and watch one do nothing, much more so than the alligator for some reason. There is something a lot more primal or prehistoric in the appearance of a crocodile than there is an alligator, both extremely beautiful though.

As a reminder, even though I mentioned it before, there are some obvious differences between the alligator and the crocodile. The first obvious one is that if you are in saltwater and see an alligator then it is probably a crocodile, if you are in the northern part of the park, in the freshwater, then you won't see crocodiles, with the exception of Nine Mile Pond. As for appearance, the alligator is a dark, almost black color (obsidian), and the crocodile is stony grey, with some light olive green coloring from time to time. However, when wet, the color differences are harder to distinguish. The snout on a crocodile is much longer and narrower than the alligator, whose snout is short and broad with a rounded tip. The alligator's eyes sit higher than the crocodile, and when the mouths are closed, you can see both the upper and lower teeth of a crocodile due to the equal width of the jawline. On an alligator, you can only see the teeth that point down, due to the uneven width of its jawline. However, that being said I have seen plenty of alligators with up facing teeth from the lower jaw, either from genetics or injury.

They both have an excellent sense of smell and good hearing. Their ears are very small slits behind the eyes, but if you can see the ears, then it's not them hearing you that you need to worry about, as you are too close already.

A visit to Flamingo should yield a glimpse of these mighty beasts, but if not, then sometimes just the knowledge that they are out there can be enough, but everyone wants to see one. At the beginning of my tours, I would usually get some type of request from someone wanting to see something. Requests would range from venomous snakes to python, alligator, manatee or a crocodile. I would say that nine times out of ten, I was lucky enough to deliver most, and in numbers. Except of course for the python, which was a lot harder to control, as discovering a python is down to pure luck.

The Florida manatee is another 'must see' creature, and a great source of tourist excitement if present. I could usually deliver at least one during the tour.

There is an apt quote from an online blog, written by a young traveler and talented journalist, Lisa Markuson:

'I have mentioned on various occasions my love of ponies, and while sadly they are not one of the species native to the Everglades, a comparably weird and endearing creature does call their brackish waters home. That elusive creature is... the manatee. I told Graham that I would tip him twenty dollars if he could find me one, and forty if he could convince it to look at me and wink. While the latter proved impossible, he did use his amazing Everglades animal attraction powers to draw not one, but two of the lumpy adorable creatures to us in the harbor at Flamingo, the southernmost inhabited point of the contiguous United States. I was

satisfied." - Lisa Markuson (*http://provincialsupertramp.blogspot.co.uk*)

The manatee (*Trichechus*), or more affectionately known as the sea cow, is a large, docile looking, marine mammal that can reach about four meters (twelve or more feet), and can weigh up to a ton or more. They really are gentle giants though, and have no sinister attributes at all. They are related to elephants, and much like their relatives, they are grey, slow moving, wrinkly, large, mainly herbivorous, and despite their size remain cuddly cute. They have flippers at the front, and a large spatulate tail, similar to the tail of a beaver, but much larger. They spend their days gliding through the warm waters, chomping and grazing on prairies of gourmet seagrass. These rich meadows grow thick and abundant thanks to the shallow waters and their access to light to photosynthesize, giving the manatee plenty to chew on.

Visitors from Australia would often call them dugong (*Dugong dugon*). However, dugongs are a separate species, with obvious differences. The snout on a manatee is rounded, and not flared like the dugong. Moreover, the tail of a manatee is round and spatulate, whereas the dugong has a Y-shaped tail much like a whale.

Both, dugong, and the three species of manatee, are members of the *Sirenia* (sea cows) order though. *Sirenia* is where the term 'Sirens of the sea' come from, as historically sailors would confuse manatee and dugong with mermaids. As far as those legends go, you would need to be out at sea for quite some time to consider a manatee as attractive as a fictional mermaid, but each to their own.

There are three species of manatee, the Amazonian, African and West Indian. The West Indian Manatee, however, has two subspecies, the Florida and Caribbean.

The Florida manatee (*Trichechus manatus latirostris*) is the manatee you will see in and around Florida, obviously. This rotund character enjoys the waters of Buttonwood Canal, and the saltier waters in the main marina. Tourists hover around these areas waiting to catch just a small glimpse of their air seeking snout or propelling flipper. Unfortunately, the marina is also home to some uncaring and idiotic boaters, who speed excessively, with little to no care for the marine life, regardless of the various warnings and speed limitations. There are many manatees exhibiting deep scarring from propeller blades, or some other unfortunate injury.

If you get the chance, it really is a wonderful experience to swim with manatees. Many people come to Florida, to pay to swim with the dolphins, which is a great experience too of course, but manatees are a completely different experience. I have swum with them a few times in the wild, and was always a fantastic and surreal time. They have a hilariously hairy face, which is like kissing your stubbly grandma, and are very playful. Much like domesticated dogs, they seem to enjoy being stroked and given attention, but then who doesn't.

A popular location for swimming with manatees is in Crystal River, Citrus County, Florida. A wonderfully beautiful place, that is a constant 72-degree spring-fed paradise, and the waters are full of these majestic and graceful sea cows.

Manatees are yet another of the endangered species found within the National Park. Their mortality rate is mainly due to cold stress syndrome, much like the American crocodile, unknowing or uncaring boaters, drowning due to water control, and even harmful algal blooms.

During the colder periods, great numbers appear around the local Homestead Nuclear Power Plant that discharges warmer waters, so keep an eye out for mutant ninja manatee, as well as crocodile that do much the same. The last source I spoke to in the National Park (in around 2011), estimated their numbers to be around the thirty-five hundred to four-thousand mark. These estimates come from the good old-fashioned method of counting from an aerial view, so they really are an approximation.

All the animals found in the Everglades are beautiful and interesting, and all live in symbiosis, apart from the invasive species, which do not belong there. Yet more and more species becomes threatened, endangered, or vulnerable all the time, and it has a serious effect on the environment overall.

Remember the words of Marjory Stoneham Douglas who said:

"The Everglades is a test, if we pass, we get to keep our planet" and it is time we started taking the test seriously.

There is plenty of wildlife in and around Flamingo, but I wanted to mention the major attractions, the manatee and American crocodile. In fact, I had many tourists who were simply not interested at all which always seemed strange to me. However, people do not come here just to see them.

There is a large campground here, which is a beautiful, yet busy spot to camp during the winter. However, it is barren in the summer, and with it being a saltwater area, is a staging ground for the squadrons of saltwater mozzies that can blacken the skies, and drain your blood.

There was once a lodge and restaurant here, with a beautiful mozzie protected swimming pool. Unfortunately, both Hurricane Katrina and Hurricane Wilma destroyed the lodge and the surrounding area in 2005. There are plans to rebuild some new type of accommodation though. I really missed the swimming pool after it was gone, as it was nice to finish a tour here, and all have a nice dip during sunset.

At the end of the car park, there is a trail called the 'Guy Bradley Trail'. This quaint little trail follows along the coast next to where the lodge once stood, and it makes its way through to the campground. This is a wonderful little trail set amongst wildlife, such as osprey, wasp nests, rattlesnakes, and a chance to sit alone at the shores edge. You can avoid other tourists, and maybe see the infamous sawfish, horseshoe crab, or watch some dolphin or shark swim past.

I suspect that Flamingo gets more visitors simply as a jumping off point into Florida Bay. Every weekend, even in the summer, tons of boaters come here to escape into the glistening calms of its shallow waters.

Florida Bay

Sheens of aqueous salt, broken only by the odd fin from a shark or ray, and where manatee gracefully chomp through meadows of seagrass, and diving osprey fly with fish in their talons embrace. Endless horizons, and serene and soulful sunsets fill the skies. Florida Bay is a simple yet beautifully complex place full of contrasts.

Florida Bay refers to the body of water that sits between the tip of Florida and the Florida Keys, extending into the Gulf of Mexico. Most of it lies within the boundary of the Everglades National Park, and so comes under federal protection and legislation. Depending on the source, its size varies somewhat, but it is around a thousand square miles or 2,600km². You certainly won't paddle or explore it in a day.

If you visit the end of the road in the Everglades National Park, the West coast of the Everglades, or the Bay side (north side, or right side traveling south) of the Keys, then the water you see forms Florida Bay. The bay averages 3-feet in depth, and ranges from a few inches to around 6-feet, or occasionally deeper in some spots. Boaters really need to beware here, as it can be deceiving.

Quoting from the National Park website:

"Boating in the Florida Bay is a task for the skilled. Treacherous passes cut through long banks of mud and seagrass that separate the shallow basins that make up Florida Bay. Safe boating requires the ability to "read the water" as well as a chart. Shallow areas are not always marked, so polarized sunglasses are a key to reading the water. Having a weatherproof copy of NOAA chart #11451 is highly recommended. Visitors should know the limits of their boat. On average, the bay is less than 3 feet deep, so knowing the draft (depth) of your boat is important."

This shallow yet expansive bay, is home to innumerable species of marine life, from manatee to crocodiles, bull sharks to tiger sharks, sting rays and eagle rays, sea turtles and hordes of various fish to name only a few.

Sitting in your kayak or canoe, in such shallow water, stroking the back of a bull shark, as it sits in the seagrass, is worth any amount of mozzie bites or sunburn. With that said, I would not recommend or condone it. Bull sharks (*Carcharhinus leucas*) are one of the most likely species to attack a human, and have some serious strength and size on their side, growing up to about 8-feet and weighing around 200lbs for a fully mature adult. However, I once heard the Florida record to be around 500lbs. The etymology of its common name 'bull' comes from its stocky stature, and aggressive manner, and has one of the strongest bites amongst the cartilaginous fish.

Mating Bull Sharks

Sarah, a close female friend of mine, and I had spent the day in the park, culminating in a sunset paddle out into Florida Bay. The day had been perfect, with blue skies and not a cloud in sight, blistering sun, and wildlife everywhere. We had already paddled through Coot Bay to Mud Lake, and had spent hours floating around Mud Lake, while laid sunbathing in the canoe with not a care in the world. You can't beat a spot of paddling with a beautiful co-pilot baring all to catch some sun.

We finished the day off by driving to Flamingo for a sunset paddle out into the bay. It was late summer, so the mosquitoes were terrible, but we had avoided any rain, and had stayed under crystal blue skies. Once we hit Flamingo, the skies started to fill with a few clouds, but that was welcome as it makes for a more beautiful sunset.

We had made our way hastily out of the marina, as the mozzies were ferocious, as they often can be in the marina due to the shade offered by the surrounding mangroves and other vegetation. We were then out in the late afternoon sun, upon a sheet of glass that seemed like it could never move, only shatter. Our boat cut through it with little ripples vanishing off behind us, as we set out south towards Murray Key. After some time of floating about, admiring the rays, various sharks and other wildlife, the sun was starting to lower, so we turned west towards Middle Ground, and the impending sunset.

We reached a point where we decided to float, and chillax in the now golden hues from the cotton candy skies that were covering the suns descent. Orange, yellow and golden rays broke through the cloud cover, and the fluffy clouds took on an added dimension. Our skin was glowing bright orange with beads of prism like sweat atop our bodies. It was a wonderful evening, and we lay there in the sunset with spotted eagle rays playing in the warm waters around us, and jumping dolphin in the distance, like the ending scene from a movie. It was perfect.

On the way back, we hugged the coastline back to Flamingo, which is in the shallow range of the bay, topping out at less than three feet deep. Bradley Key was to our right (named after Guy Bradley, the murdered Audubon warden), when all of a sudden the bow of the boat seemed to bump into something. There was a sudden eruption from the water, raining down and soaking Sarah. She was soaked to the bone, and her golden skin had turned ashen with shock, as we had stumbled into a nursery habitat for bull sharks (*Carcharhinus leucas*). This of course triggered every other animal in the water to do the same. We carried on forward, under fountains of water, mud, and seagrass, for what seemed like forever. Sarah was in complete shock and awe, yet still trying to paddle forward as she bared the brunt of the frenzy. Then all of a sudden, like a Florida summer storm, it was over in an instant, and everything was still and calm once again. There was nothing but the muddy water behind us, dripping from us, and in the boat as evidence. Sarah looked a little disheveled, yet elated from the experience. The day had been breathtaking from the start to the end.

Unfortunately, after a short drive up the road towards home, we then struck a barred owl (*Strix varia*) in the pinelands area with the car, and it didn't survive. If not for this, then the day would have been perfect.

The warm shallow waters of Florida Bay are home to many sharks, including, lemon, blacktip, sandbar, spinner, tiger, bonnethead, nurse, hammerhead and occasionally mako and even a few more. The bull shark is both fresh and saltwater though, so can be found further in to the Everglades, which is why Shark River Slough is given its name.

The bay is also home to dolphin, the most common being the bottlenose dolphin (*Tursiops truncates*), as well as found inside the Everglades in the coastal estuaries and inlets. The bay stock of dolphin number around the four-hundred mark, and they often accompany you while you are paddling through the bay. They are very playful and enjoy putting on show.

Sweet Caroline

Back in early 2000, Rustin, his girlfriend (now wife), and myself, received some news of some traumatized dolphins, the victims of naval sonar, near Marathon Key, in the Florida Keys. We went down to see if we could assist the volunteer operation to rehabilitate the dolphins, and then reintroduce them back into the wild.

One of the dolphins had sustained injuries from some fishing nets. The unfortunate dolphin also had what appeared to be some propeller damage, so a large team of volunteers was involved in its rehab, and we were fortunate enough to get involved.

We split into teams and took shifts standing in the chest deep water of the mangrove coastline, holding the dolphin afloat, and moving it around an enclosed area. The cordoned off area was about 30-feet square, and we slowly held the dolphin in our arms between two of us, and slowly moved around the water. We also had to check its heartbeat at regular intervals to make sure it was okay, and not over stressed.

We had caught the 2am shift, which was the worst, as it was bang in the middle of the night. Standing in chest deep water in the mangroves for two hours in the middle of night is not much fun. Neither is a million mosquitoes sucking the blood from your exposed skin, without any free hands to swat, or scratch for relief. No matter how immune you are to mosquitoes, two hours in the middle of the night stood in the water under the mangroves, will result in many lumps and itchy bumps. Due to the cold (yes, the Florida water does get cool in the night, especially if you are standing still, or only slowly moving around in it) we wore wetsuits, but the mozzies still found our faces and necks.

Rustin and I were holding the dolphin, and he was singing *Sweet Caroline* by Neil Diamond, Rustin that is, and not the dolphin. The dolphin then launched at Rustin and bit him in the chest:

"WTF, the dolphin just bit me!" dropping his grip, and I staggered to regain the dolphin.

I was in stitches, but we managed to get back on track quickly. He started to sing again and the dolphin attacked him again. I was laughing my head off, trying to keep hold of the dolphin. I know it doesn't sound that funny, but believe me when you are stood half asleep in the moonlit mangroves, and holding a dolphin that bites when it hears Neil Diamond, it is hilarious, and a touch surreal.

They released the dolphin after about a week, along with others, which had come in on the Atlantic side, so all was good in the end. Every time I hear *Sweet Caroline*, I am right back there in the water holding a dolphin and laughing.

Florida Bay has a lot to offer, it is much more than just a large expanse for paddling, or for the sighting of a dolphin or shark. The bay is home to many keys, from tiny to large mangrove islands. Some keys are out of bounds due to fragile rookeries, but most are available for exploration, and some are designated campsites. You will also find lone mangroves standing proud in the crimson sunsets, that one day will probably turn into a key, as the tidal debris and silt collects in its prop roots, creating more mangrove real estate.

The Bay is extensive, and takes many years to explore all its inlets, estuaries, bights, keys, and to experience all its marine wonder. Where else in the world can you float in 3-feet of water next to a bull shark, with views of dancing dolphin, osprey plummeting, sea turtles, and rays. Private islands, where you can camp and sit on the beach, watching the horizon turn ruby and the water turn to blood at sunset. No one else around for miles and the only sounds are the shore lapping at your feet, and the flocks of roseate spoonbills, or ibis flying overhead.

Aside from the keys where you can camp, there are also now chickees out in the bay if you fancy living out your own Kevin Costner movie, your very own *Waterworld*.

Though most of my descriptions of the bay have included visions of crystal clear and calm water, blazing sunshine and little foul weather, it is of course subject to some of the worst weather you can see anywhere in the world. Hurricane Andrew flattened this area in August 1992, and Hurricanes Wilma and Katrina tore their way through here and destroyed the lodge, causing extensive damage throughout.

The serene and still waters, and spotless sky, can change into a cataclysm of ferocious wind and water an instant, even without a hurricane looming through. During the summer months, you can watch the thunderheads build in the sky before you, and then open up their torrential deluge into your boat. It can rain so hard that you will need to bail out your canoe after only a few minutes.

Florida Bay is the waterspout capital of the world. A waterspout is a columnar vortex resembling a Kansas twister (tornado). They are a tornado over a body of water. Florida Bay loves to put on an aerial show, and it is not a good idea to be in a canoe if one is making its way through the bay. They can occur at any time of the year, but the summer months are the most common, and they average out to around ten a week.

Florida Bay is in distress much like the rest of the Everglades, and it was in a dire crisis back in the 80's. Today it still struggles, combating erosion, chemical toxins, algal blooms, seagrass destruction, salinity levels, altered flow patterns, and more. All of this has consequences for the wildlife, which in turn has an overall effect on the bay itself, so again it is cyclical, there is a symbiosis, and if one goes then so does many more.

Flamingo is a unique location, and Florida Bay is as beautiful as it gets. They are both, a grand culmination to the end of a day, or days in the amazing Everglades. If you manage to get to experience this wonderful place, then take a moment at sunset, look out across the bay, wonder what's out there, and go see what is out there. Breathe in the air, think of the history, and remember the sights of endangered and threatened species.

Think how you would feel if you could never see any of it again, and how this happens all over the planet every day. Species become extinct, and habitats and landscapes disappear. Would you rather stand watching the sunset over the water, with silhouettes of a thousand birds flying over ripples from sharks and dolphin?, or would you rather look out from your balcony to the lights of a bustling city?

Life is a totem pole, filled with hierarchies and echelons. In nature, we are all equal. We have all come home. It is important that we don't lose our home.

The tour has now ended. We have traveled from the freshwater sloughs of the north, to the pinelands, and through cypress forest and cypress dome, to the brackish and saltwater of the south. There has been plenty to see and experience. A few breaths lost, and plenty of memories to take away. There is just the hour-long journey home, then a nice shower and a heavenly chicken mole from Rositas, with plenty of refried beans to help you sleep and dream of the Everglades.

Don't go just yet though, I have a few more tales to tell, and a few more places to visit, but the constrictions and itinerary of a tour are over. However, there is still some stuff to see and a few more laughs ahead.

CHAPTER TEN – Tales

"A journey is like marriage. The certain way to be wrong is to think you control it." – John Steinbeck

Obviously, the majority of the book so far has been about the Everglades National Park, and rightly so, as this was where the tours were conducted. There is of course much more to see, do, and explore in South Florida. The whole of South Florida was once wilderness, and would have been what we call today the Everglades.

You are not limited to the National Park to see wildlife or explore wild places. I had many fun and interesting times outside of the park boundary. Including deserted islands, Big Cypress, Biscayne, Coconut Grove, the Hostel, and the Florida Keys, and even just traveling to the Everglades.

Traveling

You would think that the simple act of getting on a plane in the UK, and flying to Florida was straightforward. Well, nothing ever is in my life. Even the first time I arrived, I ended up having to fly home to play chaperone, though I did return promptly. No, for me, getting to Florida can involve machine guns, police, strip searches, customs interrogations and incarceration.

Machine Guns, Mayhem and Madness

In early 2000, I had encouraged my best friend at the time to come to Florida with me. To escape island life, see the world, and generally have a lad's trip abroad. He had planned to stay the three months available with the visa waiver, and go from there. His lifestyle at the time was a little more nefarious than most, with the odd brush with the law from time to time, and so he attracted police attention. Flash cars tend to do this, especially on a small island, which tends to cultivate the insular mentality.

The morning of our flight, we got a lift to the ferry, which took us from the island where we lived, to the UK mainland. When we docked, we grabbed our backpacks and waited to walk the plank as it were, and head off down the walkway onto the harbor. As we walked off, amongst the crowd ahead of us we could see armed police waiting at the end of the gangway, armed with Heckler & Koch MP5 carbines (submachine guns), and what appeared to be Glock 17's.

As we approached the police, lugging our backpacks, armed with nothing more than a camping spoon, the police surrounded us. We were both thrown to the wall, and immediately quizzed as to if we were armed. I mean, c'mon, armed police for two lads from the Isle of Wight with backpacks and flip flops, a little reactionary.

They removed our backpacks and padded us down, then handcuffed and paraded us through the station to the wagons waiting for us outside of the train station. We were both still none the wiser as to what was going on. Profanities and name-calling are never really a way to get any answers though.

At the behest and shoving of the police, we both ended up in personal vans for our trip to the barrage of farcical questioning to come.

We arrived at the station; they emptied my backpack, and listed all the contents.

"What's this?" the police officer asked whilst holding up a small red bag, with a large white cross on the front, and the words First Aid emblazoned over it.

My response to which, was to recall a scene from the 1998 classic comedy *Big Lebowski*, where the 'Dude' is attacked, and quizzed as to the nature of his bowling ball, to which he replies:

"Obviously you are not a golfer", pure cinema gold.

'It's an inflatable life raft, what does it look like?" I replied, my patience wearing thin. He was being either purposefully irritating, or just plain dumb.

Anyways, after an hour of listing every item I had with me, and watching them awkwardly jam it all back into the pack, I then found myself in a cell. My brevity and lack of co-operation probably didn't help with matters either.

I was still none the wiser as to what it was all about, and I racked my brains over every transaction concerned with our travels. Trying to figure out if something could have been wrong, but I had paid for everything on my credit card, and my friend had given me cash.

In the cell, I lay on the bed, freezing cold, with nothing to do but count hardened phlegm stains on the wall, and try to make out the illegible drunken scratches on the wall beside me. I also tried to avoid the smell of the toilet, which made 'The worst toilet in Scotland' from the movie *Trainspotting*, appear to be brand new.

After about four hours, under a blanket made from what seemed like fiberglass or horsehair, I heard footsteps and the clink of keys, and they took me for questioning.

To cut a long story short, there had been an apparent large car insurance fraud, and we were prime suspects. I cannot speak as to the innocence or guilt of my friend, but along with many others, he served a custodial sentence.

I left the police station a few hours later that day, and permitted to continue my journey. I left, and I made my way to Gatwick.

Virgin Atlantic was good I must say. I had missed my flight but they were able to get me on the next one at no cost to me. I spent the night on a Gatwick floor, laid up against my backpack, and set out the next morning, heading to Miami.

Some would say the above incident was just bad luck. Some would say it was just an experience to look back on and laugh about. I would say it was both, and just one of many.

Beef Bombs

Arriving in Miami, it was clear skies and sun ahead for me, or at least I thought. I strolled off the plane, not a care in the world, with island life behind me. I was eager to get through customs and jump in a taxi and head to Florida City. There is a simple bus exchange, but I felt I deserved a little luxury, for the 70-mile or so journey to my holiday abode, after the journey I had so far.

I went through the initial checks with no issues as expected. I picked up my luggage for the final checks, where the officer then asked me to put my backpack through a scanner, which I hadn't had to do before. As my bag went through there was a loud alarm and the flashing of a red light.

"You have to be kidding me?" I thought.

The officer asked me to empty the contents of my backpack. I couldn't believe it, initially thinking that I had been setup. However, after leaving the police station in England, the first thing I had done was repack the inept attempt the police had made, so was sure there was nothing incriminating in there. Packing a rucksack correctly is no easy feat, and takes many years of practice to get it just right. It is a fine balance of accessibility, necessity, weight distribution, and comfort.

"Do you have any beef in your bag sir?" the officer asked.

"Beef" I thought to myself, what the hell would I be doing with beef in my bag, and why are they not looking for bombs or drugs, or can bombs be made from beef?, has someone out there now figured out how to inject or snort beef? I was befuddled.

"No, I don't have any beef" I replied, as I racked my brains as to what was in my bag, and why was beef important.

I begrudgingly continued to empty the contents of my carefully packed bag, and each item catalogued for official record. Eventually I pulled out a stuff sac, which contained dehydrated camping foods. The inspector asked to look at them. He then singled out two of the packets, which had dehydrated beef in them. He confiscated them, and searched the rest of the items. He then told me that it was illegal to bring various meat products from Europe and other areas in luggage. This was due to various diseases, such BSE (Bovine Spongiform Encephalopathy) specifically, as far as the UK was concerned. Bearing in mind that this was dehydrated beef in a tin foil packet.

Anyways, it was resolved. I was once again free, and again left to repack my luggage. This time I was getting away from anyone with a gun, or the ability to stick me in a cell, and just chill in the sun, in a hammock, and drink a cold beer. Though it did bother me as to how they knew I had it in the bag, surely they couldn't detect beef in a tin foil packet.

I have done a little research. The only answer I can come up with is that sniffer dogs actually detected the beef prior to me picking up my luggage. The scanner, which is manned, picked up tin foil packets that could possibly contain beef. Still I was free, and still don't know if you could snort beef. I must get an OXO cube and try it.

In summary, I have flown from Gatwick to Montreal, and then onto Miami, to be questioned about a stabbing in the hotel room next to me. I have then flown from Miami back to Montreal. Stayed overnight, and then flown back to the UK, to make sure an ex-girlfriend arrived home safely, after falling out and breaking up. I then flew direct from Gatwick back to Miami.

A few years later, I was arrested at gunpoint, searched, and missed a flight to Miami from the UK. I was later in possession of beef bouillon, with street value of approximately £7.99. You would think that by now,

Miami might not be so appealing, or that I may consider another route to the Everglades.

Well, it wasn't all bad. I had plenty of good, almost banal and uninteresting trips back and forth. In fact, I had a good ten years until the next arrest. At least this time it was on the plane itself to add some variety, which I thought was considerate.

Arrested on a Plane

In 2007, I was in the UK after a short break from the USA. I was in full time employment as an IT Security Consultant, after recently leaving another full time job for a local firm. One morning, I woke up and decided to give up my new job, my apartment, belongings and abnegate all responsibility. I packed my bags and decided that I was going to move, and live in the USA permanently.

Another friend of mine from the island, another close friend, came with me this time. I paid for his ticket, and said that I would fund him initially, until he found a job in the USA.

I emptied my flat, booked a ticket for the next day, packed my bags, and we went. I posted my flat keys back to the proprietor, and emailed my employer to let them know I wasn't coming in again, and that I would no longer be working for them. I was still in the new probationary period and could leave at any time, and so I did. It is cathartic to leave everything behind, pack a bag, and head off to another country. It is uplifting.

After some time in the USA, things weren't working out the way I had planned, and the friendship was on tenterhooks. I changed the initial return flight and decided that we would fly back to the UK. I would then decide what I was going to do.

We landed at Heathrow. The plane taxied itself off the runway, and we approached the terminal. As we approached, a voice came over the tannoy (PA) system, informing us not to leave our seats, because the UK Police needed to board the plane. We looked out of our windows, and saw the police wagons, and police officers, moving about around the terminal concrete. Much like the incident years before, it didn't occur for a minute it was anything to do with us.

We started to joke and laugh that someone was about to be arrested on the plane, throwing around jokes about terrorists and international drug dealers. We started looking around the plane to see if we could see anyone looking shifty. Then as the plane came to a stop, the police boarded. We could see down the aisle towards the front of the plane as the police (armed police, yet again!) made a beeline direct towards where we were sitting. It still didn't occur they were heading towards me. I turned my head and looked behind to see who was behind me, and then a voice addressed me.

"Excuse me sir, are you Graham Mitchell?" the officer asked, and my heart sank.

"Yes, why what's up?" I said with a gulp, and yet another uncomfortable night in a cell flashed before my eyes.

"Please come with us sir!" he said while directing me to stand, handcuffing me, and then escorted me down the aisle.

I looked down the aisle behind me to see my friend also being ushered from the seat and down the aisle, but no handcuffs.

Once again, I was off into a van, not into the Airport holding, as this was UK police, and not the airport authorities. The van then arrived at the police station. They placed me into holding, without any formal check in. They gave me a room without a view, no minibar, no clean sheets, no cable, but at least the toilet looked clean.

Shortly after, they took me to the desk, where they checked me in. The officer asked all sorts of personal questions, none of which made sense. There was a real air of confusion, and it seemed like what I was saying made no sense to them either.

The Sergeant looked at my passport, looked back at me, and asked more questions. I asked about my belongings, and they informed me that an officer was picking them up from the airport. Shortly after, an officer arrived with my checked baggage, and placed it in the corner. Although they were not interested in it, and didn't open it or check through it.

The Sergeant then started to ask me questions about my friend. How I knew him? Who he was? I told the truth, but didn't give anything more than needed. I kept asking what was going on, but they kept telling me to be patient. They were trying to figure out what was going on, as they were acting on behalf of another police force as they were close to the airport.

I didn't have to go back in the cell, and they allowed me to wait on the bench by the arresting desk. As I waited, the Sergeant, who was actually a nice bloke, asked me about my time in Florida, what I did there? What I did at home? He told me about his vacations in Florida, and that he enjoyed it there. He kept alluding to a wrongful arrest, and that I would be leaving soon, but he didn't say anything concrete.

Finally, he received a phone call, and then instructed another officer to take me for fingerprinting and DNA.

"Right, we will get this sorted out once and for all!" he said. Smiling at me in a kind of reassuring manner, but I still didn't realize what was going on.

The fingerprints were the digital scan type, and the DNA was a swab to the mouth. They then took a photograph, and the officer returned me to the bench. I had a coffee, and told that if I needed anything from my luggage, that I could help myself.

I felt like they were grooming me, but it turned out that they were actually being very genuine, and they were all nice and accommodating people. The Sergeant told me that he didn't think I was the person they were after, and that the fingerprints, photo, and the DNA, would return the answers they needed soon. All this time, I had not seen my friend, and he was apparently still in a cell. It was all very strange.

I was given a phone a call, and so I phoned my good friend, whose dad ran a taxi firm on the UK mainland. He was waiting for me at the airport, though had probably left by now. The original plan was for him to pick us both up, and take us back to the ferry to get home. He had probably left, but I wanted to let him know what was going on.

When I spoke to my friend, he had apparently been on the phone to his father, who had been wondering where we had got to. I explained, which he found very amusing, and told me that he would get his dad to come to the police station ready for our release.

Eventually, the results of the fingerprints came back, and they informed me that I wasn't the person they were looking for. What actually happened was that my friend had used my name in an incident that had taken place about three months prior to us leaving the island for the USA. The incident had taken place on the UK mainland, and so the local police had not recognized him, which the local police would have done. It still didn't seem to make much sense to me though, as surely he had given fingerprints initially, which would have indicated that he wasn't who he said he was. It was all very confusing, and I never found out what the details of the incident were or why he assumed my identity.

Once again, I was free. My friend's father picked me up, and took me back to the ferry. We had a good laugh about the whole thing during our car journey south. I stayed at home for 10 days, catching up with people, and then returned to the USA. This time alone and free from 'friends', and their baggage so to speak. It wasn't quite as simple as that though, which you can read about shortly

This time I moved full time to the USA. I got my green card, and started to work year round as the wilderness guide, except for when the tours were slow in the summer. During the slower periods, I conducted IT Security contracts in and around Miami, and the rest of South Florida.

These tales may seem fanciful, but believe me they aren't. It is all on record somewhere. I have just been unlucky for some reason when it comes to false arrests and questioning. They say, "You are what you eat". In the eyes of the law, "You are who your friends are". *C'est la vie.*

The journey back to the USA ten days later wasn't completely straightforward either. However, at least there were no machine guns, cells, arrests, or Class A beef products.

Immigration Interrogation

My return flight to the USA was another last minute thing. I had stayed back in the UK for ten days, and towards the end, I had decided that I was going to head back once again, this time to stay and become a Permanent Resident ('Green Card Holder').

As it was a last minute flight, I had taken the cheapest option, and instead of flying direct, there was a flight change in Charlotte, North Carolina. It was a short time frame too, so I had to get from the one plane to the other pretty quickly. I detest changeovers, especially when there is little time to do so. As I went through customs, the officer asked about my intentions for the trip. They then asked me to go with an officer to a questioning room, for some routine enquiries.

'C'mon, is this for real, is there someone up there who has it in for me, I am on my own this time, there is no one else with me for it to involve them" I thought to myself. While following the officer to a questioning room, and wondering what it could possibly be this time.

I sat down, and the officer searched my luggage on the table in front of me. They asked a series of what seemed like boilerplate questions, as the officer searched through my belongings. He then put them aside and started to ask some more.

What were my intentions during my stay? Why had I travelled so frequently back and forth to the USA? Moreover, why were my stays back in the UK so short? The officer then informed me that they had received a phone call about me. The call had apparently informed them about my frequent traveling, and that I might be planning to stay and work illegally in the USA. The officer never told me whether the phone call was anonymous, or from whom. I did find that out later, but I won't go into that here.

The questioning went on for about four hours, and so I had missed yet another flight. They then released me, and formally checked me into the USA without any further problems. They were obviously not concerned with my intentions, and were just doing their job. I was able to book another flight leaving later that night, and eventually found myself back in Miami.

During my stay this time, I later had to go through the formal immigration process during my green card application. There was no mention of the issue in North Carolina, and I received my green card without issue. However, it did take some time and was expensive, and involved a lot of paperwork, interviews, and a lot of stress.

After many years of traveling back and forth, guiding, chilling, returning to the UK, and the odd wrongful arrest, I eventually became a legal Permanent Resident. I got my green card, and became the wilderness guide full time, year round, except for the slow periods. From my first flight to the USA, the hiccups along the way, many straightforward journeys in between, and some more hiccups a bit later, it all sorted itself out in the end.

I became a Permanent Resident. I later decided to retire from guiding, and return to the UK. Now I am writing this book, so you never know what's around the corner.

The Hostel

The hostel is a haven of hammocks and hookahs, with hordes of heterogeneous, homogenous, and hidrotic hippies on a hallucinogenic hiatus, all hanging in the heat. All the h's are at the hostel, where holidaymakers hide away from the hectic hustle of humanity, alongside itinerants, volunteers, full time staff and the odd hobo. They are all kindred spirits relaxing in the cool shade of the garden canopy, amongst sounds from gazebo guitars, wind chimes and waterfalls. Communal dinners, outdoor movies, lizards, and lazy lounging, swings, rope ladders, rope tree houses, campfire storytelling, Adirondack relaxing, and easy living, for the cost per night of a cheap meal for two.

The hostel is so unique. I cannot put it into words, despite my best efforts. You need to feel the atmosphere, chat to the people, smell the air, walk barefoot in the dirt, and live the life. It was my home and my haven, a gateway to a wilderness, where I lost myself and found myself. A hub for the various people that came into and out of my life, and from where I made friends and memories that will survive forever.

As a guide, there were two typical days for me at the hostel, a workday and a day off. A workday would mean stumbling from my blackened manhole, where no light entered nor escaped, and then stumble aimlessly towards the kitchen house to grab some caffeine from the dripping cocoa beans in the coffee machine.

I would then relax, facing west. The sun would melt my neck in the curvy and body-hugging Adirondack chairs underneath the cycad, sipping coffee, and I would slowly awaken, as fellow caffeine hunters passed by and went about their early morning business. Some kind chef would offer me some pancakes from the communal mix, or I would make some eggs, and then I would be ready to start my day. I would then shower, get dressed, pack the van with a cooler full of food, and then resume my relaxation until any tourists who were on my tour were ready to go. All of whom were taken care of by the front desk, while I relaxed waiting for the start.

Once everyone was ready and had signed their death waivers, they would congregate in the garden around me. I would go over any last minute questions before heading off into the wilderness.

After the tour, I would come home, empty the cooler, shower, and grab a cold beer and sit in the yard. Maybe chat around the campfire, go get some dinner, or eat communal dinner if it was on offer, and generally chillax the evening away with travelers from around the globe.

This of course would be a typical workday. There were other times when that same workday began at 0600 AM, and finished at 0200 AM, the following morning. A sunrise tour, some food, a full day tour, some food, a night walk or full moon tour, eat and then repeat.

The tour season is hectic. There is at least one tour each day of some kind, and some days it was more than one. There was occasion, usually after ten or so days back to back of tour after tour, that I would take a day off, but it was rare. I would usually wait for a quiet day, though they were rare too in the busy season.

The season is all about the hostel making as much money as it can, so that during the quiet summer months, those that remain can continue to live the easy life in the tropical paradise, and recoup ready for the upcoming busy season once again.

This hectic schedule soon changes once the summer rains hit South Florida though. Travelers stop coming through the gates, and the garden and rooms are empty. The staff lazes in front of the large TV, with buckets of ice cream, for five days straight. The only movement is from mosquitoes, fan blades, geckos and anole lizards, with the odd flood from tropical storm feeder bands. During the summer, I would also laze around. I would also head out in the wilds on my own, or with friends, volunteers, or work freelance doing IT contracts.

My days off, both during season and in the off-season varied, and were rarely ever the same, no matter what I was doing. Over the years, there was plenty of time for fun, laughs and adventure in and outside of the park. I am a bit of a prankster, and so I love to annoy people, play tricks on them, encourage others to do the same, and generally enjoy a giggle. Life in the hostel was full of frolics and antics over the years.

Budweiser, Bike Sheds and Body Sweat

The hostel has a fleet of bikes that it rents out to travelers and uses for the occasional bike tour. They are stored in a large steel shipping container at the rear of the hostel, the same as those found on the international cargo ships transporting cars and large antiquities etc.

These huge solid steel containers are virtually indestructible, impenetrable, and inescapable. Even during the colder months, they are a sauna inside, as the South Florida humidity takes hold. You become a dripping mess after only a few minutes inside, and that is with the doors open.

One day, during summer, it was very quiet around the hostel. I don't think there was anyone checked in, and the only people around were the owner, a handful of volunteers who were all pottering about carrying out various tasks or just relaxing. One of the volunteers, who I loved to play pranks on, was in the bike container. I was outside feeling playful. I think he was bringing a bike out to repair it. However, he wasn't going to get out just yet.

I slammed the heavy door shut, and pulled the latch down, then sat outside of the Pelican, which is a converted caravan used for storage of the canoe paddles and other gear. The caravan or 'Pelican' has been modified and decorated like most of the hostel attractions, resembling a jungle or beach shack with its very own decking and an add-on bamboo roof top.

I sat outside the pelican, with my feet up, soaking up the sun, my head in the shade of the bamboo, and sipped on my cold beer. The only disturbance was from the volunteers whimpering screams, and annoying banging from the container next to me. I did shout to him to keep quiet, because his noise was ruining my Budweiser. Unfortunately, he ended up staying in there a little longer than he had to.

Eventually, I decided I should let him out. As I opened the door, this pitiful looking, sweat covered, soaked to the bone, and flushed red body, came hurtling towards me. Filled with rage, he launched a punch at me. I sidestepped, and he landed face first into the grass and dirt, narrowly avoiding the large solid steel immovable trash can, that stands out in the back of the yard. His sweat soaked up every ounce of dirt from the ground, and he stood up looking camouflaged. He wore a few cuts from some broken glass, and a general look of disdain towards me. He then hurtled some expletives at me and walked off, brushing himself off, and stormed away in a huff. I finished my beer.

Later on near the kitchen house, I was recounting a strange whimpering I had heard in the back of the yard when I was chilling with my beer, and the rest of the volunteers were laughing at the story. I felt a little guilty, not a lot, but a little. In the spirit of fairness, I told him I would give him one punch and we would be even. I told him he could punch my shoulder as hard as he liked. I stood side on, to let him punch my deltoid. He punched me, but didn't hit me square, and so bent his fist back, and hurt his wrist. I was pissing myself with my laughter, but I gave him one more attempt. He went to punch me with his other hand, I moved out of the way, and he punched the open kitchen door behind me. Everyone was in hysterics. He was fuming. Ah, those were the days.

Putrid Pee & Pillow Pooh

There were some girls and a volunteer in the hostel yard; gathered around looking at something on the floor. I wondered over to see what they were looking at. They were all huddled around a small baby bird that had fallen from a great height above, and onto the limestone tiles below. I then for some reason decided that I would put it down the back of the volunteers t-shirt when he turned his back, so I did. He freaked a little, but shook it out and we put it in the bin.

He knew I was a prankster, and he knew if he engaged in a game then all bets were off, but he enjoyed a good joke too, so he was up for a little back and forth gameplay.

I later went into my room and it was a ridiculously hot day, so my room, was like a sauna. I turned on my AC. Instantly there was a putrid urine tinged effluvium filling my room, the dehydrated, wheat-flavored kind. I knew straight away, what it was, and where it was coming from.

The volunteer lived in the pelican at the back of the yard, which aside from housing the canoe livery, also provided accommodation for one easygoing traveler, or two if you are very close. I myself, spent many months living in there in previous years. It was a wonderful and comfortable place to stay. Except that if you needed a pee in the night, you either did it in a bottle, or did it outside in the hostel yard, where hostellers and families may see you, or walk to the bathroom waking yourself up in the process. I used to pee in a Nalgene bottle, and empty it in the morning. The volunteer used to pee in a jar. I knew this as I had seen it in the livery on days when he had not emptied it. This pungent, coffee brown, hot, musty discharge was just waiting for a prank to unfold. He had poured it all over my AC, which sits outside of the window, and was easily accessible from the side of the hostel.

I went straight to the utility room, grabbed some bleach and walked straight to my AC to clean it. I then went outside into the yard. I walked past the volunteer, nodded, and he nodded back. It was a kind of mutual acceptance of the beginning of the games. I then settled into a typical evening.

Now he knew, as did most around the hostel, that I had no boundaries. I do not get offended at anything, and I don't understand offence in others. So when it comes to pranks and games, I tend to go what people would say as a "little too far" at times. Seeking only to find what mileage I can get out of someone, or what buttons I can press and see if the person breaks. This particular prank didn't actually end up in what I thought was anything extreme. However, it did soon end.

One of the best things you can do when someone is expecting you to do something, is to do nothing at all. The mental anguish one experiences when awaiting a prank, is far better than the prank itself.

For a week, I didn't do a thing at all. I let the rest of the hostel volunteers and staff, build up imagery in his head about what I might do or had done in the past, and let his mind do the rest.

After a week, I am pretty sure he had either resigned himself to the fact that something was coming and he didn't know what, or that I had forgotten, and had better things to do.

So one evening, I had to go to the toilet. I took a large plastic tub with me, and I filled it with poop. I then went to the pelican where he slept, and emptied the tub under his pillow. Now I don't know what I would have preferred, either that he discovered it with his hands in the night, or how he did eventually find it. What actually happened was that it took three days for him to find it. Which meant for three days, in the heat of South Florida, my poop sat festering under his pillow until the day he found it. He was actually nonchalant about it, but the fact it took a while, and that he did find it, was all I needed. The games didn't continue, which meant everything. It meant I had won.

Firefighters & Firecrackers

As I mentioned in the opening chapter, there was already a guide at the hostel when I first arrived, and his name was Drew. Drew and I became good friends over the years, before he left to become a wildland firefighter for the National Park Service. Wildland firefighters are those brave people that fight the wildfires, which sweep across the wilderness, and endanger built up areas close to them. They also conduct the prescribed and controlled burns that help the wilderness thrive.

It was sometime in 2004, when a traveler from Washington State came to the hostel. His name was Brandon. Brandon was interesting, funny, and up for adventure, and we later became good friends. He worked as an Alaskan king crab fisherman, the ones you can see on the TV show *Deadliest Catch*. He had offered me the chance to go and work as a member of the crew if I ever wanted to, and I wish I had, but never did. You don't need any experience. Just some balls, a good swimmer in case you go overboard, and a few extra fingers, in case you lose one or two.

He had been staying at the hostel about a week, and had naturally inserted himself into the small hostel community of staff and volunteers like a regular hostel fixture. He was up for a laugh, we all got on, and we had some good times. He was, however, still a paying hosteller.

Brandon was sleeping in the gazebo in the garden one afternoon. Drew had noticed him sleeping, and he then showed me some firecrackers and asked if I wanted to have some fun. We went over to the gazebo, which is open air, but where the windows would usually be, there is a covering of mesh mosquito netting. Brandon was asleep on the cushions towards the rear, near one of the openings covered in mesh. We bent down quietly by the gazebo door, chuckling like little schoolchildren. Drew got the firecrackers out, and I think his intention was to let them go inside the gazebo to scare him. I held the two firecrackers and he lit them, he then opened the door quietly and I threw them in. I threw them towards Brandon, who was sleeping, however, one landed right on his chest. There was a sudden bang which resounded around the whole of Florida City, which most people probably assumed was a gunshot. A flash, bang, and a ton of smoke, and a shout from the gazebo, then through the mesh netting jumped a disheveled, burnt, and covered in black soot, speechless Alaskan fisherman. Drew and I broke down in tears with gut wrenching laughter. Brandon looked like wily coyote from the Roadrunner cartoons, when he would try to blow roadrunner up with a box of ACME explosive, only to find himself covered in soot and burnt fur.

Drew and I were laughing so hard it hurts my stomach to remember. We tried to get the words out to apologize but we couldn't. We were in fits of hysterics on the floor, laughing at a not so happy, soot covered paying hosteller, who was quite within his rights to phone the police. Brandon did see the funny side of it later on, but it took some time, and as I said, we later became good friends and shared a few funny trips together.

Sandals, Socks & Strange Germans

There was an amusing character from a German group staying at the hostel. He resembled Jason Biggs from *American Pie* fame. However, he was considerably taller and skinnier. From his arrival, he had worn shorts with white socks pulled high towards his knees, and a pair of Birkenstocks.

I was walking back into the hostel yard from the rear, down the driveway, and ahead of me stood the large trashcans. They are huge and heavy skips, which are difficult to move, even on the wheels. Stood by, and leaning over into one, was this funny German character. As I approached, I saw him lean even further, his legs lifted, and his feet left the floor. The next thing I saw was just a pair of skinny shins in white socks and sandals, sticking skyward from the trashcan. I was in hysterics as a pair of flailing legs were bandying around in midair. When I got to the skip to help him out, there wasn't even a sound. He just lay inside the skip, moving nothing but his legs. I asked if he was okay, and he said he was fine. I asked if he wanted a hand out, and he said that he was fine where he was, and would get himself out. I left him to it, went over to the cycad and sat down, and in the distance, his legs continued to flail. I showed everyone else, and they all laughed. He stayed this way for about 10 minutes then got out himself. He was a very strange individual.

Boo! & the Blubbering Baby

One of my favorite all time pranks, was simply scaring my good friend, Rustin. The sheer amount of laughter and tears make it my favorite.

In the hostel, there is a room called the 'Ghetto', which is traditionally the home for volunteers. In the early days, it was a dark and seedy room, with little to no character, which actually gave it its character. Rustin and I were living in the ghetto at some point back in the early days. Remember that, when I first started visiting and staying at the hostel I was on a temporary visa. I wasn't a legal resident, so I wasn't an employee. I merely assisted on the tours and volunteered at the hostel. I also stayed in the ghetto, amongst other places such as the pelican, tents, or anywhere I could lay my head if it was busy.

Anyways, Rustin had nipped out. The ghetto was almost pitch black, with a blanket covering the window, and only a small source of light coming in around the sides, just enough to see what you are doing. I decided that I would hide under the bunk bed, and when he came in, I would scare him.

I stayed committed to my cause under the bed for half an hour until he came back in. I was ready to scare him, when I realized he was undressing, and was going to go into the bathroom to take a shower, so I continued to wait patiently. I lay there, and occasionally giggled to myself, like a child.

I continued to wait patiently in the dark, under the bed, ready for the perfect moment. After about fifteen minutes, I heard the shower stop, and the door opened. Some light came in for a minute, along with his sodden footsteps along the tiles. He shut the door behind him, and the light vanished, leaving only the small light from the window coming through. He pottered about for a short while, and then came over towards the bed where I was hiding. As his wet foot and dripping leg stood next to the bed, I reached out my hand, grabbed his ankle and shouted. He absolutely crapped himself. He jumped into the air and landed as a naked, screaming, crying mess on the tile floor. I bumped my head on the wood under the bed, and the pregnant girl outside the door had jumped out of her skin too, as she banged on the door and shouted:

"*WTF*" she said with a pounding heart.

Rustin was a complete mess on the floor, blubbering like a baby. I had almost given him a heart attack. Funnily enough, I had even scared myself and my heart was racing too. He was laughing, tears running from his eyes, and I was holding my stomach as it hurt so much. The image of his wet naked body, curled up on the floor in the fetal position, trying to recover to a regular pulse was just perfect. That was so funny. I have scared many people over the years, but that was awesome. He did get me back later on though in the Everglades, with a perfect revenge.

I was walking a night tour around one of the famous hammocks in the park known as Mahogany Hammock. This is a large hammock, with a boardwalk built running through it, and comes around in a loop. Hammocks are black at night, and astronomers come here to use the car park, as there is little unnatural light pollution. This hammock is epic, in size, vegetation, and wildlife. It is a mini Amazon jungle all on its own.

There are huge rattlesnakes that frequent this area, along with tree snakes, spiders, turtles, rodents, and every other Everglades animal you can imagine (apart from the American crocodile). The only things missing that you would expect to see, because it so jungle like, are sloths and monkeys hanging from the trees. Though I am sure if someone released some they would thrive like the rest of the non-natives and invasive species in the Everglades.

Along with me were a group of about eight people, and we were walking around the trail all staying very quiet. It was dark and only the moonlight was occasionally filtering through the canopy. It was a perfect night. We did have flashlights, but were not using them, as I preferred to take in the true atmosphere of the Everglades at night. We were about halfway around, when a hand came up from the hammock floor through the side of the boardwalk, and grabbed my ankle. My heart jumped into my mouth. It was racing at like two-hundred beats per minute, and the group had all jumped and screamed. I looked over and there was Rustin, who had now turned on his headlamp, stood laughing at me from the hammock floor. He was in stitches, I was in stitches, and some of the group was laughing their heads off too. My voice had reached many octaves higher than usual. It was hilarious. It was awesome. It was his sweet revenge.

Summer Boredom

Staying on the theme of pranks, sometimes you had to do what you could to entertain yourself. If it was a lazy day around the hostel, sometimes a prank was just the thing to lift the boredom.

The hostel front desk has a nostalgic rotary phone. When you lift the receiver, it automatically forwards the call to the staff member operating the desk that day.

I was sitting outside under the cycad and relaxing, chatting to the owner and a few volunteers. I was bored, so I decided to play a joke. I used an app on my phone to ring Owhnn's phone, and make it appear as if it was coming from the front desk. She would answer, there would be no voice on the end, so she would have to get up and walk to the front desk to see who it was, as often people did this without speaking because they didn't understand the process. She would get up, wonder to the desk, and then find no one there. She would come back out, I would tell her someone just walked past the front gate, and she would sit back down to wait for the next time the phone rang.

As we sat there chatting, I would phone again from my pocket. She would get up, go back, find no one there and the process repeated. After a while, she got pissed off with this of course.

Later on, she was in the yard, and so I decided to do it again. Hidden from her sight, I phoned again. She answered. This time I spoke in a broken voice and accent, pretending I was at the front desk and that I had been there ten times already that day, and no staff had attended. She told me to wait, and then I watched her walk back again to the front desk, of course to find no one there yet again. She came out and asked if we had seen anyone, and I said I had seen someone walking around out the front. She then went searching for them.

Anyway, this went on for some time until I got bored. I did it again a few times over different days, and with different staff, and it never got old. I eventually owned up, they weren't amused, but I was.

Airports & Aluminum

There was a hosteller staying at the hostel called Carl, who just seemed to rub me up the wrong way, and he got on others people nerves too. He had been a volunteer for a short time at the hostel, and in the end, we asked him to leave.

Apparently, a good joke to play is to take a piece of cardboard, and draw the shape of a gun on it, then cut it out, and wrap it in tin foil (aluminum foil, or aluminium if you are British), and you do the same for the shape of a knife. You then insert one into the lining of a backpack of someone you do not like very much, and the other into the lining of the hand luggage, if there is some. You then send them on their way to the airport.

I heard this might have happened to him, though I have no idea who would do such a thing. I never heard from him again, but I have a good imagination.

Pool Balls and Banjos

'Last Chance Saloon' is the epitome of an American biker bar. It is a large space, with a long and large bar, wooden dance floor, pool tables, jukebox, tattoos, bandannas, leather, and plenty of sassy barmaids with matching tattoos and skullcaps.

When single girls, or groups of girls, came through the hostel, I would often use the promise of pool, and some large pitchers of beer to get them out and in my company for the evening. It was an experience for them. Although for the more timid then I would take them a little closer to home, to 'Sam's Hideaway', or to the 'Mutineer', which serves great food, including free bar food on a Monday, including pulled pork, tacos, roast chicken and much more.

Though I have built it up a little, it is not that bad, in fact 'Last Chance' is very accommodating to all those who enter, as long as no one is too loud, or too much of a troublemaker. It is just that from appearance and locale it can be a little intimidating to some, especially those from a foreign country.

When there were no girls to take with me, then I would often go for some pool and large pitchers of cold beer with friends from the hostel. I would often go here with my friend Drew, the firefighter with the firecrackers amongst others.

We had been drinking one day at the hostel and had become a little drunk already. We then decided to head down to the bar. At the time, a good friend used to be a barmaid there, though sadly, however, she has since passed from cancer, RIP.

We did the usual, and bought some pitchers of ice-cold beer, put on some tunes, played some pool, and bought more pitchers. As the night grew longer, we adopted our positions at the bar, slumped on stools, elbows on bar with hands on faces, and put the world to rights, accompanied by all sorts of liquor. The other visitors soon started to thin out, and we were left sloshed at the bar, with only our barmaid friend to keep us entertained, and with a constant flow of liquor.

After a short while, we entered the rowdy phase. This for some reason, still unknown to me today, became a bar fight that moved over to the pool tables. I remember being in the air and landing on my back on the pool table, cracking a rib on a pool ball. I hurled the ball back at Drew's head, which smashed some glass over the other side, and then our barmaid friend stepped in and kicked both of our asses. We ended up back at the bar, apologizing to her, and hugging each other, with the usual emotive slush that pours from drunken friend's mouths.

We now entered the 'must change our lives phase'. Nothing needed changing however, and we loved where we were and how things were, it was just the alcohol talking. All I really remember from that phase is that we left the bar planning to drive to Alaska as soon as we got back to the hostel. We were going to live in the woods, hunt grizzlies, and catch fish and homestead.

By the time we got back to the hostel, we were even more determined to get in the truck. We just needed to grab our gear and go. Somewhere between going to grab our gear and leaving, we entered yet another fight. Although, this time it was a drunken play fight, but not amongst ourselves, but with those we could find. It was playful to us, but a nightmare to the sober of course.

We entered the kitchen house where most of it remains a blur, but I know we started pummeling into two different friends who were asleep on the sofa. We took the banjo and guitar from the wall to use as weapons. The banjo ended up getting broken on my back, accompanying the rib damage. We smashed the guitar, we pulled over the shelves, we hurled the cushions, and finally we found the huge yellow pages, which were like six inches thick. There were loads of these, so that visitors could use them to find numbers across the USA. They made great projectiles. I know, because one hit me in the head.

There was a sudden calm and stillness. Drew had the last yellow pages in his grasp. He threw it, it missed me, and it hit the wall and slumped to the floor. His girlfriend at the time, one of the owners, was standing behind watching. Hurricane Owhnn had arrived, and with no warning. I can't remember the words, but I know his head dropped with a face like the cartoon *Droopy*, his eyes sullen, and a curled bottom lip. He followed her like a chastised dog on its way to the kennel. I didn't know if I would ever see him again, so I said goodbye. She turned and gave me the stare, and then led him away.

World Cup and Watches

During the World Cup, the hostel television room becomes a home to a large group of drunk, cheering, booing, and screaming football fans. Personally, I don't enjoy sport of any kind, either watching or playing.

I used to have a Casio watch, which was also a TV remote control. It had the facility to be able to tune itself to pretty much any TV, and then act as a remote control, much like certain apps on Android phones today. I had great fun with this over the years, and this World Cup was no exception.

They all gathered in the room, and from time to time, I would walk in to the kitchen house, stand by the sink, and point my watch at the TV. I would wait for what looked like some action, and the spirits would rise, as would the voices. You could feel the anticipation and excitement, ten or so different languages all saying the same thing:

"Go on" they would chant. Then just before it happened, I would change the channel. The same ten or so different languages, now all shouting the same thing again:

"WTF" as they frantically try to find out what happened.

This went on for days. They changed the remote control batteries, they left them out, and they started searching everyone in the room for another remote. I sat outside, drank my beer, and played with my watch. I guess I do find sport entertaining after all.

Why Are You Following Me?

I was giving a friend a lift to Ft. Lauderdale Airport to pick her mother up. Her mother was flying in to see her, and stay at the hostel for a while. As I drove down the Turnpike, I weaved in and out of the lanes as everyone does, but I wasn't speeding. In front of me was a police car that was doing the same. After about fifteen minutes, the police vehicle slowed, and dropped behind me. I paid no real attention, as I was not speeding, and I carried on driving the same as I was before. Then all of a sudden, the lights came on behind me, signaling for me to pull over. I asked my passenger if I had done anything wrong, and she didn't think I had, so I wasn't worried. I pulled over and got out of my vehicle. This was my second mistake.

As I walked back towards the police vehicle, the police officer got out of his car and immediately pulled his sidearm, pointing it straight at me. There is no standard issue sidearm to US Law Enforcement. However, I was sure that I was saying hello to his little friend, the Sig Sauer P226. I immediately threw my arms in the air, and he told me not to move any nearer, and to stay where I was.

After a few questions, it appears that when pulled over in the USA, you should stay in your vehicle and await them to approach you. The fact that I was British also seemed to amuse him, as he thought I had an Australian accent, which many people that I met also thought. My British accent mixed in with American slang, and the Southern draw, obviously changed me to an Ozzie.

Anyway, the reason I was pulled over was that he thought I was following him, because I was weaving in and out, changing lanes just like he was. Well forgive me for heading in the same direction, along with thousands of other people. He let me go, and warned me that he didn't want to see me in his mirror again, and if he did, I would be enjoying a night in a cell. Like that has never happened to me before.

Every day at the hostel had a story. Something amusing, and someone amusing, a new memory made every day. There are far too many for me to put down here. I have omitted so many that I was going to add, but there are other places to go, and other stories to tell.

If you ever manage to find yourself at the hostel, you will make your own. Even if it is just floating in the lagoon to the sound of the waterfall, a cold beer on the side, and the vermilion sunset breaking through the palm leaves. Perhaps, watching lone travelers sit in the tree house and write letters and postcards. Listen to guitars playing somewhere in the yard, with the smell of an evening meal being prepared in the kitchen. Either way, every day has a tale to tell. What will your memories look like?

The Island

White sands, calm waters, blue crabs, crocodiles, sharks, palm trees, pine trees, sunrise and sunsets, nudity, campfires, mozzies, horseshoe crabs, jellyfish, raccoons, and above all, peace, quiet and solitude.

The Island is the affectionate name given to Short Key, a key that lies just outside of the National Park Boundary, and sits between Middle Key and Main Key. These tiny islands, are not part of the Florida Keys archipelago as such, they lay just off the tip of the Florida mainland in Barnes Sound, which laps onto the shores of Key Largo.

To the west lies Manatee Bay, and to the east and down to Key Largo are the waters of Barnes Sound. Across Barnes Sound from the Islands is the toll bridge that separates Card Sound and Barnes Sound. This toll bridge is part of Card Sound Road, which is a more scenic route, with less traffic to Key Largo, avoiding the dreary metallic coffins that trundle along US Route 1.

In case you were wondering what a 'sound' is, it refers to a body of water (an inlet), lying between a mainland and an island. A sound is larger than a bay, but its exact definition is sketchy, and its etymology is arguable too.

There are a few ways to get to the 'Island', but the easiest and traditional route is to drive down Card Sound Road. Pay the toll, stop at Alabama Jacks for some conch fritters and a cold beer, and stick your canoe in the canal. You then head out into the sound, and head southwest until you hit a beach.

I always found that heading there at the last minute, at midnight after a bunch of beers in the hostel garden, and convincing someone to drive was the most fun. Night paddling, navigation, and just being in charge of a canoe when drunk is always a lot more memorable, and often leads to finding places you wouldn't normally come across.

I spent a lot of time here, on my own and with others. During one summer, I stayed here for ten days in my hammock tent. I took a cooler full of food, fished in the sound, and never saw another person, except for the odd day I canoed over to Alabama Jacks for some cold beers. Other times I spent with friends, having plenty of giggles.

It is small thin island, with white and yellow sandy beaches. There is a slightly higher inner of grass, pine, and beds of needles and marsh, pneumatophores and mangroves, with plenty of mozzies in the summer. There are also raccoons, so all food and water needs to be secure.

The paddle across the sound takes about an hour or so, depending on winds, craft and skill. It can become treacherous in the wind with white caps in the sound, so it is often wise to hug the coast where possible. You paddle over, drag your canoe up on shore, put up your hammock, or pitch your tent, and then chill in the sun. Fish, sit by your fire, sunbathe, sit on your camp chair in the water and read, watch wilderness life go by, and ponder on the big questions in life, such as how many beers you have left. It is an awesome place, and I had some great times there, especially with friends.

Psilocybin Pasta, Raccoons, Crabs and Testicles

My friend Brandon, along with another friend from Israel called Yuvie, and I, took off for a week on the 'Island'. It was a few months after the firecracker incident, and we had all become good friends, though Brandon did allude to seeking his revenge.

We drove down to the car park near Alabama Jacks, parked up and went to have a good meal and a few beers. We then set off across Barnes Sound during the tail end, and golden light of the sunset.

The water was like glass, and the boat seemed to be floating across liquid gold, as the sunsets hue reflected back from beneath us. The only clouds were on the horizon, helping to filter the sun into its beautiful colors. The only sounds were our paddles and boat gliding through the water, with the odd squeak and squawk from an aerial avian. Silhouettes of pelicans, ibis, and egrets peppered the sky, and the occasional fish flip, ray fin, and osprey plummet appeared in the water. It was a perfect paddle.

We had a few beers before setting off, but just enough to put us all in a relaxed mood. I paddled the stern, and Brandon took the bow, with our other friend Yuvie laying comfortably, sipping a cold beer in the middle of the boat, resting on the yoke (the center beam in a canoe). We filled all available space with the cooler, camping gear, and fresh drinking water. The boat was heavy, but glided easily in the calm waters, the odd correction from my paddle, and the main thrust from both the stern and bow paddling got us there quickly, with us quiet all the way.

We arrived, unloaded, set up camp and got a fire going. We then sat around the fire the first night, drinking beer, telling tales, and chatting. For supper we cooked up some hot dogs before heading off into our respective tents or hammocks, and had a good night's sleep.

The next morning I woke up at early twilight to the chirms of nearby birds. There was a dark sky to one side, and light chasing it out from the other. A light zephyr kissed my skin, with the slow waves licking the shoreline. I got up, put on a fleece, and then took my stove down to the water's edge. I boiled up some water, grabbed the coffee press, and made a pot of coffee. I sat at the shoreline, sun on my shins, sipped my brew, and waited for the day to begin.

I sat ruminating. A blacktip shark swam by, some birds flew over as if commuting to work, and the sun began lifting the cooler night air from the ocean. The steam from my coffee mug rising before my face was extremely comforting. Camping in the wilderness always seems to accentuate the tiniest of comforts and details.

After a short time, the shore now bright orange from the early sun, and the humidity kicking in, there was the familiar tent zipper sound. The others had woken up, and had wondered down to grab a coffee. We all sat there chatting, sipped caffeine and took it all in. After a short while, we went exploring along the shoreline. We gathered more driftwood for the fire, and looked to see if anyone else was camping there with us. We found a few horseshoe crabs (*Limulidae*), which is an amazing looking marine arthropod that looks like miniature tanks laying on the beach. We also gathered plenty of driftwood, found some rope, and an old BBQ grill. No one else appeared, so we were alone.

We spent most of our days doing the same routine, from the morning coffee, swimming, paddling, snorkeling, fishing, eating, drinking, and just lazing and laughing. However, a couple of days were more interesting. On one of the days, we all headed out in the canoe for paddle around the sound and the small keys where we were staying. The waters behind the key, in Manatee Bay, are delightful, and I could float there all day in the sun. It also offers some great snorkeling.

Brandon had the idea to have some crab for dinner, so we paddled around looking for crab pots, and we found a few, but most were empty. We then found one that had a few large blue crabs in them. This is illegal of course, but we were only grabbing enough for dinner, and not emptying all the pots to sell.

He pulled one of the pots up with three large blue crabs in it. I opened the cooler, and he grabbed one from the pot, and threw it in the cooler, past Yuvie who was sitting in the middle of the boat. On the second attempt, he threw a crab towards the cooler, or at least went to, and it slipped from his hand and straight into the Yuvie's crotch. The crab bolted its pincer straight down onto his testicle, Yuvie let out a high-pitched yelp before panic set in and he screamed.

'Get this f****** thing off me!' he whimpered, and we broke down in fits of laughter trying not to fall out of the boat.

The crab had locked on, and had buried the end of the claw through the light material, and into his scrotum. The ends of blue crab claws are pinpoint sharp needles. Brandon had to use a Leatherman to snap it off. I was in hysterics. He then took his testicle out, and it had two tiny holes either side with a little trickle of blood. Oh my, it was the funniest thing. We couldn't stop laughing. If you doubt that a crab can cause such damage, believe me, they can. Blue crabs are quite aggressive, and can cause injury easily if not handled properly. However, they are easy to catch and they taste great.

We did have blue crab for dinner and they were lovely, and the laughter continued through the night.

On another of the days, towards the end of the trip, Brandon said he was going to cook dinner, and make up some pasta and sauce. I chilled out in my hammock reading *'The Gold Cell'* by Sharon Olds, a wonderful collection of poetry. My other friend laid on the shoreline, in and out of sleep, with brief bouts of swimming in the sunset, trying to avoid any crabs up his shorts. We then chilled and let the darkness envelop us. We got the campfire going, and Brandon cooked up the pasta.

He was a wonderful chef, and had made some tasty dishes at the hostel, but this time he really added a kick to it. He had made up a mushroom sauce with various mushrooms, but he had hidden amongst the familiar flavors of traditional mushrooms the infamous 'shroom', or magic mushrooms. They are a potent psilocybin packed hallucinogen. Though my memory is blurry, I am sure he added more 'shroom', than regular mushroom. My memories of that night are scattered at best, but I do remember the tiny eyes of raccoons in the mangroves, which seemed to zoom in and out from small to large. I remember the sound of the waves being loud, yet I am sure there was no wind or current. We danced, we lay down, we tripped over, we laughed, we drank beer, and we built a huge fire. I kept feeling tingly, as if a small electric current was passing through my body, and tiny ants were under my skin. I felt good, but then felt depressed, then I suddenly laughed. I remember sitting on the beach thinking, but then running off down the shore.

One thing I do remember vividly, though it may have been a dream, was that I fell asleep, and I awoke in the dark and looked up to see Brandon running naked off into the mangroves. He was wearing nothing but a head torch, a machete, and a hairy butt crack. I don't know how long had passed, but then there was a shouting sound from the mangroves.

"Come here you little f*****" as he come crashing through the trees, machete in hand, chasing what he said was a raccoon.

The following morning, he was asleep naked in the dirt with a machete buried in the bark of a tree next to him. Yuvie woke up to find blood smeared down one side of his face but no signs of cuts anywhere, and I had hands covered in charcoal, and seaweed between my toes.

I can't say that I would opt for magic mushrooms again, but it was funny and relatively harmless. I suppose in a way, that was his revenge.

There were plenty of other good times spent here. One time I went with a collection of friends. They were an eclectic bunch. Three of which were musicians in a band. I awoke to see them, all three, naked in the lapping shoreline, in ankle deep water, performing one of their tunes. On the other side of me, one of the volunteers from the hostel was laid in his hammock and masturbating, and no drugs were involved this time.

There are many little keys or islands like this in and out of the park boundary, but the 'Island' is one of my favorites. I miss its smells, I miss its sounds, and I miss its feeling of wilderness solitude, even though you can see a road in the distance. Although I live on an island now, it is not quite the same.

Coconut Grove & Biscayne Bay

One of the best periods that I spent in South Florida, was living on a 53-feet tri-sail sailing yacht, in the marina at Coconut Grove for six months.

Coconut Grove, more commonly just referred to as 'The Grove', is a corner of the City of Miami, towards the south of downtown and the Miami beaches. It rather reminds me of a tiny Monaco. I am not sure why, I just get that vibe. It is very energetic, hip, and cultured, and home to Vizcaya museum and Gardens, the Miami Science Museum, and a plush and busy shopping district.

For those who enjoy TV shows, the TV series *Burn Notice* had its set situated here, in the marina where I lived, although I was staying here prior to the creation of the series. It was also, where Dexter Morgan lived, from the awesome show *Dexter*. Filming of *Bad Boys*, *Scarface*, *Meet the Fockers* and many more also took place here, and were either set in, filmed in, or alluded to Coconut Grove.

Its skyline is one of luxury hotels on one side, and the glistening waters of Biscayne Bay on the other. Biscayne Bay is where Dexter used to dispose of his bodies (fictionally of course).

The Grove is a contrast of relaxation and bustling energy, money and style, culture and history. You can see Lamborghini, Bugatti, Bentley and Ferraris, and you can see shoeless people in cut off denims riding rusty bicycles. Toothless hobos begging for a quarter, and holidaymakers eating Italian ice, gelato, or $1 dollar pizza slices. The Grove has a little of everything. Like most of South Florida, there is plenty of sun, sea, and a laid-back lifestyle. The Grove caters for everyone.

Espadrilles, Elvis and a Ferrari

OK, so life living on a boat in a Miami marina wasn't quite the same for me as it was for the 1980's Sonny Crockett. I didn't have a pet alligator called Elvis. I have never owned a pair of espadrilles, or a Ferrari. I did have some cool and creased linen clothing, a suntan, sunglasses, and I did cruise the Miami harbor and Biscayne Bay in my speedboat. Well I say speedboat, it was actually a small dinghy with a 15hp engine, which I could drop off the back of the yacht and play around in. I know the image of me in a dinghy, in a cloud of two-stroke smoke, eating a taco, doesn't quite compliment the music of a Jan Hammer soundtrack, but a man can dream.

In all seriousness though, living on a boat in a marina in Miami, should be on most peoples bucket lists. If not, then add it. I have been able to tick it off, but I wouldn't mind doing it again.

I was originally at the hostel. Sarah was there with me, and we were living together in one of the back rooms, and hanging during the day around the hostel. Sarah is American, and we had met at the hostel a year or two before.

After some time at the hostel, routine set in a little, and she needed to move on or at least get some work to fund her travels ahead. She planned to move north a little, and see what work there was around, and so off she went. I stayed at the hostel in my routine, with plans to meet up again a later time.

About a week later, she turned up back at the hostel, and talked me into going with her, as she had found a nice gig in Coconut Grove, living on a boat. I packed up some stuff and went with her. The owner of the boat had originally run it as a charter, living on it at the same time with his wife. His wife fell pregnant, and they needed room, so they moved off the boat and into the Grove. He changed to a full time job in the city, and they needed someone to live on, and look after the boat.

His plan was to run charters at the weekends, and so he needed someone to live on it, look after it, and keep it clean in the meantime. We lived on the boat, kept it clean, grilled steak under the stars on deck, relaxed in the moonlight with the sound and air of the open water, and generally had a great time. The owner would come down from time to time, bring me some Guinness and some steaks, and we would all have a wonderful evening. During the day, Sarah would head off into the Grove and other locales, picking up temporary gigs for extra money, such as promotional work and the like. We also occasionally picked up boat cleaning work in the marina. It was easy living.

On the days that she had promo work, I would laze about on the boat, sunbathing, eating frozen grapes, frozen cantaloupe and homemade banana ice cream, or take the dinghy around the harbor and Biscayne Bay.

There was a little key over the other side of Biscayne that had an old shack in the mangroves, where you could pull up in the boat, get off, grab some fish tacos and head out again, which was my regular lunch spot. I would also just head out into the middle of Biscayne Bay, and float and sunbathe, hoping not to be in the way from anything coming through at speed.

At the weekends, the owner would swing by when there was a charter lined up. We would head off down to the Keys, or across to Elliot Key, and we would spend the weekend sailing around, and having a good time. Sarah and I would help on the boat, she would play host to the customers, and in return, we were able to live on the boat, go sailing, and enjoy Coconut Grove.

We did this for a few months, before we headed off up the East Coast and further north to stay with her family. I then returned to the UK and back again to the USA to renew my ninety-day waiver.

When I got back this time, I headed straight to the Grove. I contacted the owner, and the boat was free, so I lived on the boat by myself for a few more months. It was a great experience.

I thought, as I mentioned them, that I would provide some simple tips for using cheap, fresh fruit, for hot weather delights.

Frozen Delights

If you ever find yourself in the heat and humidity of South Florida, or indeed anywhere that you fancy a frozen delight, then I highly recommend the following as a refreshing, tasty and healthy treat.

Frozen Cantaloupe

Take a cantaloupe, skin it, cube it, put the cubes in a Ziploc bag and freeze it. When frozen, take out a bag on a hot day, and suck on the cubes. They are refreshing, smooth, and delicious. The same works for mango or any fruit really. I found tropical fruits to work best.

Frozen Grapes

Take your grapes, wash them in cold water, and stick them in the freezer. Eat when frozen. The warmth of your mouth will melt them quickly. They are very refreshing and tasty. A healthy alternative to sugar filled iced popsicles and the like.

Banana Ice Cream

This is delicious, and one hundred percent natural, and requires only one ingredient, some bananas.

Take as many bananas as you like, the more you have then the more ice cream, obviously. Skin them, put them in the freezer, and when frozen take them out. Take the frozen banana and feed them into a blender or food processor, and blend until silky smooth. The result is a smooth, icy delight of all natural bananas, and tastes much nicer than any other banana ice cream you will ever try.

All of these are a welcome treat on a humid, sweat-dripping day, lying in a hammock, on a boat deck sailing to the keys, or floating in a canoe in the Everglades, as long as you take a cooler of course.

The End

This has now brought us to the end. I could talk for many more pages, about Biscayne, Big Cypress, and Dry Tortugas, more tales of the Everglades and plenty of other places of interest in and around South Florida. However, the wilderness remains out there for all to find. Go explore and appreciate. Go discover, make your own memories, tell your own tales. If you don't have a bucket list, create one, and start ticking. If you do have one, then keep ticking, and keep adding.

Life has many meanings and definitions. However, whatever else it maybe, life is full of challenges. Take up those challenges, take life by the reigns and ride it hard. Don't arrive safely at death, skid into it shouting:

"Yee-haw, what a ride!"

Final Thoughts

"I come more and more to the conclusion that wilderness, in America or anywhere else, is the only thing left that is worth saving." – Edward Abbey

I thought I had already said my goodbyes to the Everglades and South Florida. Now, since remembering and writing, I have taken myself right back to the thick of it. This textual tour was no easy task. Aside from my inept ability to write grammatically correct or interesting prose, I also struggled trying to describe things that I just couldn't verbalize. Contained in these pages is only small percentage of what I saw, felt and experienced. I have included only a small sample of images, and there are a million in my mind, that I cannot print. I have omitted hundreds of tales, and small yet wonderful moments, that would make no sense to the reader, yet meant so much to me.

I am not entirely sure I met my challenge. I am uncertain I delivered what I promised the reader, or myself. I guess if you are reading this then the chances are you reached the end. To reach an end requires commitment. Commitment comes from desire, so perhaps I did lead you here, and you had a good time. I hope so!

I now live back in the UK, and no longer work as a guide in any capacity. I left for many personal reasons, and do not plan to return anytime soon, though I am sure in the future I will find my way back there. I would love to show my daughter its entire splendor.

This book was an attempt to take the reader to a place that has to be experienced, so I am sure that I failed. If you can at least take away with you the importance of knowing that the wilderness, wherever it is, is a vital part of humanity, our planet, and the human spirit. They all exist symbiotically, like the animals and plants in these wild places. Everything is important, whether you can see it or not.

Our modern world is all about change. The irony being, that change is the only constant. We cannot change the past, or our past mistakes, but we can alter the now, which is our tomorrows yesterday. Society places a premium on beauty, yet it continues to alter that beauty when it appears naturally, to fit in with our idea of beauty, whether that is a person or our planet.

The Everglades is fragile, our planet is fragile, humanity is fragile. We collectively need to make positive changes, and strive towards protecting more of the wild places. When we destroy the wilds, and alter their beauty, we are destroying our heritage, our homes, where we once came from. Everything is connected, a chain is only as strong as its weakest link, and we are that link.

Humanity is arrogant and selfish, and our modern selves are far behind that of our ancestors. Intelligence is not about what we can build or achieve, it is about understanding and appreciating what we already have. Our world belongs to us, yes! However, we need to realize that there is more going on than we know. The wilderness is a window into what that could be, and we need to start taking more notice what is out there, outside of our protective and lazy techno bubbles, and start looking after what we have.

Nature does not need us, but we need nature. Nature does not care about us, who we are, why we are here, it has been there way before us, and will be there well after we have gone, back to its embrace from where we came.

Nature looks at us and asks:

"You are not that far gone are you?"

Sadly, we almost are. Let's protect our wild places, our wild animals, our resources. Enjoy them, look after them and appreciate them. The Everglades are a test, which is certain. We will never pass it with flying colors, but it is better to try and fail than to never try at all. We are working towards its restoration, but it will never be what it once was, and the efforts are only small compared to what's required globally.

I mean, let's take shark fin soup. It is tasteless, so why do we eat it? There is no need to eat shark fin soup, to destroy ninety-percent of the oceans sharks as we already have done. Do we think it is cool or novel to eat shark steaks? Have you checked your recommended mercury intake lately?

We are stupid, we are dumb, and we are failing our planet, our children and ourselves. I am not a tree hugger, nor am I a vegan, vegetarian, or an active conservationist. I am just not short sighted.

My time spent in the Everglades will always be with me. I met some wonderful people, and had some amazing times. I hope that they learned something on the tour. I hope you learned something on the tour. Whatever they, or you took from it, it was worth it. The Everglades are a magical place. A hidden, yet in full view look into our natural history, and a glance into our future.

I hope you enjoyed the tour, and was able to glimpse a little of what I saw. It is now goodbye from the Everglades and a goodbye from me. If you go to visit, say hello from me.

"Every Story has an end, but in life every end is just a new beginning."–
Dakota Fanning, *Uptown Girls*

Suggested Reading

Lodge, Thomas E. *The Everglades Handbook: Understanding the Ecosystem*, 3rd ed. CRC Press, 2010.

Douglas, Marjory Stoneham. *The Everglades: River of Grass*, 60th ed. Pineapple Press, 2007.

Minetor, Randi. *Everglades National Park Pocket Guide*, Poc ed. Falcon Press Publishing, 2009.

George, Jean Craighead. *Everglades*, Reprint ed. HarperCollins Publishers, 1997.

Golia, Jack De. *Everglades: The Story Behind the Scenery*, KC Publications, 1978.

Grunwald, Michael. *The Swamp: The Everglades, Florida, and the Politics of Paradise*, Reprint ed. Simon & Schuster, 2007.

Gannon, Michael. *The New History of Florida*, 1st ed. University Press of Florida, 1996.

Whitney, Ellie, and D Bruce means, Anne Rudloe, Eric Jadaszewski. *Priceless Florida: Natural Ecosystems and Native Species*, 1st ed. Pineapple Press, 2004.

Molloy, Johnny. *Paddler's Guide to Everglades National Park*, 2nd ed. University Press of Florida, 2009.

Genzen, Holly. *Paddling the Everglades Wilderness Waterway: Your All-in-One Guide to Florida's 99-Mile treasure plus 17 Day and Overnight Trips*, Menasha Ridge Press Guide Books, 2011.

Brown, Loren G. *Totch: A Life in the Everglades*, University Press of Florida, 1993.

Simmons, Glen. *Gladesmen: Gator Hunters, Moonshiners, and Skiffers*, University Press of Florida, 2010.

Index

A

Air Plants, 26, 80, 82, 97, 142, 143, 145
Alligator, 18, 30, 31, 38, 39, 42, 44, 52, 55, 58, 60, 63, 64, 65, 66, 67, 68, 69, 70, 71, 72, 74, 77, 78, 83, 84, 85, 88, 91, 92, 93, 94, 95, 96, 97, 100, 101, 102, 103, 105, 112, 119, 120, 125, 126, 127, 128, 129, 131, 132, 133, 135, 137, 138, 139, 140, 141, 143,145, 146, 147, 148, 149, 159, 160, 161, 162, 163, 164, 167, 168, 169, 170, 172, 175, 177, 179, 181, 183, 184, 186, 187, 188, 190, 191, 192, 194, 195, 197, 200, 201, 202, 212, 213, 214, 215, 260
    American, 39, 67, 68, 92, 93, 212
Audubon, 99, 206, 221

B

Big Cypress, 24, 227, 264
Birds, 15, 71, 77, 78, 81, 83, 85, 87, 88, 91, 92, 93, 97, 98, 99, 103, 104, 133, 140, 143, 146, 148, 172, 176, 177, 186, 192, 198, 200, 201, 206, 225, 241, 256
    Anhinga, 5, 29, 34, 63, 64, 66, 75, 77, 82, 84, 85, 86, 87, 91, 93, 95, 100, 103, 105, 146, 148, 170
    Cormorant, 85, 86, 87
    Crow, 198, 208
    Egret, 98, 99
    Flamingo, 205
    Hawk, 65, 94, 140, 148, 165, 166
    Heron, 98, 133
    Kite, 81, 140
    Osprey, 124, 175, 186, 207, 211, 218, 223, 256
    Owls, 109, 132, 146, 168, 221
    Stork, 85, 97, 98
    Vulture, 65, 78, 79, 80, 84, 85, 98, 100, 140, 179, 208, 211
Brackish, 7, 16, 29, 64, 69, 174, 175, 177, 183, 197, 200, 203, 215, 225
Bromeliads, 15, 26, 35, 81, 103, 132, 142, 145, 153, 164, 165, 189

C

Caiman, 39, 55, 67
Canoe, 5, 18, 28, 29, 30, 48, 61, 62, 63, 64, 69, 84, 91, 136, 138, 150, 168, 176, 177, 178, 179, 181, 184, 186, 188, 189, 190, 192, 194, 195, 196, 203, 207, 211, 219, 220, 224, 240, 242, 254, 255, 256, 257, 263
Canoeing, 5, 18, 28, 29, 30, 48, 61, 62, 63, 64, 69, 84, 91, 136, 138, 150, 168, 174, 176, 177, 178, 179, 181, 184, 186, 188, 189, 190, 192, 194, 195, 196, 203, 207, 211, 219, 220, 224, 240, 242, 254, 255, 256, 257, 263
    Coot Bay, 7, 200, 201, 203, 210, 220
    Florida Bay, 7, 16, 40, 63, 99, 183, 196, 200, 205, 207, 210, 211, 218, 219, 220, 221, 223, 224
    Hells Bay, 7, 195, 196, 197, 201
    Nine Mile Pond, 7, 69, 81, 121, 150, 174, 177, 179, 180, 181, 182, 183, 186, 190, 193, 195, 207, 211, 214
    Noble Hammock, 7, 120, 193, 195, 198, 206
    West Lake, 7, 176, 181, 194, 195, 197, 198, 199, 200
Carnivorous
    Plants, 192

Chickee, 31, 196, 197, 224
Crocodile, 28, 31, 35, 42, 67, 68, 69, 175, 177, 183, 192, 194, 197, 198, 200, 202, 203, 205, 208, 209, 210, 211, 212, 213, 214, 215, 217, 219, 254
    American, 67, 68, 69, 70, 95, 175, 207, 211, 212, 213, 214, 217, 218, 247
Crocodilian, 39, 67, 68, 69, 72, 92, 93, 182, 211, 213
Croczilla, 7, 69, 121, 181, 182, 183, 184, 185, 211
Cypress, 6, 131, 132, 134
    Tree, 132

E

Ernest F. Coe, 43, 58
Everglades, 1, 2, 3, 5, 9, 11, 12, 13, 15, 16, 17, 18, 19, 21, 22, 23, 24, 25, 26, 27, 28, 29, 30, 31, 32, 33, 34, 35, 37, 38, 39, 40, 41, 42, 43, 44, 45, 47, 48, 50, 52, 55, 57, 58, 59, 60, 61, 65, 66, 67, 68, 70, 71, 73, 74, 77, 78, 80, 82, 83, 85, 87, 89, 92, 93, 95, 96, 97, 98, 108, 109, 111, 116, 122, 124, 129, 131, 133, 134, 135, 138, 139, 142, 144, 148, 150, 157, 159, 164, 165, 166, 167, 168, 169, 171, 176, 178, 179, 182, 187, 189, 190, 191, 194, 196, 199, 202, 203, 207, 215, 217, 219, 221, 222, 224, 225, 227, 232, 247, 263, 264, 265, 266, 267, 269
    Glades, 13, 28, 34, 39, 52, 108, 111, 112, 113, 134
Everglades National Park, 11, 16, 24, 25, 33, 39, 41, 43, 47, 48, 55, 60, 61, 83, 92, 95, 108, 124, 129, 134, 167, 179, 203, 207, 219, 227, 269

F

Fish, 31, 35, 70, 77, 78, 83, 85, 92, 93, 98, 100, 102, 103, 124, 133, 139, 142, 152, 176, 182, 186, 189, 191, 203, 207, 212, 218, 219, 220, 251, 255, 256, 262
Flamingo, 7, 48, 51, 59, 73, 108, 111, 134, 179, 183, 195, 197, 202, 203, 205, 206, 207, 209, 210, 212, 215, 217, 218, 220, 221, 224
    Bird, 205
Florida, 3, 7, 9, 11, 15, 16, 21, 22, 23, 26, 29, 32, 35, 37, 38, 40, 41, 42, 43, 47, 48, 51, 52, 53, 54, 57, 58, 61, 63, 67, 68, 70, 72, 74, 79, 85, 90, 93, 94, 96, 97, 99, 104, 108, 109, 113, 114, 135, 139, 140, 146, 157, 160, 166, 167, 175, 176, 177, 183, 196, 200, 203, 205, 207, 210, 211, 212, 215, 216, 217, 218, 219, 220, 221, 222, 223, 224, 227, 230, 234, 244, 254, 269
    South, 9, 11, 21, 22, 32, 33, 37, 39, 41, 42, 44, 47, 50, 53, 54, 60, 68, 69, 79, 86, 89, 103, 104, 108, 109, 115, 131, 156, 159, 166, 176, 205, 206, 212, 214, 227, 235, 239, 240, 243, 260, 263, 264, 265
Florida Bay, 7, 16, 40, 63, 99, 183, 196, 200, 205, 207, 210, 211, 218, 219, 220, 221, 223, 224
Florida City, 21, 22, 35, 47, 48, 51, 53, 109, 230, 244
Florida Keys, 21, 22, 23, 32, 47, 48, 63, 90, 207, 219, 222, 227, 254
Freshwater, 15, 29, 40, 41, 60, 61, 68, 69, 134, 175, 211, 214, 225

G

Guide, 7, 9, 12, 15, 16, 17, 18, 19, 23, 24, 28, 29, 32, 35, 38, 44, 47, 78, 86,

87, 96, 116, 131, 136, 138, 143, 144, 154, 157, 188, 190, 203, 235, 237, 238, 243, 265, 269
Guy Bradley, 99, 206, 218, 221
   Key, 206, 221

H

Hammock, 25, 27, 41, 54, 57, 73, 74, 82, 83, 103, 104, 105, 106, 107, 109, 112, 113, 114, 115, 116, 117, 135, 157, 166, 168, 169, 177, 193, 194, 195, 196, 197, 231, 237, 247, 255, 256, 258, 259, 263
   Gumbo Limbo Trail, 6, 77, 103
   Mahogany Hammock, 247
   Noble Hammock, 7, 120, 193, 195, 198, 206
Hells Bay, 7, 195, 196, 197, 201
Homestead, 21, 166, 217
Hostel, 5, 8, 16, 21, 23, 24, 25, 26, 27, 28, 35, 47, 48, 53, 54, 61, 74, 78, 82, 104, 136, 138, 144, 155, 158, 170, 179, 186, 187, 192, 210, 227, 237, 238, 239, 240, 241, 242, 243, 244, 245, 246, 248, 249, 250, 251, 252, 253, 254, 258, 259, 261
Hurricanes, 22, 31, 32, 104, 159, 176, 187, 218, 224, 251
   Andrew, 159, 224
   Katrina, 218, 224
   Wilma, 104, 218, 224

I

Indians
   Miccosukee, 39, 197
   Seminole, 134, 197
   Tequesta, 205
Insects, 15, 26, 41, 71, 132, 133, 142, 189, 190, 194
Invasives, 100, 140, 152, 159, 161, 168, 210, 217, 247

K

Kayak, 48, 178, 179, 182, 184, 188, 201, 202, 203, 219
Keys, 6, 22, 82, 83, 103, 108, 111, 113, 220, 222, 254, 262

L

Lard Can, 196
Limestone, 26, 37, 40, 50, 53, 55, 61, 73, 83, 85, 109, 133, 149, 162, 169, 181, 184, 188, 241
Lizard, 70, 71, 77, 95, 105, 113, 132, 142, 146, 168, 238, 239

M

Mahogany, 82, 211, 247
Mammals, 15, 34, 68, 73, 92, 93, 156, 212, 215
Manatee, 35, 197, 200, 202, 203, 207, 208, 211, 215, 216, 217, 218, 219, 254, 257
Mangroves, 18, 24, 29, 31, 42, 63, 64, 82, 96, 108, 120, 123, 174, 175, 176, 177, 179, 184, 185, 186, 187, 188, 189, 192, 194, 195, 199, 200, 201, 203, 208, 220, 222, 223, 255, 258, 259, 262
   Black, 176, 199
   Red, 42, 163, 175, 176, 177, 199
   White, 176
Marjory Stoneham Douglas, 39, 43, 44, 217
Miami, 5, 21, 22, 23, 39, 47, 52, 79, 109, 136, 156, 159, 176, 200, 210, 229, 230, 231, 235, 237, 260, 261
Mosquitoes, 28, 33, 34, 49, 64, 65, 132, 169, 195, 196, 199, 200, 210, 211, 218, 219, 220, 222, 254, 255

O

Orchids, 81, 112, 166, 172
  Cowhorn, 81, 166, 172
  Ghost, 106, 166

P

Panther, 72
  Florida, 41, 57, 72, 109, 135, 139, 160
  Park, 11, 15, 16, 29, 30, 41, 43, 44, 47, 48, 49, 50, 51, 52, 55, 57, 58, 59, 60, 61, 63, 64, 65, 69, 71, 73, 74, 77, 78, 79, 80, 82, 83, 84, 87, 91, 94, 95, 96, 97, 98, 99, 101, 103, 106, 109, 111, 112, 113, 117, 132, 134, 137, 138, 139, 146, 150, 152, 155, 158, 161, 168, 169, 174, 175, 177, 178, 179, 180, 181, 185, 190, 193, 194, 197, 200, 207, 210, 211, 214, 218, 220, 227, 239, 247, 255, 259
    National, 16, 24, 32, 38, 39, 44, 48, 51, 52, 61, 79, 83, 205, 207, 217, 219, 227, 243, 254
  Pearl Bay, 196, 197
  Poison, 15, 28, 32, 44, 50, 66, 74, 90, 150, 151, 152, 157, 164, 172, 206
    Plants, 28, 44, 150, 151, 152, 164, 206

R

Reptiles, 15, 39, 67, 68, 69, 93, 95, 97, 101, 110, 156, 160, 168, 211, 212
  Alligator, 18, 30, 31, 38, 39, 42, 44, 52, 55, 58, 60, 63, 64, 65, 66, 67, 68, 69, 70, 71, 72, 74, 77, 78, 83, 84, 85, 88, 91, 92, 93, 94, 95, 96, 97, 100, 101, 102, 103, 105, 112, 119, 120, 125, 126, 127, 128, 129, 131, 132, 133, 135, 137, 138, 139, 140, 141, 143, 145, 146, 147, 148, 149, 159, 160, 161, 162, 163, 164, 167, 168, 169, 170, 172, 175, 177, 179, 181, 183, 184, 186, 187, 188, 190, 191, 192, 194, 195, 197, 200, 201, 202, 212, 213, 214, 215, 260
  Caiman, 39, 55, 67
  Crocodile, 28, 31, 35, 39, 42, 67, 68, 69, 70, 72, 92, 93, 95, 175, 177, 182, 183, 192, 194, 197, 198, 200, 202, 203, 205, 207, 208, 209, 210, 211, 212, 213, 214, 215, 217, 218, 219, 247, 254
  Reptilian, 39, 93, 133, 139, 141, 145, 148, 156, 191, 192, 213
  Snakes, 6, 41, 79, 88, 89, 90, 91, 97, 110, 111, 114, 126, 127, 128, 132, 134, 139, 145, 146, 149, 152, 153, 154, 155, 156, 157, 158, 159, 160, 161, 162, 164, 165, 166, 167, 168, 169, 170, 173, 200
  Turtle, 70, 77, 78, 88, 91, 92, 102, 103, 125, 127, 133, 146, 147, 167, 212, 219, 223, 247

S

Saltwater, 29, 48, 63, 68, 69, 70, 96, 174, 175, 199, 200, 201, 203, 207, 210, 211, 214, 218, 221, 225
Sawgrass, 5, 28, 39, 41, 44, 57, 60, 62, 65, 66, 74, 82, 83, 97, 108, 131, 135, 138, 140, 144, 149, 163, 164, 175, 177, 192
Seasons, 5, 29, 32, 33, 34, 40, 49, 50, 52, 58, 59, 60, 73, 83, 85, 87, 92, 93, 94, 101, 105, 111, 113, 115, 133, 135, 137, 138, 140, 142, 144, 148, 153, 163, 167, 189, 190, 195, 196, 197, 199, 201, 203, 207, 211, 239
Shark, 31, 41, 48, 61, 134, 213, 218, 219, 220, 221, 223, 225, 254, 256, 267

Blacktip, 221, 256
Bonnethead, 221
Bull, 7, 18, 197, 219, 220, 221, 223
Lemon, 221
Mako, 221
Sandbar, 221
Spinner, 221
Tiger, 219, 221
Slough, 61, 74, 97, 112, 161
Shark River, 41, 61, 134, 221
Taylor, 5, 41, 61, 63, 65, 83, 103, 177
Snails
Apple, 140
Tree, 109, 113, 114, 115
Snakes, 6, 15, 18, 28, 41, 42, 44, 53, 55, 65, 66, 67, 68, 74, 77, 78, 83, 88, 89, 90, 91, 93, 94, 100, 103, 105, 109, 110, 111, 112, 113, 114, 126, 127, 128, 131, 132, 134, 139, 144, 145, 146, 149, 152, 153, 154, 155, 156, 157, 158, 159, 160, 161, 162, 164, 165, 166, 167, 168, 169, 170, 173, 186, 195, 200, 203, 206, 213, 215, 247
Cottonmouth, 6, 41, 89, 126, 127, 132, 134, 139, 145, 149, 152, 153, 154, 155, 156, 157, 158, 162, 164, 165, 166, 167, 168, 169, 170, 173
Eastern Diamondback, 41, 89, 110, 111, 128, 152, 157
Python, 55, 74, 88, 93, 100, 131, 144, 152, 158, 159, 160, 161, 162, 200, 215
Rattlesnake, 89, 110, 111, 128, 148, 157
Rattlesnakes, 41, 89, 110, 111, 112, 128, 148, 152, 157, 166, 200, 206, 210, 218, 247
Spiders, 90, 109, 113, 115, 116, 247
Golden Orb, 113, 115, 116

T

Tours, 1, 5, 7, 9, 10, 12, 13, 15, 16, 17, 21, 23, 24, 27, 28, 29, 30, 31, 32, 35, 47, 48, 49, 59, 60, 65, 66, 67, 72, 73, 77, 78, 84, 91, 100, 101, 105, 111, 121, 135, 136, 137, 138, 140, 142, 143, 144, 146, 147, 148, 154, 155, 157, 158, 161, 162, 165, 168, 170, 174, 178, 181, 182, 183, 184, 186, 187, 188, 190, 192, 198, 202, 208, 209, 215, 218, 225, 227, 235, 238, 239, 240, 246, 247, 265, 267
Travel, 2, 7, 163, 227
Trees
Cypress, 6, 29, 35, 41, 89, 102, 122, 131, 132, 133, 134, 135, 136, 137, 138, 140, 141, 142, 145, 148, 153, 157, 163, 164, 165, 166, 169, 171, 174, 177, 184, 197, 225
Mangroves, 18, 24, 29, 31, 42, 63, 64, 82, 96, 108, 120, 123, 163, 174, 175, 176, 177, 179, 184, 185, 186, 187, 188, 189, 192, 194, 195, 199, 200, 201, 203, 208, 220, 222, 223, 255, 258, 259, 262
Pine, 6, 40, 41, 55, 57, 108, 109, 111, 112, 113, 117, 118, 131, 254, 255
Poisonwood, 74, 150, 151, 157, 164, 179, 180
Turtle, 70, 77, 78, 88, 91, 92, 102, 103, 125, 127, 133, 146, 147, 167, 212, 219, 223, 247
Snapping, 83, 132, 167, 169
Soft Shell, 146, 147

U

UK, 9, 22, 23, 38, 54, 163, 227, 228, 231, 232, 233, 235, 236, 237, 262, 265

V

Venom, 6, 15, 28, 41, 44, 66, 67, 83, 89, 90, 110, 112, 114, 131, 132, 139, 145, 149, 152, 153, 154, 155, 156, 157, 158, 164, 167, 213, 215

Visitor Center, 77
- Ernest F. Coe, 58
- Flamingo, 206
- Royal Palm, 60, 66, 72, 73, 74, 75, 77, 78, 82, 108, 111, 181

Volunteer, 24, 25, 144, 210, 222, 238, 239, 240, 241, 243, 244, 246, 248, 259

W

Water, 11, 15, 19, 26, 28, 29, 30, 31, 32, 33, 34, 35, 40, 41, 42, 43, 44, 47, 49, 50, 55, 58, 61, 62, 63, 64, 68, 69, 70, 71, 72, 74, 78, 83, 84, 85, 88, 89, 92, 94, 95, 97, 98, 101, 102, 104, 107, 112, 114, 120, 126, 129, 133, 135, 138, 139, 140, 141, 142, 143, 144, 145, 146, 147, 152, 153, 154, 156, 159, 162, 163, 164, 165, 167, 168, 169, 170, 171, 172, 173, 175, 177, 179, 181, 182, 183, 184, 185, 186, 187, 188, 189, 190, 191, 192, 193, 194, 195, 196, 197, 198, 199, 201, 202, 206, 207, 208, 210, 211, 212, 213, 217, 219, 221, 222, 223, 224, 225, 254, 255, 256, 259, 261, 263

Wild, 5, 11, 13, 37, 38, 47, 67, 70, 72, 73, 78, 83, 85, 88, 94, 99, 107, 109, 114, 138, 139, 147, 154, 161, 163, 195, 197, 202, 206, 217, 222, 227, 239, 265, 266

Wilderness, 9, 11, 12, 15, 16, 17, 18, 19, 22, 23, 24, 28, 29, 30, 31, 37, 38, 39, 42, 43, 45, 47, 48, 66, 74, 77, 103, 111, 117, 142, 144, 159, 170, 182, 191, 196, 197, 201, 203, 205, 227, 235, 237, 238, 243, 255, 256, 259, 264, 265, 266, 269

Made in the USA
Charleston, SC
08 August 2014